American Designs

The Late Novels of James and Faulkner

Jeanne Campbell Reesman

University of Pennsylvania Press

Philadelphia

Library of Congress Cataloging-in-Publication Data

Reesman, Jeanne Campbell.
    American designs : the late novels of James and Faulkner / Jeanne
Campbell Reesman.
    p.   cm.
    Includes bibliographical references and index.
    ISBN 0-8122-8253-1
    1. American fiction—20th century—History and criticism.
2. Knowledge, Theory of, in literature.   3. James, Henry, 1843–1916—
Criticism and interpretation.   4. Faulkner, William, 1897–1962—
Criticism and interpretation.   I. Title.
PS374.K55R44   1991
813'.5409—dc20   90-19272
                                                          CIP

This book is dedicated to my husband,
John

Contents

Preface   ix
Acknowledgments   xix

1 Contexts for Dialogue   1

2 Knowledge as Interest and Design   22

3 Failure to "Live": *The Ambassadors*   53

4 Community Versus Design in *Absalom, Absalom!*   84

5 The Negative Design of *The Golden Bowl*   114

6 *Go Down, Moses*: Dissolution of Design   149

Notes   193
Bibliography   211
Index   219

Preface

JAMES AND FAULKNER? How does one compare the creators of Lambert Strether and Ike Snopes? It is hard to imagine Henry James and William Faulkner even speaking to each other had they ever met, and neither would have been likely to acknowledge similarity, let alone a shared approach. Occasionally parallels are drawn between James and Faulkner in literary criticism, and they are often compared to the same authors, most notably Nathaniel Hawthorne, or included in the same arrangements of authors. Yet sustained comparison of their work is rare. They are arguably America's two greatest novelists, in part because of their extremely complex narrative responses to an important moral problem in American thought and culture: what can be called "the problem of knowledge." The major similarity between James's and Faulkner's narratives, particularly in their late novels, is the way the search for knowledge of the self and of other people is presented as a metafictive issue of power, authority, and freedom. The interests of James's and Faulkner's characters lead them to enact designs on other characters, yet the novels themselves ask readers for a community of interpretations instead of a single "design." *The Ambassadors*, *Absalom, Absalom!*, *The Golden Bowl*, and *Go Down, Moses*, the best examples of James's and Faulkner's handling of problems of knowledge in their late novels, demonstrate not that James influenced Faulkner but rather that each author responded to problems of knowledge in American thought in strikingly similar ways. *American Designs* describes a philosophical community of knowledge shared by James and Faulkner that addresses broad concerns in the development of the American novel. Although directed toward those who study James's and Faulkner's work, it is intended for a much broader audience as well—for theorists, teachers, and students of American literary thought in general.

American Designs addresses three major literary critical issues: the hermeneutics of the novel genre, the intense importance of this novelistic form for American literature, and the way James and Faulkner explore the novelistic designs they inherited and transformed. They are masters of their genre within a tradition that grants mastery to a willingness to fail.

Chapter 1 offers contexts for comparison by connecting James's and Faulkner's handling of problems of narrative knowledge to other sorts of problems of knowledge among literary theorists, critics, teachers, and students. At issue is the philosophical preference for knowledge defined as hermeneutics, or knowledge as a group of interpretations, over epistemology, or knowledge as a single truth. That a move toward such openness is broadly evident in the modern novel or in modern American literary thought is not a new idea, nor is the fact that James and Faulkner deliberately leave openings in their texts to be entered by the reader in interpretation. But it will be valuable to identify their philosophical and structural preference for a hermeneutic model of knowledge as a moral question.

Much has been published on James and Faulkner, and one may well question the need for more. But a broader approach will help us address James's and Faulkner's narrative experimentation as part of the same move toward the hermeneutics invoked today in the opening of the canon and the general emphasis on new voices in literary interpretation. I hope to promote possibilities of dialogue for many readers through analyses that address the similarities in these two authors' narrative structures. Much of what has already been published on James and Faulkner shares my hermeneutic emphasis—to varying degrees—and of course much does not. I refer to examples of both. Because of the need for larger contexts, *American Designs* juxtaposes and compares structures of knowledge in many areas of literary study.

Numerous critical interpretations of both James's and Faulkner's work devote close attention to the question of technique, a focus thought to be opposed to another major approach, the study of moral questions. But James's and Faulkner's notions of narrative craft, as put forward in the fiction as well as in James's prefaces and Faulkner's interviews, hermeneutically address the problem of how to speak about what were broadly defined in the past as issues of style and content. Critical appraisals of James and Faulkner that tend to split narrative technique from moral content have resulted in inadequate and reductive knowledge concerning these writers that does justice neither to the complexity of the authors' vision nor to the tradition of the problem of knowledge in American literature. Particularly in regard to Faulkner's work, one notes the construction of more and more abstract critical systems. His novels are said to be centered on everything from Aztec religion to incest taboos to the Great Mother, though his work specifically defeats such designs. Like James, Faulkner leaves the design of his work open in order to avert reduction.

James's and Faulkner's work is so complex and difficult that critics were at first awed, then began working furiously to catch up to the fiction's complexity, developing increasingly arcane approaches that too often obscure the narrative questions about knowledge these authors pose. But James and Faulkner, the masters of design, warn of the dangers of design by teaching us where our interests as readers lie. Their works direct readers' attention to matters of narrative craft instead of system as a way of knowing, asking for freedom from restrictive designs by structurally enacting ambiguity.

The most valuable critical work on James and Faulkner addresses craft as joint purpose and form. It recognizes the strategies in an author's craft for handling epistemological problems in narrative, those characterized as questions of "interest" and "design" in chapter 2 in my discussion of James's and Faulkner's careers. The best criticism, like the best literature, is an interest among other interests; it regards itself as a voice in a community of critical voices, as an interpretation among interpretations, capable of receiving a reply. Systematic designs have no place in the study of language unless they recognize their contingent, contextual, communal, conversational qualities and make their claims accordingly. A novel or any work of art is the utterance of a human being, and any statement about that utterance, no matter how abstract and theoretical, is a response, a rejoinder in a dialogue. I chose these two authors not only because they are the most complex examples of a hermeneutic philosophy of the American novel, but also because they *are* two: that is, I felt that the method of comparison as I conceived it would preclude me from offering one more critical design, one more closure, on either man's work. In *American Designs*, statements about one writer are intended to resonate with features of the other in critical dialogue.

James and Faulkner never knew each other. James of course never read Faulkner, and Faulkner would deny James. One wrote about a rarefied world of English and American wealth, the other about his "small postage-stamp" of a Mississippi backwoods county. I do not wish to suggest that James's and Faulkner's conceptions of their work were completely at one with a hermeneutic mode of analysis, or that what is meant by words such as "dialogue," "interest," "design," and "community," which will be used throughout this study, is identical for each author. The term "community," for example, can take on different meanings for these two authors. James's works are less clearly a "community" in themselves than are Faulkner's; that is, James's are all discrete novels and stories whereas Faulkner's feature settings, characters, and events that are repeated from work to work. But though their differences are clear, their similarities are profound. I have oftentimes found that exploring their differences reveals further affinities. In the use of community, for example, despite their different societies, James's and Faulkner's novels argue in much the same fashion and for much the same reasons against the isolation from meaningful community both of their sets of heroes and heroines endure, whether in a small southern town or in a European metropolis. And James's and Faulkner's worlds share a certain insularity—Faulkner's is geographical and James's is social. Their shared drive toward community is all the more urgent because of this similarity. As we turn to philosophical, theoretical, and critical means of bridging the gap between their extraordinarily articulate voices, we shall find that James and Faulkner would have had a great deal to say to each other.

James's and Faulkner's presentations of moral values in narrative structures are closely compared through analysis of novels in chapters 3 to 6. *The Ambassadors* and *Absalom, Absalom!* involve a journey for their heroes to a new place: Lambert Strether goes to discover a story, and Quentin Compson brings one with him. Both Strether and Quentin are attracted to and repelled by the knowledge they uncover, and their conclusions are problematic to say the least. Both are engaged in a collaborative effort to get at truth—Strether with Maria Gostrey and Quentin with Shreve McCannon—yet both end their stories with a gesture of repudiation. Instead of their knowledge guiding them within their communities, it seems to be a burden that alienates them. For both, knowledge comes, agonizingly, "too late, too late." And yet though Quentin and Strether fail in many senses, their imaginative transformations leave readers trying to "know" their stories in the same hermeneutic ways the authors do. This effort is the very subject of these novels.

For both heroes knowledge is recognition, in the sense of "to know again," and this is presented as a critique of our usual ways of "seeing" people. Strether finds out about the affair between Chad Newsome and Marie de Vionnet when he sees them on the river; they are "exactly the right thing" for his pictoral design—until his design doubles back on him with the shock of recognition. Quentin finally finds out about Charles Bon when he sees Clytie at Thomas Sutpen's house, but, as Shreve explains, Quentin knew even as he realized he knew. Strether moves from indifference to interest to disinterest; Quentin is never indifferent and never attains disinterest. The design he and Shreve complete with their fictions, the design Sutpen has forced on them, ultimately swallows Quentin. His "affirmation" " 'I dont hate it!' " is a fitting repudiation of the knowledge he has acquired. Not even dialogue, James's and Faulkner's typical replacement for reductive epistemologies, especially that of the visual metaphor, ultimately can save Strether and Quentin from their imaginative isolation.

Quentin's approaching suicide means the end of his struggle to know his community, but Strether's return to Woollett is more ambiguous. One can well imagine Strether saying that he does not hate Woollett; his decision to return in the end is difficult to assess. Either it represents a withdrawal similar to Quentin's or it is his imaginative replacement of both the designs of Woollett (he will not marry Mrs. Newsome) and the designs of Paris (he will not stay) with something better. Strether perhaps returns to America to redefine it for himself and to identify his newly developed imagination with the freedom of the New World—as it was to have been. But the reader is not sure whether Strether withdraws to exercise his freedom or merely to hide, to grow old, and to die. Both endings leave the fate of the hero unclear, but both firmly suggest that these heroes have nothing but knowledge by the end of their stories and that this knowledge is very dangerous.

Strether and Quentin suggest an author straining at the limits of his form, seeking some way of explaining, of rendering his private knowledge public, but at last finding that there is no entirely satisfactory way. Their struggles to know are heroic; they fail in that their knowledge, hard won through sacrifice and pain as well as delicacy and discrimination, cannot always be translated into meaningful community with other people, possible audiences and critics of that knowledge. What Quentin and Strether come to know is the culmination of a lifelong search for each of them, the victory, the epiphany, the "real thing"—at last, strangely isolating. They withdraw from sharing their knowledge into self-absorption; they enjoy only the "memory of an illusion," as Strether calls it.

In attempting to become tellers and hearers, Quentin and Strether, like their creators, find that problems of interest and design can best be addressed—if not solved—through a dialogue of hearing and telling in which a "failure" in telling occasions a rejoinder that in turn offers at least the possibility of understanding. It is as though James and Faulkner are saying in their conclusions that the imagination is the only route to understanding life but that a "free" imagination makes it very difficult for one to live in one's community *and* address it. In their last great novels, *The Golden Bowl* and *Go Down, Moses*, each author found a way of allowing revelation— artistic knowledge, in particular—to live and hear and tell within the community. Yet the marvelous "failures" of *The Ambassadors* and *Absalom, Absalom!* tell us a great deal about their authors' development of hermeneutic narrative in their late fiction.

The Golden Bowl and *Go Down, Moses* carry to the most complex and extreme degree problems of narrative knowledge in James's and Faulkner's work. The concern about knowledge in these books shows up first in their unusual structures. *The Golden Bowl* breaks into two parts, "The Prince" and "The Princess," and at the end of the book the couple is far apart even when embracing: the "break" between them is emphasized even as it is ostensibly closed up, as attested by the Princess's tears. The gap between the couple and the gap in the novel suggest the crack in the golden bowl itself—deep division barely concealed by beautiful surface. Furthermore, the radical personal gap between the Prince and Princess requires a narrative structure that will emphasize Maggie's action-in-inaction and her "negative" victory. This "negativity" makes James's great novel a looser, baggier monster than many of his critics would like to admit.

Go Down, Moses consists of chronologically disjunctive but thematically parallel short stories that form a "community" of tales and make up a novel to be read reflexively and spatially as well as chronologically. This structure is somewhat like that of the earlier *The Unvanquished*, also made up of short stories, but it is much more complex. The structures of *The Golden Bowl* and *Go Down, Moses* attempt to defeat the unifying design of a traditional novel; their characters as well as readers are relatively free in their participation in knowledge and yet are also part of a community. More than ever before in James and Faulkner, here there cannot be only one way of seeing "truth." The structures forbid singleness of vision and ask instead for multiple points of view based on the reader's negotiation of the gaps between the parts of the structures. The preference is for knowledge as a conversation rather than a single "point of view"; indeed, the problem of *having* a point of view is the subject of both of these novels.

The change from *The Ambassadors* and *Absalom, Absalom!* to *The Golden Bowl* and *Go Down, Moses* is thus a relocating of the theme of failure from the characters' involvement in plot to the author's handling of structure. Strether and Quentin transcend restrictive forms of knowledge at the end of their stories, but their transcendence also comes as a withdrawal from community in novels whose consecutively numbered chapters and overall unity of form ask for traditional patterns of resolution. Ironically, *The Golden Bowl* and *Go Down, Moses* allow greater resolution for characters' as well as readers' knowledge of plot through their more fragmented structures. Yet Faulkner's late works are optimistic in a way James's distinctly are not. James's apparently happy ending hints strongly at the essential separateness of the Prince and the Princess; Faulkner's less forced ending finds the forms of community reinstated and selfish personal design challenged to a greater degree than in *The Golden Bowl*. The reinstatement of community values in *The Golden Bowl* becomes an excruciating strain as form—in this case, marriage—is reaffirmed at great cost. Faulkner's community is reinstated, too, but its members are part of a freer and larger community altogether.

In both novels, the design of community and family relationships forms the matrix for action. Genealogy is a compelling reason for interest, and it is asserted both positively and negatively. Both books involve illicit sexual relationships within families, but both also present family and community as saving values. Maggie Verver and Gavin Stevens both maintain community, but because Maggie does what Isaac McCaslin could not do, decides she must live with the knowledge that everyone—herself, the Prince, her father—is a mixture of good and evil, she pays a terrible price. Gavin's accommodation does not cost him what Maggie's costs her, but the reader of *Go Down, Moses* knows of Isaac's painful failure, and this "negative" knowledge adds needed depth to Gavin's actions. Faulkner has to bring in a character in the fifth act, as it were, to replace his failed hero. These endings are most similar in the way both authors address the difficulty of characters' as well as authors' struggles both to have knowledge and to act responsibly on their knowledge. Even the optimistic *Go Down, Moses* contains seeds of dark contradiction that make the victory of the final story, "Go Down, Moses," problematic, just as Maggie's victory is.

Knowledge and inaction form the plots of *The Golden Bowl* and *Go Down, Moses*. Isaac learns the ways of the wilderness and does not shoot the bear; he learns of L. Q. C. McCaslin's sins and refuses to accept his patrimony. The first "inaction" succeeds, but the second fails. Maggie learns of Charlotte's and the Prince's affair, but does not act, allowing others, Fanny and Adam and Charlotte, to act for themselves and for her instead. James's concern with who knows what and how they act or do not act upon knowledge in *The Golden Bowl* is remarkably similar to Faulkner's mingling of narrative voices in *Go Down, Moses* and evokes as well

Faulkner's complicated schemes and swindles, such as the card game in "Was." The reader must work hard to attain knowledge but finds that the saving knowledge in these books leads to a particular type of inaction: the knower leaves the "known" free. Characters and readers of James and Faulkner are asked to recognize that one can say something *about* something or someone without saying what or who that something or someone *is*. The opposed form of knowledge, manipulation or the "swindle," fails for Adam, Amerigo, Charlotte, and L. Q. C. McCaslin. Maggie's forgiving knowledge sustains, but at great cost; Gavin's communal knowledge is more successful, if terribly awkward. Despite their imperfect victories, both embody redemptive features, and both respond to the "other" in dialogue instead of enforcing designs.

Through narrators, James's and Faulkner's redefined moral knowledge asks for intersubjectivity to overcome the dangers of the single view. James's novels have one narrator, seer and seen, observer and observed, but instead of relying on vision this narrator is engaged in dialogue. James's narrator seems authoritative, but James, through the narrator, goes to great lengths to avoid narrative monism, largely by examining and questioning the idea of the viewpoint itself. James's famous position behind the shoulder of his focal characters allows his narrator to focus only loosely on the minds of Fanny and Bob, the Prince, the Princess, and Charlotte, while Adam's mind is left mostly to itself. The unnamed narrator of *Go Down, Moses*, who allows Isaac, Cass Edmonds, and eventually the spokesman for the recovering South, Gavin Stevens, to tell their stories, tells other stories and adds the background music, "Go Down, Moses." These narrators fail to synthesize their roles into a single, overriding design. In *The Ambassadors* and *Absalom, Absalom!* narrators are accompanied by *ficelles* whose versions of the plot events add important interpretive voices to the narrative; in the later novels, Fanny in *The Golden Bowl* and Mollie in *Go Down, Moses* similarly promote dialogic knowledge.

In these novels everyone's point of view is to one degree or another engaged by the desire to enact a design. Even Fanny, whom one would think disinterested, is highly interested because of her guilt at playing matchmaker. *The Golden Bowl* and *Go Down, Moses* seem to argue that when subjectivity is conceived of as strictly one's own manner of operating, one is likely to sin by forcing one's knowledge onto others—because one sees others as objects to one's own subject. But when one finds, as Maggie and Gavin do, that all interests are subjective and that each has an equal position in the process of negotiation, then one has given up "seeing" people at all and has addressed the other "I," another member of the community. These narrators more than any characters are aware of the dangers of looking at other people as objects.

Yet close as the narrators of these novels come to the characters' minds, they distinguish themselves from the characters, primarily through their use of metaphors, which they employ, carefully, instead of abstract "explanations" to render a character's consciousness. Certain objects come to carry meaning all their own, but in their visual definiteness they are deceptive. In *The Golden Bowl*, the flawed gilt vessel insidiously draws all characters toward it. In *Go Down, Moses* appear Lucas Beauchamp's buried gold and his metal detector; the implements young Isaac must leave behind him when he confronts the wild god, Old Ben—his watch, gun, and compass; the gold coins and silver chalice that are Isaac's inheritance from his uncle Hubert Fitzhubert Beauchamp, metal treasure that metamorphosizes into IOU's on scraps of paper in an old tin coffeepot; and the silver hunting horn Isaac forces on the jilted black lover of Roth Edmonds. All of these objects are absent, refused, destroyed, or transformed in the book once their meaning is invoked. They are icons of knowledge that reveal but that also indicate the dangers of such revealing, for metaphors in both these novels can promote the entrapment as well as the freedom of the character to whom they refer. Addressing (or "dialogizing") these objects can sometimes disarm their designs, yet when the narrators use epistemologically "real" objects that might actually occur in the story—houses, boats, a golden bowl, or trains, a snake, a bear—the metaphor has been invoked by the narrator or by a sympathetic character. If the metaphor is fantastic, such as Adam's Palladian church or silken halter, the character to whom it is attached is unsympathetic and bound on a course of design against fellow humans. Paradoxically, the empirically real objects do not cast the shadows of design as the imaginary ones do. Design, like interest, always maintains its simultaneous, contradictory good and bad connotations, whether in life or in art. For James and Faulkner, it *always* points to art.

A new hero and heroine appear for James and Faulkner in *The Golden Bowl* and *Go Down, Moses*, protagonists who can make something out of their knowledge. In all these stories of manipulation, in which characters' motives are likely to be selfishly racial, economic, social, political, or sexual, heroes and heroines turn out to be the listeners, the comprehenders, the endurers who learn about others and about themselves. They remain free of the narrow designs of the other characters—though at their best they do not have to renounce others—and also mostly free from their own self-designs. Charlotte and Isaac are poignant, perhaps even tragic figures, but they are replaced as heroes by Maggie and Gavin, characters who approach their authors' knowledge of interest and design through dialogue with their interlocutors, Fanny and Mollie. Even as they assert their designs, Gavin and Maggie allow others a certain freedom from definition. Their ability to know in a context of community instead of personal design is the ability the reader too must develop in order to understand their stories.

These four late novels, the most complex and intriguing work of their authors' careers, are communities of knowledge for author, narrator, characters, and readers. Close attention to their hermeneutic narrative structures will allow us better to understand James's and Faulkner's particular phrasings of the question in American thought, How do I know? For these two novelists, the question is restated: How do *we* know?

Acknowledgments

THERE HAVE BEEN MANY VOICES in dialogue with *American Designs* over the past few years. At various stages, Peter Conn, Robert Lucid, Phyllis Rackin, William E. Cain, and Patrick Day provided generous and detailed responses. Earle Labor and Lee Morgan have given critical dialogue and warm friendship for many years. Mark Allen, Helen Aristar-Dry, Houston A. Baker, Jr., Wendy Barker, Wayne C. Booth, Jacqueline Brogan, Kenneth Bruffee, Alan Craven, David J. DeLaura, Daniel Hoffman, John Jopling, Paul Korshin, Elaine Maimon, Gary Saul Morson, Robert Regan, Elaine Scarry, and Robert Turner also offered advice and encouragement. Tanya Walsh and Leah Flores contributed their able and intelligent assistance in the preparation of the final manuscript.

The financial support I received from the Faculty Research Grant Program at the University of Texas at San Antonio significantly furthered my work, as did the year's leave of absence I was granted by the University of Hawaii at Manoa.

I am grateful to the staffs of the Van Pelt Library of the University of Pennsylvania; the John Peace Library of the University of Texas at San Antonio, especially Margaret A. Joseph; the William Faulkner Collection at the University of Virginia; and the Smith College Archives.

Excerpts from *Lion in the Garden: Interviews with William Faulkner, 1926–1962*, edited by James B. Meriwether and Michael Millgate, are reprinted by permission of University of Nebraska Press. Copyright © 1968 by James B. Meriwether and Michael Millgate.

Excerpts from *Absalom, Absalom!*, *Go Down, Moses*, and *The Marble Faun and A Green Bough* by William Faulkner are reprinted by permission of Random House, Inc. *Absalom, Absalom!* copyright © 1936 by William Faulkner, copyright renewed 1965 by Estelle Faulkner and Jill Faulkner Summers. *Go Down, Moses* copyright © 1940, 1941, 1942 by William Faulkner; copyright 1942 by The Curtis Publishing Co.; copyright renewed 1968, 1969, 1970 by Estelle Faulkner and Jill Faulkner Summers. *The Marble*

Faun and A Green Bough copyright © 1924 by the Four Seas Publishing Company, copyright renewed 1952 by William Faulkner.

Quotations from Henry James's prefaces are reprinted with permission of Charles Scribner's Sons, an imprint of Macmillan Publishing Company, from *The Art of the Novel* by Henry James. Copyright © 1934 Charles Scribner's Sons, copyright renewed 1962.

Working with the copy editor Trudie Calvert and the editors and staff of the University of Pennsylvania Press, particularly Arthur B. Evans, Zachary Simpson, Jerome Singerman, and Ruth Veleta, has been a pleasure.

I am deeply grateful to my parents, Evan and Jeannine Campbell, and to the rest of my family for their unwavering love and faith.

Finally, I owe thanks to my students at Baylor University, the University of Pennsylvania, the University of Hawaii, and the University of Texas at San Antonio. They have ceaselessly taught me what a community of readers and writers can be: a dialogue that leads to new discoveries, a conversation to which one is always eager to return. In response to these dialogues, I hope this book inspires other readers of James and Faulkner to greater understanding of these authors.

1. Contexts for Dialogue

THE GENIUS OF GREAT WRITERS such as James and Faulkner is always unique, yet it always lives within social and intellectual contexts. This book describes James's and Faulkner's shared context of addressing what philosophers call "problems of knowledge." In his most significant work, *Philosophy and the Mirror of Nature*, contemporary American philosopher Richard Rorty offers an intellectual context for a study of literary knowledge in American culture and literature that broadly addresses the development of modern and postmodern revisions of theories of knowing. Rorty examines the shift in American philosophy from the certainties of epistemology's subject/object knowledge toward the community of hermeneutics. In so defining epistemology, he narrows somewhat the general use of the term to mean the study of how we know, and he opposes "epistemology" to "hermeneutics" throughout his work. Hermeneutics, or the study of interpretation, is an important term in current scholarship. Neohumanism, phenomenology, deconstruction, feminism, reader-response criticism, and new historicism emphasize hermeneutics, but hermeneutics as a separate discipline has its own history and tradition. Arising in part as an attempt by nineteenth-century German theologians to interpret the Bible so as to preserve its meaning in the modern world, hermeneutics took on many forms before it appeared in contemporary American literary criticism. Rorty relates how philosophers in the American pragmatist tradition such as John Dewey and James's brother William James, reacting to the work of earlier and contemporary German hermeneuticists, gave up the search for a "foundational" philosophy in favor of something besides traditional representation. Their work is thus "therapeutic" rather than "constructive" because it asks about motives for philosophizing instead of offering a new philosophical program. In imagining a culture without epistemology and metaphysics, they have, Rorty argues, brought us to a period of revolutionary philosophy consonant with Thomas Kuhn's revolutionary science, in which scientific truth is found to be communally negotiated. Following the pragmatist tradition, Rorty himself offers, as a replacement for the certainty or grounding offered by systematic epistemological philosophies, a hermeneutics he defines through metaphors for knowledge based on the model of dialogue rather than vision. Because Rorty furnishes the critic of American literature with a theory of reading that admits many important pluralisms, his philosophical distinction is highly suggestive for readers of James and Faulkner.[1]

Throughout his other hermeneutic maneuvers, Rorty consistently attacks the ocular model of representation, the "framework" of the traditional metaphor of the mind as a mirror of nature. The "original dominating metaphor" of having our beliefs determined by "being brought face-to-face with the object of the belief" suggests, he says, that we should try to improve the quasi-visual faculty, the mirror of nature, and to think of knowledge only as an assemblage of accurate representations. But looking for a "special privileged class of representations so compelling that their accuracy cannot be doubted" means that philosophy as epistemology becomes "the search for the immutable structures within which knowledge, life, and culture must be contained . . . ," causing us to commit the moral error of substituting "*confrontation* for *conversation* as the determinant of our belief." In short, Rorty feels, we must change the way that arguments about knowledge are conducted: our certainty should be "a matter of conversation between persons, rather than a matter of interaction with nonhuman reality." Because "personhood" is a matter of "decision rather than knowledge, an acceptance of another being into fellowship rather than a recognition of a common essence," there is nothing left "for epistemology to be." In all our endeavors, he concludes, we need to "turn outward rather than inward, toward the social context of justification rather than to the relations between inner representations." What matters is not the commensurability of epistemology but "that there should be agreement about what would have to be done if a resolution *were* to be achieved. In the meantime, the interlocutors can agree to differ." This notion of "knowledge-as-conversation" suggests, as do James's and Faulkner's works, that "coming to understand is more like getting acquainted with a person than like following a demonstration." Indeed, we "play back and forth between guesses about how to characterize particular statements or other events, and guesses about the point of the whole situation, until gradually we feel at ease with what was hitherto strange."[2]

In the twentieth century, according to Rorty, "edifying" philosophers "have to decry the very notion of having a view, while avoiding having a view about having views." This is an awkward, but not impossible position:

it is the very position that James and Faulkner find themselves in as novel-ists. James, Faulkner, and Rorty seem to fear the dehumanizing idea that "there will be objectively true or false answers to every question we ask, so that human worth will consist in knowing truths, and human virtue will be merely justified true belief. This is frightening because it cuts off the possibility of something new under the sun." With this in mind, a novelist may be able to adopt "keeping a conversation going as a sufficient aim" and to address people "as generators of new descriptions rather than beings one hopes to be able to describe accurately."[3]

Rorty's hermeneutics contextualizes important responses to problems of knowledge among American literary critics, particularly three major hermeneutic themes: the derivation of values from conflicts within the Puritan tradition, the discussion of the dual attitude in American modern-ism toward technology, and the emergence in recent years of new voices from feminist critics and other reformers of the canon. Though they often oppose and contradict each other, these approaches ask moral questions by opposing hermeneutics to epistemology as ways of knowing. In this chap-ter, I present these three emphases in practical criticism as contexts for my approach to James's and Faulkner's characteristic problems of knowledge. I conclude the chapter with an additional context, Mikhail Bakhtin's "dia-logics," a current theoretical approach to the modern novel that closely addresses problems of knowledge in narrative structure.

James and Faulkner are part of a humanist tradition in modern Ameri-can literature developed as a response to historical and religious problems of knowledge. Within this tradition, American authors develop narrative structures that fail to close. Theirs is an open-ended search for American identity. Structures remain unfinished or unresolved or "disunified" in order to allow human beings a certain freedom from closed design, and they do this out of a dual reaction against both Old World tradition and New World Puritanism. This complex structural response is largely a result of the attempt both to carry forward the traditions of British literature found to be meaningful and to separate from those traditions as well, but it is accompanied and complicated by a similar ambivalence toward the epis-temologies of Puritanism.[4] In reacting against British as well as Puritan values, the American novel was and is torn between values, dualistic in its very nature. Such problems of knowledge deeply preoccupy James and Faulkner, giving rise to their hermeneutic techniques.

Responding to the presence of such polarities, Larzar Ziff, Emory Elliott, and Richard Poirier broadly trace the Puritan tradition in American literature from colonial to modern times. Ziff, in his *Puritanism in America: New Culture in a New World*, shows how in seventeenth-century Puritan America problems of knowledge characterized social thought, political or artistic. New England needed an authority to replace that of the Roman Catholic church to protect and rule the citizens, and it found such "in the Bible as interpreted by the learned," Ziff writes. Every man was encouraged "to read his Bible with his own eyes," but he was "equally required then to bring his understanding in line with the judgments of the ministry as they were expounded from the pulpit." The Puritans saw "the word" as a bridge over the abyss between God and man. The printed word was the common property of all readers, but unless it was controlled by church authority, "the word was chaos." Since membership in the elect was "ultimately verbal," Ziff emphasizes, learning was seen as the way of acquiring the means necessary to make such distinctions. Learning was essential for the preacher in colonial America because the church was "jeopardized should the highest reaches of learning be denied to its leaders," just as it was jeopardized by "the illiteracy of parishioners who cannot read their Bibles."[5] Knowledge was a dangerous—and desirable—power to have in Puritan America.

The Antinomian controversy demonstrates how conflicting attitudes about knowledge and authority in Puritan America tested the church's power and led to new ideas. The Puritan leaders' determination to quash Anne Hutchinson's claims to knowledge of God as immediate revelation resulted from their opinion, as Ziff puts it, that "the members of any civil society . . . must be subject to a control external to them."[6] The John Cotton–Anne Hutchinson group's radical claim of individual authority—absolutely unaffected by authoritative, external claims—occupies one extreme of a spectrum of models of knowledge, the other of course being occupied by the Massachusetts Puritan establishment's determination to wield "external" control over the members of society. The struggle between these ideas has long characterized problems of knowledge in American literature.

The obvious outcome of the Antinomian controversy was that because the church could no longer claim the authority over the individual conscience it once did, the state would govern society. But the Puritan conception of an external authority in matters of knowledge was later reinstitutionalized in the church, partly through the efforts of Cotton, whose views had become more authoritarian. Cotton, who came to hold that punishment could be inflicted on a sinner without his consent or approval, was challenged by Roger Williams. Williams found "monstrous" Cotton's idea that in punishing an errant believer the authorities were preventing the miscreant from further sinning against his own conscience by his error. In the view of the new Puritan establishment, which now included Cotton, the sinner was not persecuted for the *cause* of conscience but for sinning against his *own* conscience. This idea, says Ziff, which neatly seems to combine Cotton's earlier individualism with his later Puritan emphasis on the external power of the authorities, "served as the basis of security in Massachusetts in the revolutionary decades." Like its original, truth, in this reestablished Puritan view, was epistemological rather than hermeneutic. Williams's attack on Cotton, *The Bloudy Tenent of Persecution* (1644), was burned by the public hangman because it was thought to be so dangerous.[7] Though Williams's terminology was still designedly theological, his belief in freedom of thought made his ideas a communal solution to the problem of the individual and the society. One is free, not because, as in Cotton's earlier formulation, one is separate, but because one exists in a community of others, who all share one's freedom. Williams's reformulation of Cotton's early and late positions is an attempt to do what would later occupy so many American thinkers, especially writers, to reconcile the individual and the community.

"Scaffolding" in Puritan sermons represents the Puritan drive to overcome feeling with reason. A preacher announced a biblical text, extracted from it a doctrine, and explicated the doctrine by dividing it into numbered parts—then he presented numbered practical applications of it. As a design, an intellectual strategy, the scaffolded sermon is an excellent example of the way knowledge was managed by Puritan preachers: rationality did not allow anything into the sermon that did not fit in such a preconceived, systematic plan.[8] Both the Puritan sermon and the Puritan didactic poem demonstrate something of the effect such aspects of the Puritan design were to have on literature, especially in the eighteenth and early nineteenth centuries. In their retreat from the kind of knowledge suggested by scaffolding, James and Faulkner test the limits of authorial design. They seem afraid of knowledge, as the Puritans were, but more afraid of the Puritans' solutions to problems of knowledge.

Eighteenth-century authors' handling of problems of authority also reveals important intellectual influences arising from the political, cultural, and religious crises of knowledge of their day. In his study of American literature after 1945, Warner Berthoff has recognized the "remarkable persistence" of the religious element suggested that American novelists think of themselves in a "clerical role." Sacvan Bercovitch has advanced a widely respected thesis involving the importance of religious language to American authors and other thinkers. Emory Elliott, in *Revolutionary Writers: Literature and Authority in the New Republic, 1725–1810*, traces the intermingling of the clergy and the emerging authors of the eighteenth century. The set of beliefs displayed in New England Puritan rhetoric "formed the superstructure" that encloses nearly *all* American ideas, he argues; the "American identity is necessarily a religious identity." Struggles for power and authority in the new national culture took shape during the two decades after the American Revolution. By the end of the eighteenth century, novelists seem to have begun to take over center stage from the clergy in intellectual and moral questions. But they inherited their predecessors' epistemological difficulties. Because of their proximity in authority to the clergy, Elliott emphasizes, intellectuals found the question of their authority a major stumbling block. The learned clergy and the cultured men of letters, "those who had exercised the greatest degree of intellectual and cultural influence in the prewar society," were eventually left with little authority.[9]

Thus what seems obvious today as the "dissatisfaction" of American authors with the public actually began when the nation was formed and has changed very little; their limited sphere of influence today is not simply "the result of twentieth-century malaise or nineteenth-century philistinism," according to Elliott. An understanding of Ralph Waldo Emerson, Henry David Thoreau, Nathaniel Hawthorne, and Herman Melville depends, he feels, upon a study of their precursors Joel Barlow, Hugh Henry Brackenridge, Charles Brockden Brown, Timothy Dwight, and Philip Freneau. Brown in particular expresses "the terror of uncertainty" that resulted from the new distrust of authority during his day. Fearing that in reaction to the epistemological chaos after the Revolution America might become a "sterile society which worshiped only the status quo," Brown and the others remained committed to a common goal: "to bring art into the marketplace and to use literature to reveal the spiritual meaning and human interests in the practical affairs of life."[10]

Elliott draws an important connection between this perception of a need for "spirit" in literature instead of authority and the narrative forms chosen. Indeed, in the poetry and fiction of the postrevolutionary decades one recognizes early signs of the narrative ambiguities that would characterize the works of later American writers. As he notes:

By 1785, serious writers of both political parties felt that the new order of the republic would be one of fragmentation. As Madison argued in *The Federalist* #10, order would spring from a consensus that would emerge from a plurality of opinions. Accordingly, the writers realized that traditional literary forms would have to be replaced by structures that could encompass a society of discord and competing voices. The fitting literary embodiment of this disorder would be a form that was more formless.

Consensus emerging from plurality in political terms finds its analogue in narrative forms that strive for a similar hermeneutical structure. The devices of pseudonyms and personae, for example, "allowed the writer to present personal convictions as though they were really the thoughts of people more socially acceptable to the common readers than to the author himself," and this was important, for the writers would lose their audiences if they presented themselves as inflexible authority figures. Writers of the new republic, like all American writers after them, "were engaged in a task more difficult than they were capable of understanding: the negotiation of an uncharted intellectual and artistic path from a dominant religious vision of America to a new nationalist ideology."[11] This cultural plurality informs their unique failure to close or restrict the narrative structures of their novels.

Richard Poirier takes on many of the directions of Ziff and Elliott and similarly suggests a hermeneutic approach to the American novel. His *A World Elsewhere: The Place of Style in American Literature* explores nineteenth- and twentieth-century problems of knowledge in American literature and culture through the metaphor of American artists building a "world elsewhere," creating through style a freedom they found otherwise difficult to experience. Because the New World offered opportunities—both physical and spiritual—as never before, Emerson's successors build structures of language designed to replace outworn, traditional, closed forms of knowledge. (One immediately thinks of James's and Faulkner's architectural and carpentry metaphors for writing.) American authors try to create their worlds elsewhere, Poirier insists, "even when they are *sure* of failing, as Hawthorne was; they struggle for years in the face of failure, as Mark Twain did with his finest book, and as Melville did with most of his." Evolving "a style meant to liberate [their] heroes from those, like the governess in *The Turn of the Screw*, who would 'fix,' imprison, or 'know' others," the best books in American literature thus displace "many of the reader's assumptions about reality." If the fiction must give the appearance of failure to do this, Poirier insists, then so be it.[12]

Thus in Ziff's, Elliott's, and Poirier's arguments, the American author's turning away from historical "styles" or "social constraints" is done because of a desire to act—that is, American authors enact on a prose level what they are concerned about on a national, social, cultural level. This notion is important to many other critics' ideas about American writers as well. James and Faulkner are excellent subjects for such analysis: "escaping" from society by rejecting its closed, traditional epistemologies, they invoke community between themselves and their readers and thereby redeem the value of the social, much as Thoreau, one of their predecessors in such problems, attempts to do in *Walden*.

Yet how may one claim that James and Faulkner deliberately construct their novels to avoid the "dangerous" knowledge of the single interpretation, the single voice, when this deliberate building of an "open" novel is itself a design? The answer lies in the way James and Faulkner self-consciously address such issues. They are self-conscious about the problem of design as are no other authors, and though their metadesigns are themselves designs, they are not mechanical, systematically closed ones. Such narrative strategies not only grow out of the problems of knowledge in Puritan theology, but they are analogous to and partially result from a more recent problem in American thought, the problem of the machine.

Today we are familiar with protests against the machine as dehumanizing. Modernism has been described as an agonized response protesting the alienation in society caused by the machine. But we just as insistently invoke the positive side of the machine's status in our culture. This version of the machine as liberator aligns itself with democracy, egalitarianism, and the pursuit of the good life. This contradiction gives us literature in the tradition of *Walden*, a pastoral, Transcendental work nevertheless devoted to minute scientific observation and empirical structure. As the tradition of the machine in America alternately praises and damns technology, in literature one identifies the opposed American intellectual traditions of fear of thought-without-action and fear of action-without-thought.

As craftsmen, James and Faulkner are deeply affected by the dual idea of the machine; these master-makers exhibit in their modernism both horror of the hegemony of the machine and delight in its intricate workings. Their narratives, beautiful machines of rational consciousness that they are, nevertheless are structured with indeterminacies and evasions to frustrate the system-building tendency of the works. Modernism both celebrates and warns against the machine, and so do James and Faulkner. They respond to the presence of technology as one might expect humanist authors to do: with indeterminacy as antidote to system. But their ambivalence toward the machine is born of admiration for technique. James and Faulkner are important contributors to a widely documentable and widely consequential debate about knowledge and freedom in the modern technological world.

In *The American Scene* (1907) James's horror of modernity is apparent throughout his return to America after twenty years abroad.[13] The changes that had taken place, particularly in the cities, defined twentieth-century America as a culture of money and power, of industry, modern skyscrapers, and masses of poor immigrant workers. *The American Scene* bears out James's sense of what his life in America would have been had he not left, a theme that sharply defines the late story "The Jolly Corner," in which the ghost of the New York town house appears as a potent figure of American success, terrifying to James's protagonist. According to Leon Edel, *The American Scene* "was written with all the passion of a patriot and all the critical zeal of an intellectual who could not countenance national complacency and indifference" concerning the changes occurring in the country. To James America had belied its past: it now seemed "founded on violence, plunder, loot, commerce; its monuments were built neither for beauty nor for glory, but for obsolescence." America placed "science and technology at the service of the profit motive; and this would lead to the decay of human forms and human values. Older nations had known how to rise above shopkeeping; they had not made a cult of 'business' and of 'success.'" Everywhere James looked he felt that "Americans had interpreted freedom as a license to plunder."[14]

Although James found Concord much the same, when he visited Salem to see Hawthorne's House of the Seven Gables, he was saddened by the house itself, which no one seemed to care about, and by Salem's new machines. Salem's greed and materialism seemed the same as greed and materialism everywhere else. James despaired that there was no longer a viable environment in America for an artist. Peter Buitenhuis notes that after his American trip James "returned to England, convinced once again of the rightness of his original decision to live there, and sure that whatever price he might have paid for this expatriation had been well worth it."[15] That price bought James's unique view of America from abroad. Because it was an American *and* European view, it was freer from the self-interested national design that might, in James's mind, accompany the view of an

American writer in America. James found, Edel believes, that "to be an American is an excellent preparation for culture"; from his own redefined American point of view he could "deal freely with forms of civilization not our own . . . pick and choose and assimilate."[16] This was an attempt to stand inside and outside the new society of industrial America. Yet James's uniquely productive position between two worlds, Old and New, European and American, *was* uniquely a feature of the modern world. The point of view that he found "highly civilised"—he claimed that he wanted to write in such a way as to create ambiguity concerning whether he was an American writing about England or an Englishman writing about America—could not have so easily existed before the age of steamships, telegraphs, and railroads. Edel calls James's point of view a "great balancing of values, moral and material," through which the "great story of the Western world for years to come" would occur, "the New World's rediscovery of the Old, and the Old's discovery of the New."[17]

Like James, Faulkner feared the dominance of modern society by its machinery, what people would do to other people with it. There are many examples of antimodernism in Faulkner's works, perhaps most memorably in "A Rose for Emily," "That Evening Sun," *Pylon*, and *Go Down, Moses*; Dayton Kohler even claims that the center of Faulkner's work is the destruction of the people of the South by a "ruthless and competitive industrial society."[18] Indeed, it seems that Faulkner felt, as Joseph Blotner says, "disgust, loathing, and revulsion as he looked at the present and the projection of the future which followed from it." But he was not romantic about the past: "man was capable of baseness and profligacy then as now, but in his rapacity man was consuming the earth at a phenomenal rate." Yet although Faulkner saw America becoming a vast expanse of "highways and parking spaces for the age of the machine," Blotner emphasizes that he held onto an agrarian dream of small farmers.[19]

Faulkner's Nobel Prize Award Speech, delivered in Stockholm in 1950, is a powerful and widely quoted statement of his fears for the modern world. His sense of the future is both dark and desperately hopeful. If and when there is a nuclear holocaust, Faulkner says, "when the last ding-dong of doom has clanged and faded from the last worthless rock hanging tideless in the last red and dying evening," humankind will still endure and prevail because "even then there will be one more sound," that of our "puny, inexhaustible voice, still talking." It is the artist's privilege to help us endure and prevail by lifting our hearts, by reminding us of the "courage and honor and hope and pride and compassion and pity and sacrifice" that have been the glory of our past.[20] Because Faulkner calls events in modern times a tragedy, he also hints at hope, for tragedy demands an interpretation of life, and this is for him the purpose of art. Art helps us endure and prevail by running counter to the forces in the modern world that would destroy freedom and life itself. Indeed, many of Faulkner's characters—the Dilseys of the world—who do endure and prevail are outwardly defeated or even killed, but redemption speaks through whatever happens to them. As representatives of the human race they prevail over rapacity and "ultimate folly," as Blotner puts it.[21] As speakers, artists are thus endurers and prevailers too; like their heroes and heroines, they sometimes prevail through failure.

But Faulkner's dual attitude toward modernity is present even in a direct attack on machines in *Pylon*: the description of the novel's airport and its inhuman noises occurs in the context of his admiration for pilots and their technical skill. Blotner notes:

> Some of the anger, disgust, and unease that permeated these passages may have come from an unresolved ambivalence. His antimodernism was clear: electric lights were bloodless grapes, automobiles (though he owned several) were popping stinking abominations, and airplanes were "trim vicious fragile" machines, delicate, unnatural, and deadly. At the same time, however, he had been a hero-worshipper since childhood, when his imagination was stirred by the very names of airmen. In his development as an artist and thinker, he had tended to place a higher and higher valuation on the best of the past and harmony with organic nature. At the same time, on a different level, he still admired people like Wedell and Omlie [the pilots]; he wanted to be able to do the things they did. In some of his works he had used ambivalence and ambiguity profitably. Now it was unresolved, and it was probably making the work more difficult.[22]

In both James's and Faulkner's late work, ambivalence toward technology indeed makes "the work more difficult"—and more intriguing—for themselves and for their readers.

One of the strongest analyses of the machine in American literature is Leo Marx's classic *The Machine in the Garden*, which identifies ambivalence toward the machine as a typical reaction of modern American novelists. Marx begins with the famous "Sleepy Hollow" passage (July 23, 1844) from Hawthorne's *Notebooks*, in which the harmony of a natural scene is broken by the screeching wail of an approaching locomotive. This sound marks the shaping of a "metaphoric design," Marx says, which occurs in variants in American writing since the 1840s. Thoreau hears a locomotive in *Walden*;

as Ishmael explores the whale carcass in *Moby-Dick*, he describes it as a New England textile mill; Huck and Jim run into trouble when the steamboat crashes into their peaceful nighttime of rafting on the river. Marx hears the dissonance of the machine in *The Octopus*, *The Education of Henry Adams*, *The Great Gatsby*, *The Grapes of Wrath*, and "The Bear." This dissonance characterizes modern American literature; the question is what a given author will do with it. I think James and Faulkner more than anyone else knew what to do with it: their metafictive negativity allows art to confront the machine by showing through craft how problems arising from technology can be addressed by the artist's voiced human imagination. In American literature, Marx contends, neither the wilderness nor the city is the ideal; rather, there is a symbolic "middle landscape" that is "created by mediation between art and nature," a New World between the far-flung wilderness and the Old World cities. It is a midpoint in a continuum of hideous wilderness, wild garden, cultivated garden, rural life, and city, all metaphors for states of being in America. In works like James's and Faulkner's human beings exist in a moral scheme in which they must accept "a set of contraries." Such a hermeneutics, Marx's analysis suggests, "admits of no absolute solutions, and looks to an endless series of *ad hoc* decisions, compromises, and adjustments in resolving problems." The pastoral design is essentially thus a compromise, for literary works tend to qualify or call into question the "illusion of peace and harmony in a green pasture" while at the same time invoking the freedom of imagination of the green places. Marx calls this American duality a "tragic ambivalence."[23]

Marx's notion of the ambivalence of the middle landscape, Poirier's "world elsewhere," Elliott's analysis of marginalization, and Ziff's treatment of intellectual rebellion, as models for an American literary hermeneutics, all represent widely accepted critical positions in American literary studies. A third theme is a later and more socially oriented approach that addresses the earlier concerns about knowledge but offers a different emphasis for studying James and Faulkner as hermeneutic writers. But I am not speaking here of another theme in itself: I am referring to the recent multitude of challenges made by American critics to the American literary canon. Nineteenth- and twentieth-century American literature by women, for example, has enjoyed unprecedented analysis. In the context of America as an expanding community, feminists, along with minority critics, have offered far-reaching new approaches in American literary criticism. In emphasizing texts as addressed to and by the "other," in arriving at critical practices to reflect the diversity of relationships among writers and readers, and in going beyond traditional, Western, white, male-dominated ways of "knowing" people, many current critical approaches address the cultural emphasis on freedom of interpretation for American identities. The methodologies offered by these approaches should be described as "hermeneutic." As James and Faulkner and other modernist authors developed their complex hermeneutics, so these later approaches similarly direct us to hermeneutic "openings," particularly in redefinitions of what literary community itself *is*. "Canon-reformation" these days is thus perhaps not so much a departure from as a development in traditions of American thought. It might be thought of as an action that follows and fulfills structures worked out in fiction a few generations before.

Developments in feminist and minority criticism and theory are widely discussed and widely available, and so, instead of restating those general facts here, I offer a small community of three contemporary American women scholars who analyze related aspects of American hermeneutics. I intend this to be suggestive of the larger arena of socially oriented hermeneutic criticism in general. Though they do not necessarily dwell on James and Faulkner, their approaches reject epistemologies James and Faulkner also explored and rejected. Carolyn Porter describes in the American literary tradition a process of "reification" of artist and hero that makes their shared position as "observer-participants" so problematic. Anne Norton argues that the national intellectual context itself must be viewed as pluralistic. Finally, Wendy Barker offers a reading of Emily Dickinson's poetry that shows how, through inverted light and dark imagery, Dickinson reverses our usual assumptions about "knowing" people. These critics are concerned with what knowledge is and what sort of society a given form of knowledge arises in and helps create. Despite their differences they display a broad but distinctive intellectual notion of hermeneutic community very similar to James's and Faulkner's.

Porter begins her study of the American hero, *Seeing and Being: The Plight of the Participant Observer in Emerson, James, Adams, and Faulkner*, by explaining that the oft-noted self-contradictory nature of Emerson's view of the transcendental visionary poet versus the neutral scientific observer arises because the seer, like the observer, occupies a place in the world he presumes, godlike, to watch. Emerson's wish " 'to be and see [his] being at the same time' " culminates, Porter finds, in the figure of Thomas Sutpen, who demonstrates the "depth of the reifying process in the American history which his career both reenacts and exposes." Porter departs from the American tradition of freeing the American hero from society as described in "classic" American authors by D. H. Lawrence, R. W. B. Lewis, Richard Chase, and Irving Howe, as well as Poirier. Relying on Georg Lukács's *History and Class Consciousness* as a source for her concept of reification, Porter analyzes James and Faulkner among others as writers who, following Emerson, portray humans alienated from themselves in a process "generated by the developing autonomy of a commodified world of objects which confronts man as a mystery." Distanced from the products he labors to make, the laborer becomes passive in the capitalistic world because his role in manufacturing has become "mystified." Imprisoned, Porter says, in a contemplative stance, heroes find that when the supposedly logical and objectified world suddenly seems to operate irrationally, the psychological contradiction generated becomes insurmountable.[24]

Porter's analysis powerfully conveys how novelists have shown the hero's relation to problems of community, particularly when community is economically stratified. The "classic" American hero as frontier independent could thus be said to adopt a tragic stance not because he *chooses* to seek his freedom outside the boundaries of community but because certain economic epistemologies have forced him to. Sutpen is an excellent example of such an entrapped male, embarking on his design in reaction to designs placed on him. But as we shall find, though Sutpen's and other such heroes' entrapment in individualism is a result of their entrapment by forces within their societies, in presenting stories like Sutpen's, James and Faulkner offer hermeneutic solutions to the problems of epistemology in American identity by presenting a new model of community. And Porter's ideas could be extended to include the makers of books as well as the characters within them; James's and Faulkner's sense of their own "commodification" helped lead them to fictive as well as personal attempts to thwart reifying designs.

Anne Norton, in *Alternative Americas: A Reading of Antebellum Political Culture*, finds that because of its ethnic heterogeneity, America is primarily a setting for contradictory traditions rather than a single epistemology. Norton, a political scientist, argues that the ostensibly dominant Puritan—which she terms "Northern"—tradition is not wholly applicable to many constituencies in America, particularly women, blacks, and Indians. She describes a "Southern" model for a countertradition that challenges the hegemony of New England Puritanism. Created in conflict with another continent, America was an "experiment in the capacities" of human beings rather than representative of a manifest destiny or any setting for the culmination of history. "In this many-voiced claim—to universality, to singularity, to the beginning and the end, to initiation and culmination, to comprehension and incomprehensibility, to unruliness and imperial rule—Americans have spoken themselves into being," she states. The ever-expanding nature of America means that those who would understand the society must comprehend these contradictions: its bipolarities, its government by checks and balances, its two-party system, its dual inheritance of Enlightenment and Reformation, its English versus Indian, Puritan versus Cavalier, white versus black, North versus South, East versus West, man versus woman, are "doubled and redoubled, [creating] a network of meaning through the articulation of difference." Norton allies the South with the feminine, the ambiguous, the heterogenous and characterizes the North as male, epistemological, and hegemonous. She argues that the contradictions raised by southern tradition were undervalued in the past because of the overemphasis on the Puritan tradition from the great scholars who have written about it.[25]

Although I find Norton's application of the labels "closed" North and "open" South problematical, she rightly emphasizes that the "peripheral" in our "dominant cultural, political, economic, and social structures of American nationality" must be reevaluated. Among past critics and historians, she points out, "devaluation of domesticity, and an intolerance for ambiguity" were encouraged, and indeed insisted upon, by the "academic segregation of studies concerning blacks, Indians, women, the working class," and others. She concludes:

> The reevaluation of values that confronted academia, and America, in the sixties began to redress this. In the immediately succeeding years, however, attention to the heretofore-neglected periphery was facilely dismissed as mere fashion. It is not. The recognition of the role of the other in the definition of identity, the role of difference in the articulation of meaning, is essential to an understanding of collective identity.[26]

Besides its obvious applicability to James's and Faulkner's own dualities and ambivalences about America, Norton's dualistic characterization is suggestive for reading their novels because it reexamines the entire notion of "community" in American political and artistic thought. Through fiction such as James's and Faulkner's, one finds, as Norton would expect, that "speaking" oneself "into being" can replace being defined.

Among women writers, the insistence on dualism in place of monism, dialogue instead of monologue, and ambiguity and relativity rather than a single truth often defines the female voice as a hermeneutic one, particularly through imagery. Metaphor, which by its very openness resists closure of meaning, supplies many women writers with image patterns that generate rich ambiguity for narrators and readers. A pronounced use of hermeneutic imagery in American literature is to be found in the poetry of Emily Dickinson, particularly in a specific image pattern: the reversal of our usual assumptions about light and dark imagery. As Wendy Barker argues, in Dickinson's poetry light does not represent that to which the speaker aspires; instead, darkness is the preferred setting for problems of knowledge. In Dickinson, sun and light, identified with male values, are described as the burning rays of a relentless eye of cruel, judgmental knowledge, while darkness and even confinement are settings for these women speakers' healing dialogue with readers. Dickinson suggests that darkness is illuminating to those who flee the barren life of the single eye, the institutional view of knowledge of the self foisted on female speakers and heroines by their cultures.[27] Indeed, "voice" itself comes to be an escape from the polarities of light and dark, of rigid male and female roles. Through her speaker's voice, Dickinson develops a feminist hermeneutics that violates traditional notions of truth. Her words seem fantastic if viewed from within traditional cultural notions of knowledge, for they are direct and indirect social commentaries addressed through the fantastic mode. But Dickinson's speaker is a voice attempting to engage a monologic culture, indicating just how that culture may free itself from restrictive epistemologies through dialogue. Barker's analysis of light and dark conflicts may thus be extended to address voice as a counter to the certainties of many visions. In Dickinson's work as well as James's and Faulkner's, vision often results in closed epistemologies, while voice attempts to ensure freedom as well as community.

The major American critical developments I have briefly addressed are very different, and all their assumptions are not shared, but they indicate a similar direction—toward literature's unique role in engaging the "other" in dialogue rather than in design. The hermeneutics operating in practical criticism and cultural studies is accompanied, not surprisingly, by an emphasis on hermeneutics in contemporary theory, most especially as demonstrated by the current interest in Mikhail Bakhtin. As Rorty furnishes a philosophical context for comparing James and Faulkner, Bakhtin's ideas on the novel supply a theoretical one. Although past critics have read Bakhtin's work mostly in relation to Russian literature and to other theoretical positions, many are finding that his work suggests specific approaches to reading American literature, particularly in its analysis of problems of knowledge in the novel. Bakhtin's definition of the modern "polyphonic," "dialogic" novel made up of a plurality of voices that avoids reduction to a single perspective indicates a concern about the dangers of knowledge on his part that strongly suggests such concerns in the American novel, and his ideas reveal the novel as America's most characteristically hermeneutic genre. Bakhtin most closely addresses moral problems of knowledge in the novel in his *Problems of Dostoevsky's Poetics* and the four essays of *The Dialogic Imagination*.[28]

Bakhtin's description of what he calls the novel's "carnivalized" quality closely fits James and Faulkner. Bakhtin argues that Fyodor Dostoevsky, for example, writes out of a rich and complex tradition of seriocomic, dialogic, satiric literature that may be traced through Socratic dialogue and Menippian satire, Apuleius, Boccaccio, Rabelais, Shakespeare, and Cervantes. In the modern world this carnivalized antitradition appears most significantly in the novel. Just as the public ritual of carnival inverts values so as to question them, so may the novel call into question assumptions about closed meanings. Bakhtin claims that the novel carnivalizes through diversities of speech and voice reflected in structure. As Michael Holquist points out, rather than seeing the novel as a genre alongside others, such as epic, ode, or lyric, for Bakhtin it is a "supergenre" that has always been present in Western culture, always breaking traditional assumptions about form. Holquist explains that " 'novel' is the name Bakhtin gives to whatever force is at work within a given literary system to reveal the limits, the artificial constraints of that system. Literary systems are comprised of canons, and 'novelization' is fundamentally anticanonical." The novel, Bakhtin argues in "Epic and Novel," is "the only developing genre."[29]

Although the novel has existed since ancient times, its full potential was not developed until after the Renaissance. A major factor was the development of a sense of linear time, past, present, and especially future, moving away from the cyclical time of ancient epochs. Whereas the epic lives in cyclical time, the novel, especially today in an ever more complex and ever more "modern" world, is oriented to contemporary reality. "From the very beginning, then," says Bakhtin, "the novel was structured . . . in the zone of direct contact with inconclusive present-day reality. At its core lay personal experience and free creative imagination." In its contemporaneity, the novel is "made of different clay [from] the other already completed genres," and "with it and in it is born the future of all literature." Bakhtin adds that the novel may absorb any other genre into itself and still remain a novel, and that no other genre can do so. It is "ever-questing, ever examining itself and subjecting its established forms to review."[30]

Bakhtin's best-known idea is what he calls "dialogicity," and this notion moves past genre to describe language. According to Bakhtin, the person is always the *subject of an address*. One cannot talk about him; one can only address oneself to him." One cannot understand another person as an object of neutral analysis or "master him through a merging with him, through empathy with him." The solution, dialogue, "is not the threshold to action, it is the action itself." Indeed, "to be means to communicate dialogically. When dialogue ends, everything ends." Bakhtin's principles of dialogue of the hero are by no means limited to actual dialogue in novels; they refer to a novelist's entire undertaking. Yet in a polyphonic novel, dialogues are unusually powerful. In such dialogues, as in Quentin's and Shreve's in *Absalom, Absalom!* "the replies of the one touch and even partially coincide with the replies of the other's interior dialogue." A deep bond of words is formed by one hero with the "internal and secret discourse of another hero."[31]

James's and Faulkner's novels carry out Bakhtin's principles of the freedom of the hero, special placement of the idea in the polyphonic design, and the principles of linkage that shape the novel into a whole—including multiple voices, ambiguity, multiple genres, stylization, parody, the use of negatives, and the function of the "double address" of the word both to another word and to another speaker of words. His discussion of Dostoevsky's work in particular time and time again suggests James's and Faulkner's. Bakhtin describes how Dostoevsky builds indeterminacies into his polyphonic design, introduces multiple voices, renders ideas intersubjective, and leaves his novels "unfinished"—all to leave his characters "free." As in James's and Faulkner's novels, this offers no help to the reader who would "objectify an entire event according to some ordinary monologic category."[32] Faulkner uses multiple voices as subject, purpose, and structure in the "story-telling" of *Absalom, Absalom!* and *Go Down, Moses* to achieve a dialogic polyphony that makes statements about the authority and responsibility of author, narrator, and reader. Bakhtin's work addresses James's narrative ambiguity, unfinishedness, and openness—his amazing negative passages in *The Ambassadors* and *The Golden Bowl*—by suggesting how and why an author should want to ask so strongly and so often for the reader's interpretation of the story.

Most important for a comparison with James and Faulkner, Bakhtin describes how the novelist may voice a moral concern through narrative technique, particularly the power of knowledge to enact a design on that which is known. As Bakhtin argues, to think about other people "means to *talk with them; otherwise they immediately turn to us their objectivized side*: they fall silent, close up and congeal into finished, objectivized images." For this reason, the author of the polyphonic novel does not renounce his own consciousness but "to an extraordinary extent broaden[s], deepen[s] and rearrange[s] this consciousness . . . in order to accommodate the con-sciousnesses of others," and he does not turn other consciousnesses, whether character or reader, into objects of a single vision.[33] As Bakhtin asks in "Author and Hero in Aesthetic Activity," an early essay, "What would I have to gain if another were to *fuse* with me? He would see and know only what I already see and know, he would only repeat in himself the inescapable closed circle of my own life; let him rather remain outside me."[34]

By allowing characters their free speech, then, James or Faulkner may thus ensure that he himself does not perpetrate a narrowing design using his knowledge of the characters, a design that would violate them by restricting their freedom. To do this the author must create a "design for discourse" that allows the reader to interpret the characters' actions and words without the direct intervention of the author. Such "dialogic opposi-tion" means that the greatest challenge for an author, "to create out of heterogeneous and profoundly disparate materials of varying worth a uni-fied and integral artistic creation," cannot be realized by using a single "philosophical design" as the basis of artistic unity, just as musical po-lyphony cannot be reduced to a single accent. For Bakhtin polyphony thus gives characters some of the attributes of the author: in a polyphonic novel the hero's discourse lies on a "single plane" with the author's discourse, with no epistemological difference between them. Contrasting this po-lyphony with novels in which the hero is the "voiceless object" of the "ideologue" author's "deduction," Bakhtin describes such intrusive narra-tors as those of many nineteenth-century British novelists, who reassure readers at suspenseful moments not to fear, that "our hero" will survive the current trying event. In the polyphonic novel, "there are only . . . voice-viewpoints." Through characterization, Dostoevsky structurally drama-tizes "internal contradictions and internal stages in the development of a single person," allowing his characters "to converse with their own dou-bles, with the devil, with their alter egos, with caricatures of themselves."[35] This helps explain the presence of paired characters in Dostoevsky's work, and it suggests a reason for their presence in James's and Faulkner's work as well. James's constant call to "dramatize, dramatize" takes on new meaning when viewed in light of Bakhtin's notion of drama as juxtaposition of diverse and unsynthesized elements of character. And dialogicity in characterization leads to particular structures. A polyphonic novel seeks to "*juxtapose* and *counterpose* [forms] dramatically," to "*guess at their interrelationships in the cross-section of a single moment*." Not "evolution" but "*coexistence* and *interaction*" characterize such structures, as in *The Golden Bowl* and *Go Down, Moses*, broken into parts left unbridged.[36]

In remarking on the freedom and independence of Dostoevsky's characters and structures, Bakhtin sounds strikingly similar to James as a young book reviewer, who noted that an artist's concern should always be with a reader who must be introduced to an atmosphere "in which it was credible that human beings might exist, and to human beings with whom he might feel tempted to claim kinship." To do this the artist does not "describe" but "conveys," James wrote. Once a character is launched, his creator must not, as Edel puts it, "finger his puppets as a child besmudges a doll, he must endow them with their individuality and with life."[37] Faulkner, as is well known, had a habit of referring in interviews and speeches to his characters as if they were real people; he said he had known them for a long time, had watched them grow older, and had no idea what they might do next. The design of such authors as James and Faulkner is thus a design-as-antidesign. They show an extraordinary self-consciousness about their roles as designers and about the moral obligations that position calls for in their relationships with characters and readers, with the "others" in their own lives as well as those of their characters. Bakhtin's ideas of how such authors regard their characters always suggest a similar regard for readers, and this multivalent concern with design—occurring as it does for characters, narrator, author, and reader—constitutes the most telling connection between Bakhtin's theories and James's and Faulkner's work. The most characteristic aspect of these authors' handling of the moral question of freedom is precisely that the freedom is, paradoxically, a result *not* of an individualistic, unconditioned "freedom of the self," but rather *membership* in a dialogic and thus free community.

James's and Faulkner's polyphonic novels are in large part written in response to the same closures of nineteenth-century novels Bakhtin describes. Obviously, the particular development of characterization and structure they have in common with Dostoevsky exists within a shared hermeneutic tradition—a community—of the modern novel in which polyphony of various sorts is used to achieve a certain interpretive freedom for readers. In the development of genre, then, as well as national tradition, James and Faulkner address similar problems of knowledge in very similar ways. It seems to me that their work argues for the late nineteenth- and early twentieth-century American novel as the most developed and developing hermeneutic novel, and I would go so far as to say that, despite their distance from Bakhtin in cultural terms, their work represents the most powerful and complex workings out of his theory of the modern novel after that of his great study, Dostoevsky.[38] Bakhtin's ideas are very useful in interpreting American novels, and the problem of knowledge is the place to start.[39]

More than ever today in our communities plurality is replacing hegemony, no matter what the subject at hand.[40] Specific analysis of James's and Faulkner's extreme preoccupation with the necessity of dialogue with the "other" will help dialogize these larger cultural developments, and vice versa. James, Faulkner, and the new "voice-viewpoints" invoke the very idea of "community." *American Designs* shares with Bakhtinian, feminist, and cultural/historicist approaches the call for dialogue instead of monologue. I shall dwell to a considerable extent on how James's female *ficelles* direct readers of *The Ambassadors* and *The Golden Bowl* toward hermeneutics and how Faulkner's black and women characters dialogically enact his most characteristic moral principles in their struggles for freedom from the epistemologies of a white male culture. Like Melville's Queequeg and Twain's Jim, these characters and others like them continue to redefine American community. The hermeneutic characters, narrators, and overall structures were always James's and Faulkner's models for knowledge, but they never existed apart from their community of contexts.

2. Knowledge as Interest and Design

AS FAR AS ONE CAN TELL, neither Henry James nor William Faulkner ever used the terms "epistemology" or "hermeneutics," and one is somehow grateful that they did not. They do, however, use two key words over and over again to describe problems of knowledge, especially the moral problem of knowing people: "interest" in James and "design" in Faulkner. Though James frequently uses both words and Faulkner dwells more on "design," both authors characteristically express their preference for hermeneutics over epistemology in their narrative structures through what may be described as a dialogue of interest with design. We thus move out of the broad realm of the contexts for knowledge in James's and Faulkner's work suggested in chapter 1 to a specificity located at the level of the individual word. Interest and design generate a broad discussion of the problems of knowledge in James's and Faulkner's careers.

In his *Keywords: A Vocabulary of Culture and Society*, Raymond Williams annotates what he considers to be the most important words for understanding Western culture. Among those words, "interest" receives extremely detailed attention. "Interest," Williams says, is a "significant example of a word with specialized legal and economic senses which, within a particular social and economic history, has been extended to a very general meaning." The root word in Latin, *interesse*, meant to be between, to make a difference, or to have concern, but in Latin and Old French it later developed other meanings ranging from a compensation for loss to a transitive use for investment with a right or share. Most uses of "interest" after this "referred to an objective or legal share of something, and the extended use, to refer to a natural share or common concern, was at first usually a conscious metaphor: 'Ah so much interest have [I] in thy sorrow / As I had Title in thy Noble Husband' [*Richard III*]." The "now predominant sense of general curiosity or attention, or having the power to attract curiosity and attention" began only in the nineteenth century. We now use "interest" as "concern" in two senses: we feel concern for someone; we also speak of a business concern or company. Because of the mingling of economic and "humane" sets of definitions for "interest," the objective sense of the word derived from the formal and legal uses "is not always easy to distinguish from the later more subjective and voluntary senses." The distinction is formalized only in the word's negatives, "disinterested" or impartial and "uninterested" or uninvolved. Throughout *Keywords* Williams concentrates on this phenomenon of economic, legal, or political words taking on usages in personal, behavioral contexts; in regard to "interest," he emphasizes that "it remains significant that our most general word for attraction or involvement should have developed from a formal objective term in property and finance." "Interest" thus means power in two quite contradictory ways and demonstrates how a term for human relations can become "saturated with the experience of a society based on money relationships."[1] Over and over again in the late novels of Henry James the word "interest" demonstrates these tensions of meaning, economic and personal. Indeed, the paired interests of love and money, both expressed in terms of power, are the most characteristic Jamesian subjects.

Just as the original economic sense of "interest" developed another meaning referring to human relations, so "design" is a term borrowed from the arts by persons who speak of a "designing woman" or someone with "designs" on someone or something. In James and Faulkner, but particularly in Faulkner, the word "design" is used in such a way as to invoke both its meanings simultaneously. As "interest" occurs in James's work with what Bakhtin would call a "sideways meaning," so "design" in Faulkner's work relates both to the actions of the characters as they affect each other—that is, the characters' "designs"—and the action of the author on the characters and readers, the "design" of his work of art.

According to the *Oxford English Dictionary*, "design" occurs in sixteenth-century English and French as " 'designe, purpose, project, priuat intention or determination' (Cotgr.)," as well as the other meaning, more like that of the sixteenth-century Italian word "designo," " 'purpose, designe, draught; model, plot, picture, ponrtrait' (Florio)." The artistic sense of "design" was taken into French and "gradually differentiated in spelling, so that in mod. F. *dessein* is 'purpose, plan,' *dessin* 'design in art.' Eng. on the contrary uses *design*, conformed to the verb, in both senses." The *Dictionary* lists examples and derivations for these two basic meanings: (1) "A mental plan," and (2) "A plan in art."[2] These are the two senses of design that James and Faulkner evoke meaningfully in their fictions. Paired with "interest," "design" powerfully describes characters' relations with each other and with readers as well.

In James's work, the meaning of interest generally involves a character who is said to be "interested" in someone else's "case," as Kate Croy and Merton Densher of *The Wings of the Dove* are interested in Milly Theale's case, or as Mrs. Newsome of *The Ambassadors* is interested in Chad Newsome's and Lambert Strether's cases. Interest usually leads to tampering with someone's freedom. Characters judge others abstractly. They objectify personalities into figures; they use others for selfish aims. As Edel writes, "Henry James tells us that in our world there are persons who show no respect for the sanctity of the individual, who freely meddle in the lives of other individuals, who are blind to the tender vessels of feeling that are children and adolescents, and who use them cruelly as pawns in the clumsy game of their own muddled lives."[3] This is the "interest" of which Baglioni in Hawthorne's "Rappaccini's Daughter" warns Giovanni:

> "[Rappaccini] *has* seen you! he must have seen you!" said Baglioni, hastily, "For some purpose or other, this man of science is making a study of you. I know that look of his! It is the same that coldly illuminates his face as he bends over a bird, a mouse, or a butterfly; which, in pursuance of some experiment, he has killed by the perfume of a flower; a look as deep as Nature itself, but without Nature's warmth of love. Signor Giovanni, I will stake my life upon it, you are the subject of one of Rappaccini's experiments! . . . I tell thee, my poor Giovanni, that Rappaccini has a scientific interest in thee. Thou hast fallen into fearful hands!"[4]

But interest, of course, also has its positive aspects; James writes in "The Art of Fiction," an essay that argues for characters' freedom of expression as a key artistic value in the development of the novel, that "the only obligation to which in advance we may hold a novel, without incurring the accusation of being arbitrary, is that it be interesting."[5]

For most characters in James and Faulkner, interest simply *causes* design. Faulkner's sinners habitually carry out what he calls "designs" on other people: the great design of slavery that damned the South; Thomas Sutpen's grand design on the land, on his family, and on Miss Rosa Coldfield; Quentin Compson's designs on Caddy; the evolving economic design of Flem Snopes and his kinsmen on Yoknapatawpha County; and the genealogical design of L. Q. C. McCaslin on his descendants. It may be that some of Faulkner's "designers"—people whose self-interest has become their sole motivation—are innocent of the effects of their designs and especially innocent of the dangerous nature of design. As Sutpen explains to General Compson: " 'You see, I had a design in my mind. Whether it was a good or a bad design is beside the point: the question is, Where did I make the mistake in it?' " General Compson calls Sutpen's statement evidence of a perverse innocence "which believed that the ingredients of morality were like the ingredients of pie or cake and once you had measured them and balanced them and mixed them and put them into the oven it was all finished and nothing but pie or cake could come out."[6] Whether through a blind innocence of the moral laws that control the actions of everyone else in their societies or out of conscious evil, Faulkner's most morally reprehensible characters commit the sin of destroying individual freedom by forcing their knowledge of others onto them in the form of designs. Only through achieving a certain "disinterest" do James's and Faulkner's characters rise above selfish design.

The relationship of interest and design is a well-documented pattern in literature and of course is not limited to American writers, though it finds its fullest expression among them. The goal for James and Faulkner and for their characters, narrators, and readers is not to renounce all interests and designs, for that would be to cease to live, but to arrive at a particular sort of moral "disinterest." This disinterest does not mean withdrawal from involvement with one's community. The modern eagerness to avoid conflating "disinterested" and "uninterested" has obscured "disinterest": rescuing "disinterested" from use as a careless synonym for "uninterested" makes it mean "impartial" or "detached." This is incorrect. As David Bromwich has pointed out, disinterested persons have no vested interest in what they undertake to judge; their thoughts "will not be swayed by prejudice, by tormenting fears or habitual associations." Yet such persons *will* have been personally involved, have been intellectually and emotionally engaged. A biographer, for example, may feel reservations about the subject "so strong that he wishes he had written about something else instead," but he may still be disinterested. "But if *disinterested* is taken to mean 'neutral,' it follows that ten disinterested biographers" should arrive at the same opinion of their subject. This idea "is a fair account neither of why we read books and think about lives, nor of how our knowledge advances," Bromwich notes.[7] In James's and Faulkner's works, "disinterest" simultaneously invokes the double meanings of "interest" and "design" and thus metafictively dialogizes the closed designs of money and power. On their part readers combine an "interest" in something—a passionate response to art—with a "disinterest"—a personally unbiased view—for a truly critical apprehension of art, responding to the interpretive openings in the texts.[8]

Thus as Hawthorne in his Preface to *The Blithedale Romance* and James in his Prefaces suggest, the problem of interest and design is a complex authorial issue. Hawthorne, James, and Faulkner ask, In what sense does the author, through his narrator, control the destinies of his characters? The negative connotations of interest and design suggest the enacting of interested designs on other people; the positive meanings indicate the creation of poetic design that through disinterest redeems design. Obviously the issue of knowledge in James and Faulkner is at work in several areas; it begins with the obsession of the characters in these authors' novels with knowledge, but, as one soon realizes, the process of knowing as interest and design occurs in the narrator's relation to the story, the author's relation, and the reader's relation to all. It expands to address relationships among readers—including readers as critics and teachers. In each case, interest, a powerful force of vision and imagination, can be engaged in a dialogue with design. Singleness of vision on any level is inadequate and possibly dangerous. What is needed is a collaborative knowledge, a community of voices—a hermeneutics in which dialogue occurs in a disinterested way.

The disinterest in James's and Faulkner's work is like that hinted at in *Roderick Hudson*: "How become involved in life—an remain uninvolved?" Each man devised personal as well as fictive strategies: James's European and thus for him disinterested point of view on America, for example, is comparable to Faulkner's dualistic status as a southern and American writer. In their development of narrative disinterest both writers seem to have been inspired by the work of James's father, Henry James, Sr. James, Sr.'s, "continual self-questioning and . . . unfinished search for complete inner harmony," as Edel puts it, accord with similar features of his novelist-son's work, and the influence is both intellectual and personal. Edel conjectures that James's life, personal and artistic, was "a long search to understand this perversely ambiguous world of his childhood."[9] Quentin Anderson addresses James, Sr.'s, influence, especially as it appears in *The Sacred Fount, The Ambassadors, The Wings of the Dove,* and *The Golden Bowl,* attempting "to place James as a moralist, a moralist of a particular sort, who emerged from a particular scene." Influenced by his father, James believed that "literature was the vessel and the exponent of the noblest qualities of life, of the qualities we seldom bluntly name, of courage, of justice, of charity, of personal honor, of that without which these things stagnate, the generous imagination." James was assured by his father that through literature he could "connect his general moral intention with other men's commonplaces."[10] How like Faulkner this sounds, both the notion of the self as a vessel for morality, and the listing of these values Faulkner called "the verities of the heart."

Henry James, Sr.'s, influence on William James was somewhat different—perhaps more scientific. But although William complained to his brother about the difficulty of interpreting the language in such novels as *The Golden Bowl*,[11] particularly his method of narration by seemingly endless elaboration of reference[12]—charges to which Henry promptly responded[13]—in William's philosophy of pragmatism there are also strong analogies to Henry's hermeneutics as expressed through interest and design, particularly the search for disinterest. The case for William's influence on Henry is well known and widely available; indeed, the idea popularized by Edel in his biography that they were personal enemies is balanced by study of their intellectual connections. What is less obvious is that Faulkner's connections to James, Sr., come through the direct influence of William, who was also important to modern American writers Nathanael West, Robert Penn Warren, Robert Frost, and Hart Crane. As Victor Strandberg notes, he appealed to the American artist "as a pragmatist, a pluralist, and an advocate of the varieties of experience," sharing "the general affinity of the American artist for immediate experience in preference to any doctrinaire ideology by which experience may be interpreted"—in a word, disinterest.[14] The appropriateness of Rorty's philosophical arguments for reading James and Faulkner, based as they are in American pragmatism, is heightened by awareness of the influences on these writers by James, Sr., and William James. These influences occur within an American tradition of questions about epistemology.

Yet in regard to problems of knowledge as interest and design, the most important shared influence on James and Faulkner is Nathaniel Hawthorne. Because before 1800 most major American thinkers approached the problem of knowledge, like other human problems in early America, as a theological issue, later, the theological question How do I know God? broadens to How do I know myself and other people? and becomes central in Hawthorne's work. Hawthorne's fictions, though saturated with the vocabulary of theology, engage questions of knowing, of certitude, and of design as secular, psychological issues. Like the theologians, Hawthorne is concerned about the limits of knowledge and the dangers involved in crossing those limits. He is the first American novelist to make the hermeneutics of narrative a constant concern.

One of the most intriguing connections among Hawthorne's, James's, and Faulkner's complex versions of America is how their similar reactions to the Civil War suggest important reasons for much of their chosen fictive ambiguity. James tells us in his critical book *Hawthorne* that when his generation saw their "best of all possible republics given over to fratricidal carnage," all their illusions were dispelled because the "affair had no place in their scheme." The "convulsion" of the war "left a different tone from the tone it had found, and one may say that the Civil War marks an era in the history of the American mind. It introduced into the national consciousness a certain sense of proportion and relation, of the world being a more complicated place than it had hitherto seemed, the future more treacherous, success more difficult." The times demanded a new sense of critical awareness, of qualification, a sense of doubt, a willingness to tolerate uncertainty; the times demanded artists like Hawthorne, James, and Faulkner, who explore knowledge with the disinterest that fits a modern view of the world. James's passage continues:

> At the rate at which things are going, it is obvious that good Americans will be more numerous than ever; but the good American, in days to come, will be a more critical person than his complacent and confident grandfather. He has eaten of the tree of knowledge. . . . He will remember that the ways of the Lord are inscrutable, and that his is a world in which everything happens; and eventualities, as the late Emperor of the French used to say, will not find him intellectually unprepared.

James turns to Hawthorne's bitter disappointment at the Civil War, which in part explained his refusal to give positive support to the Union. Hawthorne even wrote an article for the July 1862 *Atlantic Monthly* trying to imagine how Southerners felt with an invading Northern army in their towns, to which the editors added a qualification deprecating his views. James concludes that Hawthorne's dualistic position is "interesting as an example of the way an imaginative man judges current events—trying to see the other side as well as his own, to feel what his adversary feels, and present his view of the case."[15]

The relevance of the Civil War to Faulkner's work requires little emphasis. Like James, Faulkner saw the war as a turning point in American life, an apocalypse that introduced the modern age to America. His work allows for redemption after suffering and suggests that the war was a necessary purgative, a chance to make a better future. For Faulkner, slavery was America's colossal cultural failure to distinguish right from wrong, its original sin, and yet it was a fall that could enable people to relearn "truths of the heart." As it did for Hawthorne and James, the war caused Faulkner to assess critically his role as an artist in society.

Many connections between Hawthorne and James are well documented in criticism.[16] James responded among other things to Hawthorne's struggles with the romance mode and with the restrictions of allegory.[17] Hawthorne's influence tends to make authors question their authority, particularly in his portraits of heroes torn by epistemological doubt and in his narrative structures. Hawthorne's Dimmesdale, Coverdale, and Kenyon are ancestors of James's characteristically troubled young heroes attempting to make difficult choices concerning relationships with others in the community.[18] Some characters are better able to accept these difficulties in James's and Faulkner's work; such a character is Maggie Verver of *The Golden Bowl*, whose imagination eventually approaches the author's own breadth of understanding.

Hawthorne's careful juxtaposition of the narrator's point of view with those of the other characters allows him to dramatize the dangers of knowledge. His figures of the modern scientist, usually depicted as a cold, reductionistic manipulator of other people, as in the case of the designing characters Chillingworth of *The Scarlet Letter* and Aylmer of "The Birthmark," are challenged by the fictional format in which they appear, for as in James's and Faulkner's work, these characters' reductive knowledge is opposed by the knowledge displayed by their narrators.[19] Hawthorne evolved such a narrator out of concerns such as those he expresses in the Preface to *The Blithedale Romance* about the author's responsibility to his characters, particularly the danger that the author will design on them in the closed, systematic way in which these characters design. He worries that the "category" his "beings of the imagination" inhabit will on one hand be too close to that of "actually living mortals" and on the other hand will appear too "fictitious," rendering the "paint and pasteboard of their composition" too "painfully discernible."[20] One wonders how much Hawthorne's prefaces may have inspired James's famous discussions of the role of the artist; in any case, by putting himself in his reader's place, Hawthorne foregrounds his uncertainties about his authority as author and predicts James's.[21]

Malcolm Cowley claims that of all classic American authors Faulkner most resembles Hawthorne. Terence Martin extends the comparison, referring in particular to Hawthorne's exploration of the meaning of an ancestral past, his sense of community, his concern over the danger of abstraction, and his treatment of the artist and society. These constitute an important legacy for Faulkner, in whose work, as in Hawthorne's, the estrangement from community actually invokes the value of community.[22] The issue of the artist's position in society and the metafictive response to that concern in fiction intrigued James in his reading of Hawthorne, and Faulkner too seems most influenced by Hawthorne in his own exploration of the artist's communal role. When James comments on Hawthorne's *House of the Seven Gables*, he might as well have been speaking of Faulkner:

> What Hawthorne designed to represent was not the struggle between an old society and a new, for in this case he would have given the old one a better chance; but simply, as I have said, the shrinkage and extinction of a family. This appealed to his imagination; and the idea of long perpetuation and survival always appears to have filled him with a kind of horror and disapproval. Conservative, in a certain degree, as he was himself, and fond of retrospect and quietude and the mellowing influences of time, it is singular how often one encounters in his writings some expression of mistrust of old houses, old institutions, long lines of descent.

And yet Hawthorne had a "lurking esteem for things that show the marks of having lasted." In this duality he is "an American of Americans," James says,[23] pointing to the artist's role, whether his or Hawthorne's, or Faulkner's, of remaking society, of reinventing "community." Because in Hawthorne's day—the very early to mid-nineteenth-century America in which Faulkner often sets his stories—writers faced unusual demands to achieve a certain complex knowledge of America and of their roles in it, art seemed to inhabit an uncertain moral territory. Yet its ambiguous status made possible a revision of the way moral values were to be expressed in what would become modern literature. This ambivalence toward the past and present further contextualizes the seemingly antagonistic cultural viewpoints that sustain the tension of Hawthorne's and Faulkner's stories and novels[24] and points as well to the authors' own questioning of their roles as artists both in and out of community.[25]

A striking allusion to Hawthorne occurs in James's restaging of *The Marble Faun*'s Colosseum scene in his "Daisy Miller," and there are other examples scattered throughout James's fiction. Faulkner alludes directly to Hawthorne in his poems and novels. In *As I Lay Dying*, for example, there is the play on names with characters from *The Scarlet Letter*: Jewel suggests Pearl, the Rev. Mr. Whitfield the Rev. Mr. Dimmesdale (white field, dim dale). But what became Hawthorne's legacy to both James and Faulkner moves well beyond allusion, and it is most evident in *The House of the Seven Gables*. This "failed" novel reveals through its awkwardnesses Hawthorne's attempt to handle questions of knowledge in fiction that would be much more effectively addressed by James and Faulkner. Like Herman Melville,

Hawthorne was writing at the time of Transcendentalism, Jacksonian democracy, massive economic and industrial expansion—and, like his friend, he wrote against the grain of all this positivism. As Melville memorably puts it in his review of Hawthorne's *Mosses on an Old Manse*, he and Hawthorne seek to "say NO in thunder" to counter the current YES-saying of their day.[26]

Obsessed with the effect of the past on the present and doubtful of the New World Dream, Hawthorne dramatically displays his ambiguous attitude toward his role as an artist in *The House of the Seven Gables* in its confusing happy ending: a book full of dark complexities is suddenly resolved by a sentimentally easy ending, supposedly suggested by the author's wife, Sophia, who was tired of reading depressing books like *The Scarlet Letter*. The ending metafictively calls attention to the same problems of authorship that James and Faulkner so powerfully address in their prefaces, interviews, and fiction, but Hawthorne's ending is much different from those James and Faulkner evolve, for Hawthorne's attempt at simultaneous resolution and interpretive freedom for the reader does not work. Under cover of a traditional ending, Hawthorne casts many strange doubts: Is the curse of the Maules really over? Can the characters be happy living in the late Judge's mansion? Does good fortune change the fact that Clifford does not love his adoring sister Hepzibah? But the main doubt the conclusion raises concerns Holgrave's sudden and complete reversal of values. He who said he would tear down all the houses every twenty years, who said inheritance was the root of evil, who roamed around the world for all these years—would he settle down forever into cozy domesticity with Phoebe? Awkward as they are, these puzzling doubts leave the way open for the reader to approach the text actively and critically. The conflicted ending fits these characters' tendency to see each other as various "versions" of identity; that is, Phoebe is a very different person to Clifford from who she is to Hepzibah, or, better, Clifford is described very differently by Phoebe and Hepzibah. Despite the awkwardness, through presenting these multiple versions, Hawthorne's narrator urges readers to take responsibility for interpretation, to "remake" the text by undermining or qualifying their sources and conclusions.[27]

James addresses Hawthorne most directly in *Hawthorne*, his first book and the first critical book about an American author published in Great Britain.[28] As Faulkner's cycle of poems, *The Marble Faun*, is an early tribute to a literary predecessor, James's study is an immediate indication of the significance of Hawthorne for James. Indeed, *Hawthorne* is not a book about Hawthorne only but one in which James expresses certain things about himself: for the most part, he indicates that he, unlike Hawthorne, has transcended America's provinciality. James's condescending tone and emphasis on the poverty of Hawthorne's cultural environment are in part an attempt to justify the path James chose to follow. The tentative, personal aspect of this book reveals in its contradictions James's difficulty in understanding his own newly developing position as a writer. For example, James clearly values Europe for its contributions to the development of the American artist but also finds that Hawthorne's virtues as a writer in *The Scarlet Letter* and *The House of the Seven Gables* reside in great part in the novels' local quality, their "New England air." James calls Hawthorne's work "charming," "soft," "natural," and "childlike," but he is strongly aware of "troubling depths," of Hawthorne's "haunting care for moral problems" and for "the deeper psychology."[29]

Indeed, throughout *Hawthorne* James turns to Hawthorne's ambiguity, and he is often ambiguous himself. Such contradictions disclose the importance of a hermeneutical version of knowledge for each author. According to James, Hawthorne "was not a man with a literary theory; he was guiltless of a system." Furthermore, Hawthorne has "none of the apparatus of an historian, and his shadowy style of portraiture never suggests a rigid standard of accuracy." Nevertheless, James recognizes, "he virtually offers the most vivid reflection of New England life that has found its way into literature." James particularly admires Hawthorne's avoidance of cliché and cant in his portraits of Americans. For the most part, Hawthorne, unlike many of his predecessors and contemporaries, disdains colloquial American dialects. His characters "are not portraits of actual types, and in their phraseology there is nothing imitative. But none the less, Hawthorne's work savours thoroughly of the local soil—it is redolent of the social system in which he had his being."[30] The comparison with James himself is obvious. Hawthorne seeks in his own "realism" to avoid designing reductively on his characters; nevertheless, they are "redolent" of a particular community. Hawthorne and James were both writing about an American community that was and is in the process of being defined, and their techniques reflect this experimentation.[31]

James describes Hawthorne as "silent, diffident, more inclined to hesitate—to watch, and wait, and meditate—than to produce himself, and fonder, on almost any occasion, of being absent more than of being present." This quality appears in all his writings, but particularly for James in his *Diaries* and *Notebooks*:

that delicate and penetrating imagination which was always at play, always entertaining itself, always engaged in a game of hide-and-seek in the region in which it seemed to him that the game could best be played—among the shadows and substructions, the dark-based pillars and supports of our moral nature. Beneath this movement and ripple of his imagination—as free and spontaneous as that of the sea-surface—lay directly his personal affections. These were solid and strong, but, according to my impression, they had the place very much to themselves. [32]

James undoubtedly felt a strong sense of kinship between his imagination and Hawthorne's, for here he seems to believe he has the ability to penetrate Hawthorne's mind and heart, and he could not but be aware of his own developing imagination—"delicate and penetrating" as well as isolated—as he described Hawthorne's.

James sympathetically points out that Hawthorne was poor and solitary, and he "undertook to devote himself to literature in a community in which the interest in literature was as yet of the smallest." Even in his own time, James asserts, it is "a considerable discomfort in the United States not to be 'in business.'" A young person who launches himself or herself in a career not belonging to "the so-called practical order" has "but a limited place in the social system, finds no particular bough to perch on." But rather than being regarded as an idler, the artist or author also sometimes receives exaggerated homage, for in America the arts and their practitioners are held in "extreme honour." But this indiscriminate attention does not encourage good writing, for celebrityhood, as Hawthorne's and James's literary descendants would discover, is isolating rather than communal:

> The best things come, as a general thing, from the talents that are members of a group; every man works better when he has companions working in the same line, and yielding the stimulus of suggestion, comparison, emulation. Great things, of course, have been done by solitary workers; but they have usually been done with double the pains they would have cost if they had been produced in more genial circumstances. The solitary worker loses the profit of example and discussion.[33]

In assuming the need for a literary community and in sympathizing with Hawthorne's lack of one, James invokes a literary community between them as he seeks his own place in the world of literature.[34]

In *The Ambassadors* the dual portrait of the artist Hawthorne in Lambert Strether and in his friend Waymarsh furnishes the reader of James with an important example of problems of authority. Hawthorne's tenure as a diplomat in Great Britain was of great interest to James. When the new consul came to Europe, first to England and then to Italy after his diplomatic term expired, the tone of his *Diaries*, according to James, is "often so fresh and unsophisticated" that the reader thinks of Hawthorne as a young man; but something of the "reflective" and "melancholy" element reminds us that the simplicity of his work is not the simplicity of youth but of inexperience. Hawthorne seems provincial in Europe, but James responds with understanding: "I know nothing more remarkable, more touching, than the sight of this odd, youthful-elderly mind, contending so late in the day with new opportunities for learning old things, and, on the whole, profiting by them so freely and gracefully." Through Waymarsh/ Hawthorne, James seems to fault Hawthorne when his work occasionally succumbs to "his constant mistrust and suspicion of the society that surrounded him, his exaggerated, painful, morbid national consciousness." Americans such as Strether and Waymarsh, placed "on the circumference of the circle of civilisation rather than at the centre," develop, whether they like it or not, a "sense of relativity" in place of the "quiet and comfortable sense of the absolute, as regards its own position in the world, which reigns supreme in the British and in the Gallic genius."[35] It is this "sense of relativity" that allows James to think as he does about America and the rest of the world. And he owes that sense, in large part, to Hawthorne.

When the young Faulkner had completed his first book, *The Marble Faun* (1924), his future father-in-law was considerably taken aback by his use of Hawthorne's title. Blotner reports that "he had asked Bill about it. Faulkner's only answer was, 'Who's Hawthorne? The title is original with me.' Major Oldham walked away from the conversation convinced of Faulkner's innocence of the New England writer and his work." Others also expressed concern that when someone asked for *The Marble Faun* in a bookstore he or she would get Hawthorne and not Faulkner. Blotner adds that most Oxonians felt the poems themselves "didn't make sense."[36] But as James's *Hawthorne* demonstrates his early debt to Hawthorne, Faulkner's *Marble Faun* directly and indirectly acknowledges Hawthorne's influence and demonstrates characteristic concerns about problems of the artist's knowledge that would become so important to the late novels.

Faulkner's poetry has recently received wide attention with the first publication of a lengthy cycle of love poems called *Vision in Spring*.[37] Faulkner often said that he saw himself as a failed poet; indeed, he revised and improved his early poems as late as 1933, well after he had published *The Sound and the Fury*.[38] In his earliest writing days Faulkner published so many poems in the University of Mississippi student newspaper, the *Mississippian*, that parodies of his work also began to appear there. He once sent in a submission with a letter to the editor counterattacking a parodist, and the letter was published with the Jamesian title, "The Ivory Tower."[39] These early self-conscious efforts to develop the voice of the artist suggest the epistemological problems of the later poems of *The Marble Faun* as well as the later fiction.

In one of the earliest poems, "L'après-midi d'un faune," a lover is frozen in the form of a marble faun. He can only lament his state as his beloved, a nymph, flees from him, perhaps toward another. In a 1921 "marionette" poem called "Two Puppets in a Fifth Avenue Window," Faulkner plays with the forms of clothing dummies whose postures mimic emotion. In the third stanza of the poem he addresses passersby, telling them that they too are puppets at the mercy of outside forces. Already the idea of the faun as a puppet, a character conscious of his own immobilizing design, is prominent in Faulkner's artistic imagination, and this idea is the central theme of the poems of *The Marble Faun*. In "subject, style, and idiom," Blotner notes, the poems of *The Marble Faun* exist in the oldest formal poetic tradition. They are pastoral eclogues, linked together by observations on the seasons of the year and pervaded by a melancholy arising out of meditations on mutability as voiced by the marble faun.[40] The poems suggest a young artist voicing his problematic self-consciousness, his problem as an artist of knowing and being known.

In a 1925 review of *The Marble Faun*, John McClure of the New Orleans *Times-Picayune* wrote that there are fewer than a dozen really successful long poems in English, and a young poet using this form is predestined to fail: "The most he can hope for, even if his name be Keats, is to fail with honor. Mr. William Faulkner, a Southern poet from whom we shall hear a great deal in the future, has failed, it seems to this reviewer, but with real honor."[41] George P. Garrett, Jr.'s, 1957 essay is still one of the best discussions of Faulkner's poetry, including *The Marble Faun*. Garrett calls *The Marble Faun* a highly complex literary exercise. Though the poems are, as Phil Stone says in his preface, "the poems of youth," Garrett finds that they were promising in more ways than was evident when they were first published: "The book fails, but the principal cause of failure is in the almost impossible task which the young poet set for himself," the blending of rigid formal structures with an expansive mythology. Indeed, "the writing of serious pastoral poetry in our time has been restricted by the lack of an adequate pastoral idiom."[42]

The odd and uncomfortable combination of traditional and experimental forms in Faulkner's pastoral poetry is partially a result of his attempt both to use the art-noveau pastoral forms of the French symbolist poets Stéphane Mallarmé and Arthur Rimbaud and to make those forms flexible enough to accommodate his American pastoral, just as James had to subordinate symbolist forms in his early work to accommodate his voice. Garrett finds that the structure of *The Marble Faun*, "separate poems joined together by a common subject and both external and internal devices," demonstrates Faulkner's early awareness of problems of structural unity. "Concern with form has marked Faulkner's work from the beginning and throughout a career noted for variety and subtlety of structural experiment," he continues. If there is continuity in Faulkner's verse, "there is, as in his prose, a restless experimentation, an attempt to achieve, within the limitations which he demanded for verse, new variations on the oldest themes."[43] Faulkner's failure to find such an idiom in poetry led him to succeed more nearly in the experimental forms of his novels. Even at this early stage, he was realizing and struggling against the limits of literary form, of closed designs, of the imagination. It is as though the artist/faun laments his own identity when he fails at formal design but laments as well how such design has failed him. *This* marble faun is an American.

In the concluding section of the first poem in *The Marble Faun* cycle, the faun says:

> The sky
> Warms me and yet I cannot break
> My marble bonds. That quick keen snake
> Is free to come and go, while I
> Am prisoner to dream and sigh
> For things I know, yet cannot know,
> 'Twixt sky above and earth below.
> The spreading earth calls to my feet
> Of orchards bright with fruits to eat,
> Of hills and streams on either hand;
> Of sleep at night on moon-blanched sand:
> The whole world breathes and calls to me
> Who marble-bound must ever be.[44]

This plaintive verse strongly suggests some of Faulkner's later preoccupations with knowledge: how does the artist, from his "marble-bound" isolation, speak of the "things I know, yet cannot know"—that is, cannot tell? The artist in these poems finds himself marble-bound by imposed form, just as Hawthorne did, and burdened by this awareness; the faun's separation arises from the simultaneous knowledge of identity and loss.[45] Yet Faulkner, following Hawthorne, is anything but marble-bound in his novels. It was the enforced design of lyric poetry that was too much for him, for such a form would not allow the freedom of development of narrator and character as occurs in the novel. As Hawthorne struggled against the imposed forms of realism and romance—so very painfully in a novel like *The Marble Faun*—so Faulkner faced the limitations of authorial design in his art.

Set in a Hawthornian garden near a Hawthornian wood and featuring one of Hawthorne's memorable characters, the faun, Faulkner's poems allude to Hawthorne's works directly in several ways. Not only do Hawthorne's Donatello and Faulkner's faun share their artful status in the authors' fiction as human and inhuman, mortal and divine, natural and artificial, but their difficulties invoke the artist's knowledge of good and evil, of past and present, of self and other, of dream and reality—and most important, of the artist's own doubtful status in a community. About one-third of the way through *The Marble Faun*, a poem begins:

> Upon a wood's dim shaded edge
> Stands a dusty hawthorn hedge
> Beside a road from which I pass
> To cool my feet in deep rich grass.

In this sheltered setting, like a Hawthornian Sleepy Hollow or Blithedale bower,

> . . . quietude folds a spell
> Within a stilly shadowed dell
> Wherein I rest, and through the leaves
> The sun a soundless pattern weaves
> Upon the floor. The leafy glade
> Is pensive in the dappled shade,
> While the startled sunlight drips
> From beech and alder fingertips.[46]

Besides the "hawthorn hedge," there are several intriguing suggestions of Hawthorne in these passages. Echoes of Hawthorne's dark green places, especially the woods of "dappled shade," look forward to the woods of

"The Bear," presenting the American wilderness as a place of transformation. But these poems are set in a garden, and the gardens in Hawthorne share with the transformative woods an eerie, unreal quality and a pensive, dreamy reflectiveness, as in the garden of "Rappaccini's Daughter." But as was also true in James's case, perhaps even more important here than the obvious direct connection to Hawthorne is that Faulkner and Hawthorne resort to a common pastoral rhetoric, however compromised, to deal with certain questions about knowledge in their novels. These authors share this American tradition of a middle ground.

Faulkner occupies a pastoral middle ground in other writing from his early period, for like Hawthorne, when Faulkner turned to the community of America, he often turned pastoral. "The Hill," for example, which appeared in the *Mississippian* on 10 March 1922, is an eight-hundred-word sketch in which a roughly dressed figure—an itinerant laborer—climbs a hill and sees a hamlet in the valley, as well as the natural landscape before him, but the beauty of the scene barely affects the "featureless mediocrity" of his mind: "Here, in the dusk, nymphs and fauns might riot to a shrilling of thin pipes, to a shivering and hissing of cymbals in a sharp volcanic abasement beneath a tall icy star," but the exhausted laborer is "mesmerized" by the "devastating unimportance" of his destiny. He has "a mind heretofore untroubled by moral quibbles and principles, shaken at last by the faint resistless force of spring in a valley at sunset." The laborer sees "the entire valley stretched beneath him, and his shadow, springing far out, lay across it, quiet and enormous. Here and there a thread of smoke balanced precariously upon a chimney. The hamlet slept, wrapped in peace and quiet beneath the evening sun, as it had slept for a century; waiting, invisibly honey-combed with joys and sorrows, hopes and despairs, for the end of time." The similarity is striking between this sketch and the famous passage in Hawthorne's "Ethan Brand" describing the pastoral scene the morning after Brand's death. Faulkner's sketch especially suggests a kinship to Hawthorne's complex pastoral in its exploration of the role of the artist. The man in "The Hill" represents the artist, perhaps, choosing what vision of America to convey in his art. Like Hawthorne's, Faulkner's pastoralism recognizes the futility of the pastoral vision, but also its beautiful necessity. "The Hill" is another important early attempt to locate its author within American literature.[47]

In the Epilogue to *The Marble Faun*, the speaker mourns:

May walks in this garden, fair
As a girl veiled in her hair

And decked in tender green and gold;
And yet my marble heart is cold
Within these walls where people pass
Across the close-clipped emerald grass
To stare at me with stupid eyes
Or stand in noisy ecstasies
Before my marble, . . .[48]

The tragedy of the artistic vision, these poems suggest, is also the tragedy of withdrawal from the world. Forever a cognizant part of society and forever an impotent observer cut off from society, the artist/faun offers his poems as his only way of connecting with his community, but does not know whether the poems will speak to anyone as he wishes them to. In poems like *The Marble Faun* the American artist's anxiety about design is dramatically expressed. Such fears were always present for Hawthorne, James, and Faulkner and for their characters. But the Hawthornian influence is not a design on James and Faulkner; they dialogize the Hawthornian influence and transform it into their own explorations of the role of the American artist.

In Hawthorne's day, before the development of mass market magazine publishing, interest and design as problems of authority for the artist were more or less anchored in particular issues of plot. But what Hawthorne experienced as the peculiar difficulty between writer and public blossomed into much greater concerns for James and Faulkner, who saw the evolution of the modern American author as a celebrity. Problems of authority for these authors became even more pronounced. And James and Faulkner, more than most writers, were conscious of the dangers of being a celebrity. In the story "The Papers," for example, James attacks the design of celebrity when he has Maud remark of another character, " 'It is genius to get yourself so celebrated for nothing—to carry out your idea in the face of everything. I mean your idea of *being* celebrated. It isn't as if he had done even one little thing.' "[49] One might also point to stories such as "The Lesson of the Master" and "The Tree of Knowledge" as examples of what Peter Conn calls James's concern with "the emptiness of a 'life' lived solely in the pages of the daily press, and the reduction of life thereby to nothing more than public entertainment."[50]

Edel surmises that the dangers of authorial design were so great—related as they were to dangerous personal design—that James's very identity was in danger of being overcome. Gilbert Osmond "is what Henry might, under some circumstances, have become." James could be like

Osmond, when, on occasion, "snobbery prevailed over humanity, and arrogance and egotism over his urbanity and his benign view of the human comedy." Perhaps the most accurate way of describing this identification with Osmond, Edel continues, "would be to say that in creating him Henry put into him his highest ambition and drive to power—the grandiose way in which he confronted his own destiny—while at the same time recognizing in his villain the dangers to which such inner absolutism might expose him. In the hands of a limited being, like Osmond, the drive to power ended in dilettantism and petty rages. In Henry's hands the same drive had given him unbounded creativity." Osmond and Isabel Archer represent two sides of Henry's personality, "two studies in egotism." Isabel, "generous high-minded creature though she is, in pursuit of an abstraction she calls 'freedom,' insists self-centeredly (in spite of grim warnings from all her friends) that she has found it in Osmond." Thus behind masks of freedom and power, James's reader encounters dependence and egotism. According to Edel, James seems to be asking: "How was one to possess the power and arrogance of one's genius and still be on good terms with oneself and the world? . . . Above all, how enjoy one's freedom and not make mistakes in the exercise of it?"[51]

This position proved to be difficult for James. He angrily "cut" a former friend, Vernon Lee, whose writing he had assisted, because she drew an overly familiar portrait of him in one of her tales. William James, who had visited her in Florence, declined another visit because, as he wrote to her, using a friend for "copy" implied on her part a disturbingly objective way of dealing with other human beings. Although she was penitent, Henry never again met her until once in 1912, at the home of a friend.[52] This is a single, very personal example, but the issue of authorial design goes well beyond the personal for writers in modern America. One may everywhere observe the phenomenon of the design of an author's public self affecting the work, overlaying the work as a mask of personality through which readers attempt to view the fiction and the writer: in Jack London, Mark Twain, F. Scott Fitzgerald, Ernest Hemingway, and Norman Mailer. James and Faulkner are similar to these other modern writers but move beyond them in their self-consciousness about the dangers of the design of artist/hero and ability to construct dialogic metadesigns to address these dangers.

Yet once, and quite grandly, James seriously misjudged his public: his ill-fated attempt at being a playwright. But as Faulkner attempted the medium of poetry and failed "successfully" (that is, discovered important novelistic applications), James gained from this failure at the midpoint of his career certain dramatic techniques for later fiction that revitalized his novels. Walter Isle has argued persuasively for a pattern in James's career rooted in this failure: Isle traces important changes in James's skill and complexity, moving from the long novels of the 1880s through the dramas and experimental novels of the 1890s, culminating in the major phase after 1900. In *The Other House*, *The Spoils of Poynton*, *What Maisie Knew*, *The Awkward Age*, and *The Sacred Fount*, James consciously experimented with techniques gleaned from his failure as a playwright. His earlier *The Princess Casamassima*, *The Bostonians*, and *The Tragic Muse* had not sold well, and he experimented in the short novels that followed because of his sense of losing an audience for these works and in the theater. His desire for success as a playwright was an attempt at popular fame; his dramas failed because he relied heavily on formulaic plots derived from successful French plays of the time—a set of formulas James thought would bring instant acclaim in the West End. These formulas demonstrated his fascination with form, with the "well-made play," but they limited character development and moral ambiguity, and James abandoned them in favor of his typical attraction to human character and its freedoms. He thus did not follow Henrik Ibsen, but returned to the novel, rejecting closed systems of symbols. But his strongest motive in all this, Isle claims, "seems to have been the dual desire for success and communication with some kind of audience, and the drama is the medium which provides the closest personal contact an artist can have with an audience."[53] Like T. S. Eliot in his plays, James's playwrighting was in part a dialogic attempt to cut across social stratifications to address a wider audience than he had hitherto been able to reach.

James's tenure as a playwright gave him new knowledge of point of view, dialogue, and broad human themes evident in the later novels. More and more he emphasized the conflict between the individual and society. The disappearance of the author, the heightening of ambiguity, and the shift from what is said to how it is said, all characteristics of James's major phase, are apparent in works of this middle period, particularly in the stories that present many of James's artist- or writer-heroes, such as "The Lesson of the Master" (1888), "The Real Thing" (1892), and "The Figure in the Carpet" (1896). As in the play *Guy Domville*, the heroes of these stories are preoccupied by the relationship between the artist and his public and are always questioning their own authority as artists.[54] At the point when he developed his "indirect vision" in narrative to avoid a reductive authorial interest, James chose once and for all his characteristic subject, how people's interests lead them to commit the sin of design, and his characteristic public stance, novelist instead of popular playwright.

Faulkner once said, " 'I found out that not only each book had to have a design, but the whole output or sum of an author's work had to have a design.' "[55] Faulkner's Yoknapatawpha allows him to use the same characters in several books in a loose metadesign of personalities, of "human hearts in conflict" with other human hearts. Faulkner avoids closed design by refusing to privilege plot or theme over characterization; indeed, in its inherent openness and ability to be transformed, character in Faulkner furnishes dialogic structure that can never be closed or silenced. Even minor characters in his work profoundly attract the reader's understanding. As Faulkner put it, these characters are all " 'quite real' ": " 'They are in my mind all the time. I don't have any trouble at all going back to pick up one. I forget what they did, but the character I don't forget, and when the book is finished, that character is not done, he is still going on at some new devilment that sooner or later I will find out about and write about.' "[56] Faulkner's major concern is not with manipulating his characters or documenting their development but with engaging in a relationship with them. To him his characters " 'are people, and they have grown older as I have grown older, and probably they have changed a little—my concept of them has changed a little, as they themselves have changed and I changed. That they have grown. I know more about people than I knew when I first thought of them, and they have become more definite to me as people.' "[57] Faulkner's readers thus discover seemingly uncharacteristic characteristics in Bundrens or Compsons or Snopeses because they "get to know" them "as people" and not as literary stereotypes.[58]

Faulkner's determination to leave his characters free is paralleled by his efforts to do the same for himself. Characteristically his concern about the public design of "author" takes the form of extreme misstatement on his part. For example, he denied that he had ever read James Joyce when he was accused of having done so at a Charlottesville, Virginia, writers' conference—then he recited from memory Joyce's "Watching the Needleboats at San Sabba" from *Pomes Penyeach*. Faulkner said over and over again in interviews that he was not a "literary man"; his simple critical terminology did not seem to grow very much during his career, and he never liked talking as a literary critic would talk.[59] In his early career Faulkner enjoyed the freedom of anonymity, but by his middle career the design of author he felt placed upon him was a heavy burden for his art. By his late career, it seems that Faulkner had better worked out the problems of design the artist faces and could enjoy a his hard-won freedom to create.

Faulkner wrote to Malcolm Cowley in 1946 to say he wished all the best for the republication of *The Sound and the Fury*, but he did not want to write the introduction himself. Earlier he had pleaded against an introduction for the combined edition of *The Sound and the Fury* and *As I Lay Dying*, asking his editors to allow the novels to be presented unintroduced.[60] He also did not want to revise to correct the book's inconsistencies because he believed they proved that the book—as well as his creative genius—was still alive. Invoking openness of interpretation and freedom for the author, characters, and reader, Faulkner told Cowley that he did not care much for facts.[61] Many years later, Faulkner seems to have felt the same way, especially about the revision of *The Hamlet* to accommodate the new volumes of the *Snopes* trilogy.[62] Cowley has argued that Faulkner never produced one "wholly satisfactory" novel,[63] but this deliberate failure suggests more than just a refusal to design systematically on his characters. Through such "inconsistency," Faulkner, like James, protects his own freedom by paradoxically inviting his community into dialogue with him and his text. Faulkner's authority over the text is a denial of the concept of authority.

Like James, Faulkner was often angered by the difficulties of life as a celebrity. For example, in 1947, after he spoke in English classes at the University of Mississippi, he heard of a plan by some students to publish their notes of his talk, as well as of a press release from the school. His response was severe.[64] He was plagued throughout his residence at Rowan Oak with trespassing curiosity-seekers, but sometimes, when these people turned out to be sincere or humble enough, he talked to them and even offered them beer and showed them around. He tried on those occasions to connect himself with his public. Too often, however, a quiet interview turned into a story that would dismay him once it was published.

Because of a certain unfavorable article in *Life* magazine[65] and stories in *Newsweek* and *Time*, Faulkner wrote an essay attacking contemporary American mores, "The American Dream: What Has Happened to It?" He saw his own experiences as symptomatic. The American Dream was supposed to be a sanctuary for freedom from the old hierarchies of power, he felt, but the dream had been lost. He named others, such as Charles Lindbergh and Robert Oppenheimer, who were vulnerable to the designs of the contemporary press.[66] Faulkner blamed his society's creation of celebrityhood on its worship of the machine: a culture that exalted the machine over people was doomed. In a letter to the editor of the *New York Times*, he spelled out his concerns for a culture that places the machine above the person; he argued that it is our notion of the infallibility of the machine as opposed to the failures of humans that will make our culture a dystopia.[67] Faulkner's and James's notions of failure as a theme were thus powerfully conditioned by their reactions against the designs of "success" in their modern society.

The relation of the artist to characters, narrators, and readers is a fitting subject for genres such as the preface and the interview. James's prefaces for the New York Edition of his work and Faulkner's interviews characterize the problem of knowledge in fiction and the attendant issue of the artist's relationship to the public as a question of "craft." In discussions of their works, they propose to address the problem of the artist's relation to community through the model of craft as something unpredictable, human, open to innovation, and unsystematic. For James and Faulkner, "craft" seemed capable of protecting artists and their characters and readers from the dangers of closed mechanical designs of all types, freeing all of them for their best discoveries.

Both James and Faulkner thought of their work as unfinished, and both were inveterate revisers. James, in the Preface to *The Golden Bowl*, wishes he could "dream the whole thing over" and hopes the unrealized form he missed in his works "may sufficiently seem to hang about them and gild them over—at least for readers, however few, at all *curious* about questions of form." He invites the reader to "dream again" the works "in my company" with "the interest of his own larger absorption of my sense." The author weaves his "web" in the confidence of invitation. "Re-visions" of a text are "alert winged creatures" ready to take off to "clearer air." And the characters partake of this communion as well: in *The Golden Bowl*, James says, the composition resulting from the juxtaposition of two points of view forms "the moral of the endless interest" of the tale. The appeal is to variety, a "certain indirect and oblique view of my presented action" in the form of a narrator whose "criticism and interpretation" contribute to the "intensification of interest" in the story—the particular case *and* some individual view of it.[68] Bakhtin would call James's narrator "dialogically" juxtaposed with author, characters, and reader.

James is always the working craftsman in his prefaces. The inherent complexity of his craft, R. P. Blackmur comments, is precisely James's avoidance of a closed "platitude of statement":

[James] enjoyed an excess of intelligence and he suffered, both in life and art, from an excessive effort to communicate it, to represent it in all its fullness. His style grew elaborate in the degree that he rendered shades and refinements of meaning and feeling not usually rendered at all. Likewise the characters which he created to dramatise his feelings have sometimes a quality of intelligence which enables them to experience matters which are unknown and seem almost perverse to the average reader.[69]

But James defended his "super-subtle fry," as he calls them, on the grounds that they are "ironic": "operative irony . . . implies and projects the possible other case, the case rich and edifying where the actuality is pretentious and vain."[70] To accomplish this, James used the devices of what Blackmur calls the "indirect approach" and the "dramatic scene" throughout his work. These devices are not, as the names suggest, opposed, nor do they cancel each other out. The indirect approach allows for

> the existence of a definite created sensibility interposed between the reader and the felt experience which is the subject of the fiction. James never put his reader in direct contact with his subjects; he believed it was impossible to do so, because his subject really was not what happened but what someone felt about what happened, and this could be directly known only through an intermediate intelligence.

The dramatic scene is the principal device James uses to give the indirect approach a form, and it closely resembles that of the stage play.[71]

In the Preface to *The Portrait of a Lady*, James's notion of the novel as the freest of genres is elucidated. James says that in *Portrait*,

> we get exactly the high price of the novel as a literary form—its power not only, while preserving that form with closeness, to range through all the differences of the individual relation to its general subject-matter, all the varieties of outlook on life, of disposition to reflect and project, created by conditions that are never the same from man to man (or, so far as that goes, from man to woman), but positively to appear more true to its character in proportion as it strains, or tends to burst, with a latent extravagance, its mould.

In the famous "house of fiction" passage, James further expands his idea of the "extravagance" of the novel. In this fascinating description, James imagines a world of multiple viewpoints in which a singular, objective, empirical meaning simply would not make sense. "Seeing" life, James suggests, is like a collection of views from diverse windows rather than a single perspective. The artist who realizes this accordingly endows his work with "his boundless freedom and his 'moral' reference." This architectural metaphor, which also occurs frequently in his fiction, is repeated in other parts of the Preface to *Portrait*. Like Faulkner's carpentry metaphor, it defines fiction writing as a craft rather than a predictable system, and in so doing it also makes a moral statement about freedom of imagination.[72]

James closely addresses the narrative problem of design and antidesign in describing the crucial scene in *Portrait* when Isabel walks by the door of the drawing room and sees Madame Merle and Osmond in the room. James stresses the importance of understatement to such a scene: "It is dreadful to have too much, for any artistic demonstration, to dot one's i's and insist on one's intentions, and I am not eager to do it now; but the question here was that of producing the maximum of intensity with the minimum of strain."[73] Similarly, in the Preface to *The Princess Casamassima*, James seems to hear a monitoring voice that asks for

> "plenty of bewilderment . . . so long as there is plenty of slashing out in the bewilderment too. But don't, we beseech you, give us too much intelligence; for intelligence—well, *endangers*; endangers not perhaps the slasher himself, but the very slashing, the subject-matter of any self-respecting story. . . . Give us in the persons represented, the subjects of bewilderment (that bewilderment without which there would be no question of an issue or of the fact of suspense, prime implications in any story) as much experience as possible, but keep down the terms in which you report that experience."[74]

Sounding very much like Hawthorne in the Preface to *The Blithedale Romance*, James finds that "extreme and attaching always the difficulty of fixing at a hundred points the place where one's impelled *bonhomme* may feel enough and 'know' enough—or be in the way of learning enough—for his maximum dramatic value without feeling and knowing too much for his minimum versimilitude, his proper fusion with the fable." James describes in his Preface to "Daisy Miller" another form of antidesign, a "charm" that disrupts the systematic design of a story. "Daisy Miller" qualified itself in *Cornhill Magazine* and afterward as "A Study," but Daisy's charm changed her case study into something else. Between the first version of the story (1878) and the two later ones, James made extensive revisions that radically poeticize Daisy and make her a much more sympathetic and admirable character, and he removed the subtitle "A Study." As James relates, "My little exhibition is made to no degree whatever in critical but, quite inordinately and extravagantly, in poetical terms. . . . [And] my supposedly typical little figure was of course pure poetry, and had never been anything else."[75] Similarly, Milly Theale of *The Wings of the Dove* requires "liberty, liberty of action, of choice, of appreciation, of contact," and through the "merciful indirection" of successive narrative centers, he notes, he approaches her "circuitously . . . at second hand, as an unspotted princess is ever dealt with."[76] In contrast to the narrator's care, characters, when they fail to consider other interests, commit reductive personal design—as another "Princess," Maggie Verver, discovers in *The Golden Bowl*.

The design and antidesign of *The Ambassadors* receives extended treatment in its Preface. James wants to "account" for Strether's " 'peculiar tone' " in the "Live" speech, James's inspiration for the novel, where he imagines there is

> a certain *principle* of probability: he wouldn't have indulged in his peculiar tone without a reason; it would take a felt predicament or a false position to give him so ironic an accent. One had n't been noting "tones" all one's life without recognising when one heard it the voice of the false position. The dear man in the Paris garden was then admirably and unmistakeably *in* one—which was no small point gained; what next accordingly concerned us was the determination of *this* identity.

James thus takes his story from Strether's *voice,* and this voice is the antidesign, for it works against the abstract stereotypical designs—the "probabilities"—that also generate the character of Strether. Possessed of Strether's nationality, one could all too easily guess the effect of Paris on him:

> He would have issued, our rueful worthy, from the very heart of New England—at the heels of which matter of course a perfect train of secrets tumbled for me into the light. They had to be sifted and sorted, and I shall not reproduce the detail of that process; but unmistakeably they were all there, and it was but a question, auspiciously, of picking among them. What the "position" would infallibly be, and why, on his hands, it had turned "false"— these inductive steps could only be as rapid as they were distinct.

But Paris does not simply act on Woollett: the two communities interact in Strether's knowledge. Because Strether undergoes "a change almost from hour to hour," James allows an openness in his narrative that defeats design—and that defeat is the main subject of *The Ambassadors*. The author's design in *The Ambassadors,* based on character and not plot, must fail to close: Strether had come with a view "that might have been figured by a clear green liquid, say, in a neat glass phial; and the liquid, once poured into the open cup of *application,* once exposed to the action of another air, had begun to turn from green to red, or whatever, and might, for all he knew, be on its way to purple, to black, to yellow. . . . The *situation* clearly would spring from the play of wildness and the development of extremes."[77]

Faulkner's concerns about craft in his interviews are remarkably like James's in his prefaces. In his face-to-face dialogues with his interviewers he addresses the relation of the artist to society as an issue of craft, of narrative problems of design and antidesign, and of "failure." Overall, despite his troubles as a celebrity, Faulkner in his interviews displays a desire for community, for interaction with his audience, just as James does at a somewhat greater remove in his prefaces.

Faulkner presents himself in his interviews as a member of what he terms the "humanist school" of writers. He says he prefers to write about people rather than to construct patterns of symbols, and he is much less tongue-in-cheek on this topic in his interviews than may at first appear. He believes that the artist can achieve the role of "humanist" only by speaking in his own voice, inviting the reader to respond. Exasperated by an interview with the *New York Times,* he asserted: " 'I write about people. Maybe all sorts of symbols and images get in—I don't know. When a good carpenter builds something, he puts the nails in where they belong. Maybe they make a fancy pattern when he's through, but that's not why he put them in that way.' "[78] He often uses carpentry as a metaphor for the creation of this language and for writing in general, describing himself as an "honest craftsman" and comparing his narrative techniques to cabinetmaking, much as his character Cash Bundren of *As I Lay Dying* builds his moral sense by reference to his carpentry. Faulkner's interviews present his notion of writing as a craft by emphasizing fictional identity as an unfinished process, always in need of revision.

Faulkner's notorious lying about his personal life is an important part of his insistence on the freedom of identity. In the early interviews he begins with a fairly simple fiction, for example, about his service as an air force pilot in Canada during World War I, but by the time of his last few interviews, this service involves his being shot down behind enemy lines in France, hanging in his harness for hours, sustaining a head injury, and at last being rescued. He reportedly claimed that he had a steel plate in his head from this injury. In fact, of course, Faulkner never left Canada during the war and probably did not even get to fly planes more than a couple of times, if at all. And he lied about more than the war. He also said, for example, that he attended school only through the sixth grade.[79] Why did this man, who was recognized as the greatest author of his day, need to lie so ridiculously about himself? Faulkner's likes are related to his notion of fiction as a "failure"; both help us interpret the life and the work hermeneutically.

As Plato defined fiction as fundamentally a lie, novelists like Faulkner exploit the fictionality of their fictions—as Twain notably does with Huck Finn's constant lying—making lying an important artistic and even moral category. James B. Meriwether and Michael Millgate speculate that

> indifference and a need to save time were not the only elements in Faulkner's attitude toward the proliferation of errors in accounts of his life and career. Presumably there was a certain amount of enjoyment too, since the extent of error could be a measure of how well privacy had been preserved. And a number of wildly untrue (or, as he might have put it himself, unfactual) legends about Faulkner obviously derive, at least in part, from the subject's own love for yarn-spinning. . . . For most of his life William Faulkner obviously regarded his own experiences as something to be shared with the public only in the form of fiction.[80]

Faulkner's "lies" and "failures," as means of protecting himself from designs of art and celebrity that threaten his artistic freedom, were an art form he obviously enjoyed.

Yet Meriwether and Millgate also emphasize that Faulkner's "pessimism about America's treatment of her public figures . . . did not prevent him, during the last years of his life, from repeatedly taking stands, as a public figure and as an American, that paradoxically involved the sacrifice of his privacy." Beginning with his acceptance of the Nobel Prize in 1950, he emerged from behind the barrier he had worked so hard to create because he

> clearly accepted, along with the . . . Prize, a measure of responsibility as a public figure, and clearly he had decided to include among his professional duties, as part of his last years of work as a writer, the speeches and public appearances he made, here and abroad, the teaching he did at Nagano and Virginia, even when they diminished the time he could otherwise have spent writing novels.

He traveled around the world and spoke at home as well. He characteristically made responsibility to others the subject of a speech, arguing that to be a human being among other human beings meant carrying out one's duty to be responsible to others if one wished to remain free oneself.[81] Individual freedom, he felt, existed *only* in the context of a community of equally free individuals: one must be "completely free in spirit." Yet freedom, "true freedom, extends only to where the next individual's freedom stops. That is, to be completely free is not to be completely ruthless, completely heedless. He must be free within a pattern of responsibility always."[82] Responsibility, Faulkner said, helps the artist, like anyone else, to avoid designing on the freedoms of others.

Faced with newspaper reporters questioning him on his works, Faulkner repeatedly replied, " 'I'm not a literary man; I'm just a farmer.' " But being a literary man, Cynthia Grenier, an interviewer, explains, "and being a writer are two different things to him, and Faulkner does admit to being a writer and will, sometimes, talk about his craft." Faulkner's manner, "which is a combination of shyness and defensiveness," places the interviewer on her honor "not to probe the forbidden areas—'literary' analysis of his works, symbolic content—but to seek rather to make contact on a human level."[83] Faulkner's personal desire to throw off such imposed designs as "literary man" accompanied by his sense of responsibility to his characters and readers "on a human level" promotes his work's freedom from design.

The Nobel Prize Award Speech is a main source of Faulkner's oft-quoted hope that through common struggle human beings will not only "endure" but "prevail," but Faulkner returned to his solution, individual freedom within communal relation, many times in his interviews. In Manila, he said:

> Man shall endure through fitness of character and intellect. It will be because man has a soul. He has a capacity to invent, he has created machinery to be his slave; but his danger is that he will become the slave of that machine he has created. He will have to conquer that slavery, he will have to conquer and control his machinery because he has a soul. Through his intellect, he has capacity to believe that all men should be free, that all men are responsible to all other men, not to the machinery but to all races, to the family of mankind.

Indeed, the "family of mankind" is Faulkner's constant novelistic subject. The artist "can't live forever. He knows that. But when he's gone somebody will know he was here for his short time. He can build a bridge and will be remembered for a day or two . . . but somehow the picture, the poem—that lasts a long time, a very long time, longer than anything." Despite the "tragedy . . . or at least the tremendous difficulty—of communication," people keep on trying endlessly to express themselves and to make contact with other human beings, Faulkner emphasizes. He claims to have tremendous faith in humanity in spite of faults and limitations: humanity "will overcome all the horrors of an atomic war," and we shall never destroy ourselves. We shall "keep writing on pieces of paper, on scraps, on stones," as long as we live. Because of this urge to communicate, humanity "is noble" to Faulkner "in spite of everything."[84]

Faulkner applies his notion of art to politics as well, and thus connects his art with his community in yet another way:

> I love my country enough to want to cure its faults and the only way that I can cure its faults within my capacity, within my own vocation, is to shame it, to criticize, to try to show the difference between its evils, its good, its moments of baseness, and its moments of honesty, integrity and pride. . . . Just to write about the good qualities in my country wouldn't do anything to change the bad ones. I've got to tell people about the bad ones, so that they'd be angry enough, or shamed enough to change it.

Is this why he takes up the extreme cases? asks the interviewer, to which Faulkner answers, "One never loves a land, a people, or even a person not because of what that person or land or place is but despite what that person or place is. That perfection, you'd have a great admiration for it, but no warmth for it, not enough warmth to want to change it or amend it."[85]

Like James, Faulkner identifies a willingness to fail as the mark of the great artist. When asked to list the five most important contemporary American writers, Faulkner gave his now-famous ranking: "1. Thomas Wolfe—he had much courage, wrote as if he didn't have long to live. 2. William Faulkner. 3. Dos Passos. 4. Hemingway—he has no courage, has never climbed out on a limb. He has never used a word where the reader might check his usage by a dictionary. 5. Steinbeck—I had great hopes for him at one time. Now I don't know." In an interview with Harvey Breit in the *New York Times Book Review* in 1955, Faulkner remarked that he rated Hemingway fourth because after Wolfe, Faulkner felt he himself "tried the most," but Hemingway "stayed within what he knew. He did it fine, but he didn't try for the impossible. . . . I rated those authors by the way in which they failed to match the dream of perfection. . . . This had nothing to do with the value of the work, the impact or perfection of its own kind that it had. I was talking only about the magnificence of the failure, the attempt to do the impossible within human experience." This distinction— between doing the possible and attempting the impossible in writing—was to be raised by Faulkner again and again in his career.[86]

Sounding like a somewhat more animated James in the Preface to *The Golden Bowl,* Faulkner told Grenier: " 'If I could I would write all my books again, and I think I could do them better. But I don't think I'd be satisfied with them. I don't think any author can be satisfied with his work. If he were, there'd by nothing left for him to do but cut his throat.' (Draws finger across throat.)" For Faulkner being a writer means "you have to keep on trying, but still it's not good enough." Indeed, failure is *the* success of Faulkner's career:

> I think the reason that any writer continues to write is that the job, the story, the poem, the book, which he has just finished, did not tell the truth that he was moved by in such a manner as suited the dream, the aspiration to tell that dream. So he writes another book, a poem or story. So, as long as he lives he will continue to write because once he matches that dream and he has set that truth to light as he dreamed that he had hoped he would, then nothing remains but to stop. The Nobel Prize did not change my own belief that what I have done was not what I could do or might do someday.

Success for Faulkner is precisely "to go under when trying to do more than you know how to do. It's trying to defy defeat even if it's inevitable."[87] Four marvelous "failures" of James's and Faulkner's are *The Ambassadors, Absalom, Absalom!, The Golden Bowl,* and *Go Down, Moses.* By failing at design in these books, these two artists address the American philosophical problem of the freedom of the individual within the community. For all who are involved with the text, knowledge in James and Faulkner is *both* free and social, both designed and undesigned, interested and disinterested: it certainly "fails" and it thus certainly succeeds.

3. Failure to "Live": *The Ambassadors*

IN THEIR CONCERNS about the limits of knowledge for characters and readers, *The Ambassadors* and *Absalom, Absalom!* represent the epitome of narrative structures James and Faulkner used for most of their careers, and within these limitations, they carry the problem of knowledge as far as they can without giving up their unity. They present characters who cannot fit their knowledge into their communities, and they ask questions about meaning that cannot be answered through their structural forms. The conclusion of *The Ambassadors*, for example, which will come up many times in this discussion, has been scrutinized in volumes of analysis. Some readers follow F. O. Matthiessen's suggestion that Strether is left empty in the end and "does nothing at all."[1] This underemphasizes Strether's addressing knowledge as he uniquely does in the conclusion; he has gone beyond the "Living" of Paris and Woollett and is doing what is required to fulfill his new sense of life. For Strether, life comes to occur in the context of an open morality based on the dynamics of human relationships, and thus his future must also be "open."[2]

Indeed, *The Ambassadors* presents itself as a book about broadly conceived relationships, including the relationship between the Old and New Worlds. At fifty-seven years of age James, in writing *The Ambassadors*, returned to the international theme for which he first became known. Edel claims that this novel "spoke for the central myth of Henry James's life. He had long before decided that his choice of Europe was wise, that Woollett and Mrs. Newsome—that is, the U. S. A.—could not offer him the sense of freedom he had won for himself abroad." James had to choose and to accept exile. Had he "stayed at home life would have been, for him, less ambivalent," yet this ambivalence had made possible his life of art and involved him in a constant balancing of the good and the bad aspects of America and Europe. It had precisely "enabled him to be Henry James, the Master—and to write *The Ambassadors*."[3] Such a cultural dualism conditions stimulating uncertainties—as Strether is torn between versions of America and versions of Europe, so readers are faced with metafictive questions of how to "read" their own versions of Strether. Perhaps the reason Strether withdraws at the end is that James withdraws, refusing to reenter America with Strether, even imaginatively. This novel does not yield the answer to Strether's and James's epistemological and moral dilemmas because it does not ultimately offer a reconciliation between the demands of personal freedom and those of the community. Conclusion is "just out of reach."

James was conscious of Strether's resemblance to himself. This "poor friend" would have accumulated character and imagination, yet this "would n't have wrecked him." But James goes on to say that his hero would not be a perfectly imaginative man, but a "comparative case"—and the comparison, one is given to understand, is with the Master himself:

> This personage of course, so enriched, would n't give me, for his type, imagination in *predominance* or as his prime faculty, nor should I, in view of other matters, have found that convenient. So particular a luxury—some occasion, that is, for study of the high gift in *supreme* command of a case or of a career—would still doubtless come on the day I should be ready to pay for it; and till then might, as from far back, remain hung up well in view and just out of reach. The comparative case meanwhile would serve—it was only on the minor scale that I had treated myself even to comparative cases.[4]

How strongly the "luxury" of the future Maggie Verver is suggested, particularly her idea in *The Golden Bowl* that a "point of view" must be "paid for." Despite the major scale of *The Ambassadors*, then, Strether's imperfect knowledge would characterize the novel throughout.

This indeterminacy contrasts with the symmetry of the novel's twelve parts. In the Preface, James admits that the story's elements "continued to fall together, as by the neat action of their own weight and form, even while their commentator scratched his head about them; he easily sees now that they were always well in advance of him. As the case completed itself he had in fact, from a good way behind, to catch up with them, breathless and a little flurried, as he best could." James's notion of chasing after his story suggests that *The Ambassadors* formed itself according to its own designs, and by according the story its own power of creation, James deemphasizes his own touch. Despite the smooth, balanced unity—the "monotony"—of its twelve parts, and, according to James, despite *The Ambassadors*'s having been "all conveniently, 'arranged for' " in the *North American Review* (1903), it is not a "monotonous" book with a "note absolute." James found ways to counteract the unity of *The Ambassadors*, to interfere with its overriding design, and these negative devices become the mode of the story. The author "had been open from far back to any pleasant provocation for ingenuity that might reside in one's actively adopting—so as to make it, in its way, a small compositional law—recurrent breaks and resumptions," and he made up his mind to "exploit and enjoy these often rather rude jolts." Furthermore, close as the narrator was to be to the hero's adventure, his "gropings" for knowledge rather than his conclusions would predominate. James's "large unity" was thus to be inclusive but not systematic: it was to leave "recurrent breaks" and offer the particular view (Strether's), the narrator's and characters' views of Strether, *and* the reader's view, the knowledge "*a fortiori* for ourselves, unexpressed."[5]

James adopted he narrative point of view in *The Ambassadors*, he explains, out of concern for such "discriminations." One surrenders the "romantic privilege of the 'first person,' " which would have made Strether "at once hero and historian." The first person has the "merit of brushing away questions at a sweep," but "one makes that surrender only if one is prepared *not* to make certain precious discriminations." Strether has "conditions to meet . . . that forbid the terrible *fluidity* of self-revelation." Thus the seemingly ordered and symmetrical structure of the book—the similar lengths of the chapters, the placement of major events in the pivotal Parts Fifth and Eleventh, the neat balancing of Strether's introduction to Maria Gostrey with that of his departure from her—is undercut by the ambiguity of narration and the unfinishedness of the conclusion. *The Ambassadors*'s straining against its own system makes "discrimination"—discrepancy and difference—more important to the meaning of the book than "system."[6] Bakhtin would share James's excitement over the novel's polyphonic possibilities: "It is not that the particular production before us exhausts the interesting questions it raises, but that the Novel remains still, under the right persuasion, the most independent, most elastic, most prodigious of literary forms."[7] In *The Ambassadors* James's novelistic ability to raise "interesting questions" that cannot be exhausted even by the book's complex discrimination offers a "disinterest" as the moral model for community, and it does this, as Bakhtin would expect, through its polyphonies of knowledge expressed as a dialogue of interest and design.

Interest is the motive for most of what occurs in *The Ambassadors*, and the story largely involves what happens when Strether's interests—his economic and social interests in Woollett as well as his emotional and imaginative interests in Paris—collide. In the end, Strether renounces all interests save that of his own redefined imagination. Chad has an interest in advertising; Marie de Vionnet is interested in Chad; the Newsomes have business interests to protect. Maria Gostrey interests Strether, and she in turn is interested in him. The word "interest" occurs over and over again in *The Ambassadors*, taking on various shades of meaning all related to the association of interest in money, in a business or estate, with interest in love, the feeling of concern or the power to attract concern. For example:

He had "taken up," by what was at the time to be shrinkingly gathered, as it was scantly mentioned, with one ferociously "interested" little person after another.[8]

"They're the best friends he has in the world, and they take more interest than anyone else in what concerns him." (125)

"Almost any girl he marries will have a direct interest in his taking up his chances." (127)

He had started as if to bring her, leaving the other objects of his interest together. (145)

It was beautiful, the way Chad said these things, and his plea was now confessedly—oh, quite flagrantly and publicly—interesting. (163)

Patient and beautiful was her interest. (213)

Their presence gave a distinction to Chad's entertainment, and the interest of calculating their effect on Sarah was actually so sharp as to be almost painful. (316)

It was part of the deep impression for Strether, and not the least of the deep interest, that they *could* so communicate—that Chad, in particular, could let her know he left it to her. (387)

Strether assumed, he became aware, on this reasoning, that the interesting parties to the arrangement would have met betimes, and that the more interesting of the two—as she was after all—would have communicated to the other the issue of her appeal. (407)

[Maria] couldn't therefore but feel that, though, as the end of all, the facts in question had been stoutly confirmed, her ground for personal, for what might have been called interested, elation remained rather vague. (412)

Strether becomes aware of the many meanings of interest in many settings. One of the most telling is when he learns of Marie de Vionnet's past:

> The girl at the Genevese school, an isolated, interesting, attaching creature, both sensitive, then, and violent, audacious but always forgiven, was the daughter of a French father and an English mother. . . . It was in any case [Miss Gostrey's] belief that the mother, interested and prone to adventure, had been without conscience, had only thought of ridding herself most quickly of a possible, an acutal encumbrance. (158)

Maria and Strether find Marie "interesting"—spiritually engaging as well as personally fascinating, and her uncaring mother "interested"—worldly and soulless. Strether also learns that he, too, may be an object of interest: "Strether looked at her a moment with a light perhaps slightly obscured. 'I think that must be why the hero has taken refuge in this corner. He's scared at his heroism—he shrinks from his part.' 'Ah, but we nevertheless believe that he'll play it. That's why,' Miss Barrace kindly went on, 'we take such an interest in you. We feel that you'll come up to the scratch' " (327). Not only do Mrs. Newsome and Marie de Vionnet artfully manipulate Strether in the fulfillment of interests, but nearly everyone is a manipulative "ambassador" of some personal interest or interests. Strether has represented Mrs. Newsome to her son Chad; he has also represented Madame de Vionnet to Woollett. The Pococks are sent by Mrs. Newsome as ambassadors to Strether, Chad, and the Europeans. Madame de Vionnet presents herself to the Americans as an ambassador of France. Miss Gostrey is an ambassador to all and for all, including herself. Even the concierges and bellmen of this novel are ambassadors—everyone is intrigued with everyone else as they pass messages, ideas, and meeting plans on to others. It is a story of power, and Strether's power eventually lies in retreating from such designing behavior.

In the end Strether rejects personal interest as he sees it reflected in the designs of other people, but he retains his own imaginative interest, which he will not, one is sure, act out on other people in closed designs. Indeed James seems to argue that only when interest acts through the disinterested imagination—as in the artist's metadesign—is it prevented from doing harm. Money, love, and power are games of interest from which Strether totally withdraws but with which his narrator engages the reader by putting into action, as it were, what Strether so painfully learns by the end of the book.

In giving up his interests, Strether will live on "the pure flame of the disinterested" (294) for the rest of his life. Strether says he admires such a quality in Mamie Pocock, "but [Mamie] would always be the person who, at the present sharp hour, had been disinterestedly tender" (309). But the most important model Strether has for his development of imaginative disinterest is Maria Gostrey, who appears in the book almost as soon as Strether himself and very nearly has the last word. Disinterest has no easy place, however, in the society either of Paris or of Woollett, and like Maria Strether will seem different from others and hence isolated in his disinterest. But if we take into account the reader's developing moral response of disinterest, then we recognize that Strether is not alone—his readers' evolving disinterest metafictively supports his odd position between knowing and not knowing.

At the beginning of *The Ambassadors*, Strether feels thoroughly designing and designed upon, like "Woollett in person" (21). He is there in Europe for the Newsome interests; his own interest is as a fiancé to Mrs. Newsome, if, that is, he succeeds in his mission. But as many readers have noted, in the first paragraph of the book—underscored by the many negative constructions there—his readiness to go over to the enemy is an immediate denial of Woollett. In Chester he hopes Waymarsh is delayed; he feels personally free for the first time in years. "Before he even knows what it is like," Strether has defected, as Charles Thomas Samuels aptly comments.[9] Indeed, Strether begins to sound very soon as if he does not want to marry Mrs. Newsome, as when he contrasts her with Maria as a stiff Queen Elizabeth and an alluring Mary Stuart. Strether senses the imaginative freedom he will enjoy in Europe, for his New England background seems to have severely limited his imagination.

Strether finds that there are "more opinions" in Paris than in Woollett, where there were "only three or four." People in Paris even seem to have invented opinions "to avert those agreements that destroy the taste of talk. No one had ever done that at Woollett, though Strether could remember times when he himself had been tempted to it without quite knowing why. He saw why at present—he had but wanted to promote intercourse" (120). Diversity, variety, a dropping of inhibitions excite Strether as he engages in the conversations of Paris; his adaptability allows him to find in Europe not a new way of life to adopt as his own but a freedom to live his life and exercise his imagination as never before. As Elsa Nettels has argued, he does not actually convert from Woollett to Paris, for that would be merely to find another design to live by, but in the end he eludes both. Indeed, as Nettels stresses, Strether's triumph may be said to be constituted by his loss of his own romantic illusions about Paris and about Marie de Vionnet and himself even more than by his new notion of Woollett.[10]

But in learning about design Strether commits designs—indeed, he could not learn other than from failures. From the beginning, for example, he romanticizes Chad: his design is corrected only when he eventually realizes Chad's shallow opportunism. In describing Chad as he first sees him in Paris, Strether thinks "of old, Chad had been rough," and "all the difference" now is that Paris "had retouched his features, drawn them with a cleaner line. It had cleared his eyes and settled his color and polished his fine square teeth—the main ornament of his face; and at the same time that it had given him a form and a surface, almost a design, it had toned his voice, established his accent, encouraged his smile to more play and his other motions to less" (104). Chad furthermore has an "air of designedly showing" his smooth surface (107), and he finds a willing audience in Strether, who determines to help first Chad and soon thereafter Marie de Vionnet.

From their first meeting, Strether romanticizes Madame de Vionnet's past (158). He sees her as a remnant of the French Empire, or even as Cleopatra, "when in addition to everything she happened also to be a woman of genius" (188). His declaration that he will "save" her is obviously a bit of gallantry he enjoys (177). "Seeing her through" becomes Strether's responsibility to Marie, and at first he does not think deeply enough about the awful responsibility this design entails.

One of Strether's other projects for helping others is his plan for Bilham to marry Mamie Pocock. To him their marriage is a " 'thread we can wind up and tuck in' " (318). But designs of "helping" in this novel can be deceptive and even dangerous, as is apparent in Marie's desperate helping the Pococks enjoy Paris: her homage to Sarah, her offering up of her daughter, and her pretended flirtation with Jim are aspects of her helping. Although Strether exclaims about how Marie helps *him* (328), her help is a design. And Mrs. Newsome, who is all "moral pressure" (341), thinks *she* is helping everyone.

Chad functions in society by making others help him. In a conversation with Strether late in the book, Chad suggests that he is willing to sacrifice Marie so that Sarah and Mamie and his mother will "like" him. In spite of Strether's saying that " 'more has been done for you, I think, than I've ever seen done—attempted perhaps, but never so successfully done— by one human being for another,' " Chad is not sure whether or not he still wants Marie's help (358–60). He is not sure how that fits into his designs but thinks he is sure how Strether does. Strether sees himself as "passively" helping Chad (339), but in contrast to Chad's selfish passivity, Strether's becomes in the end a negative capability. Strether, with his "perceptions and his mistakes, his concessions and his reserves, the funny mixture, as it must seem to them, of his braveries and his fears, the general spectacle of his art and his innocence," is for all the ambassadors of the novel "a common, priceless ground for them to meet upon" (399). Strether allows Chad to use him because Strether's "art" consists in recognizing his role for what it is. Strether is a failure, but he has also been a sacrifice.

Strether quickly gains a deeper knowledge of design when the Pococks arrive in Paris. Jim Pocock sees Strether's time in Paris as having been spent in escapades and adventures, and he thinks Strether and Chad are only out for a good time. Because he has no conception of the values at stake, Jim provides an entirely new design on Strether's behavior. As Strether says, " 'He wouldn't have expected it of me; but men of my age, at Woollett—and especially the least likely ones—have been noted as liable to strange outbreaks, belated, uncanny clutches at the unusual, the ideal' " (284). When Strether sees himself as Jim sees him, it draws him up short: he realizes that his actions may be interpreted as stereotypical designs over which he has no control.[11]

Objectifying designs often present themselves in *The Ambassadors* in economic metaphors for human relations. Waymarsh, Strether is sure, will "quite fail" to "profit" by Maria (16). Strether assures Maria, who listens "with all her interest," that if Chad will " 'pull himself together and come home, all the same, he'll find his account in it' " (42). Strether believes he is acting in Chad's economic interest, but " 'I'm acting with a sense, for him, of other things too. Consideration and comfort and security—the general safety of being anchored by a strong chain. He wants, as I see him, to be protected. Protected, I mean, from life' " (50). Being protected from life also includes being properly married, Strether muses. At this early point, Strether is acting just as Chad wishes him to; sadly, Chad, consciously or not, plays on Strether's paternal feelings for his dead son. But "protection from life" is as wrongful a goal as *merely* "Living," Strether comes to realize.

When Strether first meets Chad in Paris he finds he cannot "compute" Chad's "value" or predict what Chad will say (103). But when Strether discovers, or rediscovers, Chad's moral shallowness, the initial thrill is replaced by a dull recognition. Strether learns that Chad knows how to use surprise as a tool, as when he plans to "spring" Jeanne and Marie on the Pococks as the possessors of "some form of merit exquisitely incalculable" (134). How sad it is that their incalculability is part of Chad's calculating schemes, and that he never knows their merit because he sees only the bottom line.

Paying is an important economic theme in *The Ambassadors*. As Strether pays the café bill, Bilham pays Strether with information about Chad and Marie. In a later scene, Chad says to Strether, " 'You talk about taking the whole thing on your shoulders, but in what light do you regard me that you think me capable of letting you pay?' " In response, "Strether patted his arm, as they stood together against the parapet, reassuringly— seeming to wish to contend that he *had* the wherewithal; but it was again round this question of purchase and price that the young man's sense of fairness continued to hover." In an odd role reversal, Chad points out that Strether must " 'give up money' " if he continues to support Marie. He even almost tells Strether that in the event of Strether's being cut off—" 'Oh, you mustn't *starve!*' "—he will promise "the elder some provision against the possibility just mentioned." Strether is willing to accept his " 'absence of an assured future,' " but he realizes that Chad will not do likewise. It is Madame de Vionnet Chad really refuses to "repay" in his plans to become a financial success. Money, quite unmistakably, is at the bottom of things in *The Ambassadors*, but next to Strether's awakened imagination—his sole guide at the end of the book—Chad's financial ambitions and his debts seem tawdry. Chad does see what he "owes" Marie—"he was indebted for alterations, and she was thereby in a position to have sent in her bill for expenses incurred in reconstruction" (163)—but he is prepared to trade her in for his fortune in business. Like the rich young cad that he is, Chad Newsome does not pay his bills.

Until the conclusion Strether seems fated to take over Chad's "debt" to Madame de Vionnet, but his personal education resides in his learning what it would mean to do that. Strether cannot help but think that "somebody [should be] . . . paying something somewhere and somehow, that they were at least not all floating together on the silver stream of impunity" (395). When he gives up Mrs. Newsome, he feels "as if he had sold himself, but hadn't somehow got the cash" (249). Strether then sacrifices his personal interest in Marie. Finally, his "extreme scruple" with Maria Gostrey in the end is that "he wished so to leave what he had forfeited out of account. He wished not to do anything because he had missed something else, because he was sorry or impoverished, because he was maltreated or desperate" (410). Strether will live on his "accumulations" and will recognize where they came from (423), but his accumulations are only those of the imagination. Unlike Chad, Strether finds this enough.

To combat the closures of designs, *The Ambassadors* develops negativity, avoidance, and ambiguity. From the first paragraph onward (and the first paragraph contains six "not"'s in as many sentences), negative events, sentence constructions, and values fill the book. Negativity works by stopping an explanation, thwarting design, and leaving open possibilities—thus preserving interpretive freedom. The narrator tells us that Strether's "double consciousness" allows him to display "detachment in his zeal and curiosity in his indifference" (4), and this disinterested discrimination informs all the negative values in the book.

The most obvious gap in *The Ambassadors* is, of course, the unnamed article manufactured in Woollett, but the negatives in this novel merely begin there. In a book so full of dialogues between characters, many important ones are unnarrated: Waymarsh and Miss Barrace's, Waymarsh and Sarah's, Marie and Jim's (what an interesting conversation that must have been), and Chad and Marie's. The narrated dialogues, too, are characterized by gaps: at Strether and Maria's first meeting, they accept each other instinctively with a complete "absence of preliminaries" and begin talking right away, though "nothing had actually passed between them" (5–6). Maria even claims, " 'there's nothing I don't know' " (13). The first paragraph of Chapter II is also thick with negatives: "He had none the less to confess," "he knew almost nothing about her," "she was not a stranger," "it was a blank," "professed himself unable to fill," "no recollection of Miss Gostrey." There are "abysses" in *The Ambassadors*: " 'I don't want your formula—I feel quite enough, as I hinted yesterday, your abysses' " (26); " 'Lord, what abysses!' " (44); " 'We're abysmal—we but may we never fill up!' " (295). Toward the end, Strether's "supposing nothing" leads him to "suppose everything" (389). Earlier, he confessed that what he stands to lose in the whole business is " 'Nothing!' " and " 'Everything' " (52). He *has* to judge " 'Everything!' " (292), but eventually he learns to judge nothing.

Strether learns about the value of judging "nothing" and "everything" from one who thinks of him as a mentor, "Little" Bilham, who is empty of personal design and thus at peace: " 'Little Bilham had an occupation, but it was only an occupation declined; and it was by his general exemption from alarm, anxiety, or remorse on this score that the impression of his serenity was made' " (87). He came to Paris to learn how to paint, but like Lance Mallow in "The Lesson of the Master," his high standards of taste kept him from taking his own work seriously. Frederick Crews calls Bilham's unwillingness to be a painter "something more than a personal inadequacy." Bilham "is content to exchange most of the ordinary comforts of life for the privilege of collecting knowledge passively, of seeing Life as a disinterested spectator." He is thus "mentally active by virtue of being uncommitted to a

narrowing form of life. His 'activity' is the exercise of his expansive imagination, which he refuses to compromise."[12] Perhaps Strether learns from
Bilham rather than Bilham from him.

Strether also learns from Maria's negativity, for which she does not
give a clear reason except the oblique comment, " 'My absence has helped
you—as I've only to look at you to see. . . . You're not where you were.
And the thing,' she smiled, 'was for me not to be there either' " (227).
Through her absence Maria assists in Strether's growth by allowing his
illusions of Marie to be tried out and to fail. Hers is a negative confidence, a
negative possession of Strether—she fails to design on him in the end, just
as he fails, he explains, to "get anything" out of the whole affair for himself.
I shall return to the importance of Maria's "negative capability" later in this
chapter.

Mrs. Newsome confronts all the characters even though she never
appears in person. She "arranged perfectly for [Strether's] absence," and
even in Europe, her tone fills the air: "It struck him at the same time as the
hum of vain things" (57). Mrs. Newsome cannot appear in the narrative: in
her absence she is menacing, but her presence would be too much altogether. Hers is a very different sort of absence than Maria's, not a freeing
sort of negativity. Strether's initial appeal as a character lies in his contrast
with Mrs. Newsome—and by the end his moral and aesthetic delicacy and
discrimination set him forever apart from the Mrs. Newsomes of the world.
Strether's notion of freedom as the goal of community allows him to
attempt imaginatively to redefine America, while Chad, on the other hand,
complements his mother's boosterism with his false advertising.

Negativity also points to the lack in Strether's past and present life. In
Chad's apartment, in the city of Paris, in Europe itself, "the actual appeal of
everything was none the less that everything represented the substance of
his loss," reminding him of "the youth he had long ago missed—a queer
concrete presence, full of mystery, yet full of reality, which he could handle,
taste, smell the deep breathing of which he could positively hear" (350).
Chad, in his youth and vigor, in his smoking on balconies and in his love
affairs, easily makes Strether feel a lack in himself. But negativity, by
creating narrative mystery, more often assists in the creation of community.
In a tense scene between Strether, Marie, and Sarah Pocock, Strether must
learn to look for "things visible through gaps," to hear words not spoken:
"He guessed that, for five seconds, these words were on the point of
coming; he heard them as clearly as if they had been spoken; but he
presently knew they had just failed" (268). Later, after a talk with Marie, he

thinks of "what he didn't say—as well as what *she* didn't, for she also had her high decencies," but "it ended in fact by being quite beautiful between them, the number of things they had a manifest consciousness of not saying" (281). The "absence of full knowledge" (245) generates interest both for Strether and for the reader, and it comes to stand for the entire novel's structure of knowledge.

Avoidance is a variation of negativity. Many things are described "as if," and very often "inquiry [falls] short" (41). Characters have an "interest in waiting" (48) or maintain a "critical silence" (54) or "decorous silence" (93). Some characters are "all indirect" (81), especially Miss Barrace and Mr. Bilham. For a long time Strether is lost in confusion, wondering "what things mean": " 'Oh no—not *that!*' was at the end of most of his ventures. This was the very beginning with him of a condition as to which, later on, as will be seen, he found cause to pull himself up; and he was to remember the moment as the first step in a process" (80). Strether's fear of knowledge is relayed in the narrator's mode of avoidance. In often saying that Strether was to see something later or to know it at a future time, the narrator demonstrates a version of avoidance, postponement. Like negativity, avoidance thus allows freedom to take over from closed design. Indeed, though the narrator refers to Strether as "our friend" (205), even he does not know all of Strether that the reader knows because the reader's knowledge is, of course, the only one open to revision. The narrator makes judgments of Strether available to the reader only as possible evaluations, not absolute views, to assist the reader's own continual revision.[13] Thus the hero, narrator, and author of *The Ambassadors* provide hermeneutic models for the reader's own metadesigns.

As Bakhtin leads us to believe, avoidance in a novel like *The Ambassadors* informs its very syntax. When characters in *The Ambassadors* speak, particularly Strether and Maria, they do so in ways that ask for completion rather than offering it. Ruth Bernard Yeazell tells us that "it is in the very shape and form of the Jamesian sentence that the terror of full consciousness most makes itself felt." Even in moments of discovery Strether's mental syntax is one of hesitation, denying the push of full consciousness or recognition. Strether has been "sensing more than he can allow himself to know," as do many James characters, and our excitement comes from the "tension between Strether's resistance and the almost inexorable coming of the recognition he fears." The very rhythms of James's late style "enact this relentless unfolding of awareness; in the language itself we sense the peculiar tone with which the knowledge—half-dreaded, half-desired—thrusts itself upon the conscious mind." Yet James's characters' resistance to experience is in direct proportion to their "vast susceptibilities," Yeazell adds.[14]

Narrative ambiguity characterizes almost everything in *The Ambassadors*; the novel itself could be described as Strether's double consciousness made useful. When Strether tries to inflict his designs on other people—Chad and Marie in particular—he fails at understanding and is betrayed by design. But when he realizes he can "know" other people without wishing them to conform to his knowledge, he has learned much. Marie stirs up "the old ambiguities" (189) for Strether, and Sarah resorts to "an ambiguous flushed formalism" (264) in her dealings with Marie. But Marie's and Sarah's ambiguity approaches falsehood, whereas Strether's comes to be an honest regard. In the end, the "fair shade of uncertainty" (412) preserves freedom, but throughout the book there exists a theme of education out of mystification, from Miss Barrace's " 'ah, ah, ah,' "s and Bilham's euphemisms to Maria's absence from Paris and the thorough-going ambiguity of the last pages. *The Ambassadors* is, as Samuels writes, "James's rueful study of a man who had reached middle age without comprehending life's moral ambiguity." Strether adjusts to his disillusionment, "even going so far as to support the morally ambiguous figure who was its cause," and this gesture places *The Ambassadors* "at the summit of James's wisdom." Except for Maggie Verver, "no other Jamesian protagonist comprehends life with such poise." In contrast, in weaker books, Samuels concludes, "James cannot decide whether the world is good or bad." In *The Ambassadors* the world is both: to think otherwise in James's terms would be childish.[15] Method thus from the beginning is an instrument of meaning, especially through negativity, avoidance, and ambiguity. *The Ambassadors* always approaches meaning and never actually supplies it, always provokes interpretations and then asks for even more complex understandings.

In many of James's and Faulkner's works, designs of knowing are often described in terms of seeing. *The Ambassadors* thoroughly revises what its characters usually mean by "seeing" the truth about someone else. Strether's eyes are nearly invisible at first—"His eyes were so quiet behind his eternal nippers that they might almost have been absent without changing his face" (8). In this scene they are "unseeing," in contrast to Maria Gostrey's "sidelong glances." Then, as she reads his name on his card she sees him in a way he is not able to see her: "Ah, it was too visible! She read it over again as one who had never seen it. ' "Mr. Lewis Lambert Strether" ' —she sounded" (10). Strether senses her seeing him and "sounding" him: his being a New Englander, he admits, " 'sticks out of me, and you knew, surely, for yourself, as soon as you looked at me'" (11). But like Maria Strether seeks "the sharper sense of what they saw" that afternoon. She watches him "with all her kindness. 'That means simply that you've recognized me—which *is* rather beautiful and rare. You see what I am'" (12–13). A bit further on, Maria replies to his "'You see more in it [Chad's affair] . . . than I'" with "'Of course I see *you* in it!'" and Strether responds, "'Well then, you see more in me!'" (48). All of this early "seeing" becomes even more complicated as the story unfolds. Seemingly invoking Rorty's judgment against the reductiveness of the ocular metaphor, "seeing" occurs throughout this novel as an epistemological metaphor that soon reveals its limitations.

Just as Maria first thinks they completely see each other, Strether quickly finds that he is capable of seeing Maria as a stereotype, an unattached but attaching American woman in Europe living more or less off of the stray Americans she meets, befriends, and guides through their travels. He learns, however, the dangers of such "seeing" through a design. An important discussion of Strether's changing vision of Maria occurs in Chapter XVIII. Strether realizes he does not want to devote himself to her: "It was the proportions that were changed, and the proportions were at all times, he philosophized, the very conditions of perception, the terms of thought." Strether stops seeing her in one way and begins to see her in another, and Maria for awhile comes to figure "as but part of the bristling total—though of course always as a person to whom he should never cease to be indebted." This description sounds eerily like Chad's attitude toward Madame de Vionnet, and it warns the reader that Strether too might be capable at this point in the story of making the mistake of seeing others in terms of a personal design: "It would never be given to him certainly to inspire a greater kindness. She had decked him out for others, and he saw at this point at least nothing she would ever ask for" (234). The initial forms of "seeing" on both their parts are displaced by their later conversations.

In *The Ambassadors* Strether's and James's imaginations must constantly confront problems of surface and depth, appearance and reality, fiction and life; these metafictive issues are raised, for example, in the strongly visual metaphors that characterize the two theater scenes early in the novel. In the first, when Maria and Strether attend a play, for Strether "the publicity of the place was just, in the matter, . . . the rare, strange thing; it affected him almost as the achievement of privacy might have affected a man of different experience." Being out in public with Miss Gostrey changes the way Strether looks at their relationship by giving it a different design, and the particular social and economic world around them helps create this design: "It was an evening, it was a world of types, and this was a connection, above all, in which the figures and faces in the stalls were interchangeable with those on the stage" (37). The connection between the actors and the audience is made even stronger in the second theater scene in which Chad strides onto the "stage" of the theater-box (93). We have been prepared for Chad already, of course, because in the first play there was a "bad woman, in a yellow frock, who made a pleasant, weak, good-looking young man, in perpetual evening dress, do the most dreadful things" (38). Strether does not adopt this description, although it coincides with the Woollett view of things; the dramatic stereotype, especially the visual one, comes to appear to him a dangerously reductive thing. That the play represents Woollett makes one suspect the designs of art as well as society: Strether clearly has more to rise above than just the provincial opinions of Woollett. A more widespread problem has presented itself.[16]

Unlike the rest of the Woollett contingent, what "seeing" earlier meant for Strether comes to mean something less reductive to him, a rejection of the certainty of vision in favor of dialogic knowledge. He learns by noting the others' failures of vision, but his own vision must fail for this to occur. It is easy to see others' failed vision: Sarah Pocock "had come in the pride of her competence, yet it hummed in Strether's inner sense that she practically wouldn't see" (247). The failure to see Madame de Vionnet on the part of Mrs. Newsome and Mrs. Pocock is their greatest failure, Strether decides. It is what makes him realize that he does not belong to them any more: "Yes, they would bridle and be bright; they would make the best of what was before them, but their observation would fail; it would be beyond them; they simply wouldn't understand" (257). Mrs. Newsome's vision extends across the ocean—Sarah feels "the fixed eyes of their admirable mother fairly screw into the flat of her back" (315)—but to Strether she knows nothing. Strether says he is " 'interested *only* in [Mrs. Newsome] seeing what I've seen. And I've been as disappointed in her refusal to see it as she has been in what has appeared to her the perversity of my insistence' " (369). Strether desperately wants Woollett to see what he sees, though it is ultimately neither Chad nor Madame de Vionnet whom the Pococks and Newsomes fail to see but Strether himself.

Chad's failure to see Marie places him in the Woollett camp, for in Strether's opinion, as Crews says, "anyone who cannot see the full importance of Madame de Vionnet's gift is sadly deficient in imagination. Strether has placed Mrs. Newsome and Sarah on this list, and . . . he finds that he must include Chad himself." Yet though Strether believes that no one, including Chad, is doing justice to Marie, on the other hand, Chad's blindness makes Strether think that perhaps her achievement has not been so great after all. With all of these epistemological difficulties, no wonder Strether decides to leave for a quiet day in the country.[17]

In the river scene, in the middle of Strether's delightful "painting" of a couple rowing on the river, occurs the "sharper arrest" of Chad and Marie in the flesh. Chapter XXXI opens with "What he saw was exactly the right thing" (382), except, that is, for the identity of the subjects of the picture. Like Mrs. Newsome and Sarah, who probably would not worry much about a young man's escapades in Europe unless he happened to be "our Chad," Strether finds an aesthetic beauty in the scene until he realizes that he is connected to the people in it: "It was a sharp, fantastic crisis that had popped up as if in a dream." Strether sees further than he wants to. Seeing, too, that they nearly cut him, that they hesitate before they recognize him, that they quickly fabricate a tone and an explanation, that "amazement and pleasantry [fill] the air . . . superseding [the] mere violence" of their ignoring him "on the assumption that he wouldn't know it," Strether realizes that Chad and Marie, "out there in the eye of nature," are willfully blind: "He awaited them with a face from which he was conscious of not being quite able to banish the idea that they would have gone on, not seeing and not knowing, missing their dinner and disappointing their hostess, had he himself taken a line to match." This blindness of others, as well as his own, has "darkened his vision." Instead of an honest confrontation, Strether and the guilty couple are all "surface and sound" concerning their "charming chance" at running into each other. This scene is justly famous: when Strether thinks that he will escape, and perhaps even has escaped, from the problems of seeing other people in terms of designs, he suddenly finds his education in imaginative vision dramatically expanded.

Although Strether has come to Europe "to find out all" (130), for most of the book (until the river scene) he resists knowledge he does not wish to accept; as Bilham tells him, he is very difficult to tell anything to unless he wants to know it (139). Strether must pull down the barriers in himself before he can learn more than he is accustomed to learning, and one of the most important of these barriers is "his odious ascetic suspicion of any form of beauty," which he knows he must rid himself of before he will know "the truth of anything" (133). The river scene reveals his error in placing perfection before reality, but his problems in this context occur throughout the novel: it is the typical Hawthornian, Jamesian, and Faulknerian problem of the artist in society. Strether's capitulation before beauty is often cited as the subject of the scene in Gloriani's garden, but the scene is highly ambiguous as to what Strether's declaration " 'Live all you can' " might mean. Chapters X and XI find Strether in the magical garden of the old sculptor Gloriani, whom he meets. He also is introduced for the first time to Madame de Vionnet and her daughter. What he sees and hears there impresses him enormously, but especially as he "sees" the "terrible life" (136) in Gloriani's eyes as a terrible knowledge. Strether's vision of such a knowledge changes him for good. In the ancient garden, amid the splendor of the past, he starts to fashion his future. The irony of the old man on the bench in the walled garden urging his young friend to "Live" is that inasmuch as he may realize now what "Living" might mean in its joys and its sorrows, he also knows he is far past such "Living." But he is not past a new understanding, as we later learn, and this reliance on imagination characterizes Strether's eventual development of an "art" of living.

The "Live" speech has received a great deal of attention.[18] The characteristic Jamesian theme of "too late" is here presented more strongly than in the later river scene. Strether advises Bilham: " 'Live all you can; it's a mistake not to' " (149). Strether's advice seems attached to a "new" self, but perhaps what he speaks of also represents what he has known all along and has not been able to say. Tortured by the sense of something missing in his life, Strether comes to Paris to find out what it is. But his life is no less a "failure," he says, for his knowing it is—or is it? Does Strether's imaginative grasp of his condition and the conditions of those around him "save" him? He is left at the end with nothing but knowledge, and if that is a victory, then Strether is a triumphant hero. But underneath the buoyancy of his exhortation to young Bilham sounds the note of his own sorrow, and readers cannot help but recall this painful irony in the conclusion of the novel. It is the sorrow of the artist figured by the marble faun—first to be alive and yet forever detached from life, and then to know it.

The "Live" speech is often connected to Strether's growing awareness of the sexual "living" Chad and Marie are presumably engaged in. Indeed, at the heart of the knowledge of *The Ambassadors* is sexual knowledge. The barely hidden sexual urge informs the actions of the characters, but none of them (except Jim Pocock) ever admits it. Chad and Marie's physical relationship is only hinted at, though Marie is described, especially by Strether, as sexually expressive, and she is thought by Woollett to be a "dangerous woman." Woollett's fear of her power is quite marked, but on their side, the Woollett contingent is no less sensual, though they are better at hiding their feelings. Waymarsh at first carries on with Miss Barrace, then with Sarah Pocock. Sarah's vehement denouncement of Marie hints at repressed sexual feelings on her part. Indeed, not only does she spend time with Waymarsh, but everyone senses her suppressed power. As Jim tells Strether about Sarah *and* Mrs. Newsome, " 'They wear their fur the smooth side out—the warm side in. Do you know what they are? . . . They're about as intense as they can live' " (261). Jim's crude ideas about "living it up" send him in search of the burlesque show. The only more or less nonsexual characters are Mamie and Bilham—they keep their feelings for each other between themselves and, in so doing, make all the other characters seem guilty of bad taste. The members of this community are thus all seeking sexual knowledge, are all hoping to find love, are all constantly thinking about each other in sexual terms. The language of repression—"something un-reconciled . . . breaking out," a sense of "privation" (362–66—argues for the deep unexpressed urgency of their feelings.

Strether is powerfully attracted both to Maria and to Marie, and his feelings are confused. His character is in danger at times of being inter-preted as a *senex amans*—Strether tells Maria, " 'I'm not,' he explained, leaning back in his chair, but with his eyes on a small ripe round melon—'in real harmony with what surrounds me me. . . . It makes—that's what it comes to in the end—a fool of me' " (428). But Strether develops an understanding of human sexuality which is more comprehensive and less selfish than those of any of the other characters by overcoming his New England aversion to sexual expression and learning the power and value of Marie's passion, especially as he contrasts it with Chad's churlishness. Chad's sexual knowledge is not Strether's, nor is his "Living." Indeed, as Strether becomes aware of the depth and importance of sexual feelings in everyone around him, he learns how sexuality, like everything else in *The Ambassadors*, often becomes subsumed by personal design. Strether sees Chad "in a flash, as the young man marked out by women. . . . There was an experience on his interlocutor's part that looked at him from under the displaced hat, and that looked out moreover by a force of its own, the deep fact of its quantity and quality, and not through Chad's intending bravado or swagger. That was the way men marked out by women *were*" (105). At first Strether is eager to learn just how to be a man marked out by women. He slowly recognizes his own sexual attractions as well as his attractiveness, but he also notes Chad's selfish abuse of Marie's affection and realizes that

Chad's sexuality should be addressed according to the communal standards by which he comes to judge every other human act. Although one cannot help but wonder how many years it has been since Strether has faced romantic problems like this, it turns out that he knows more about human relations of all kinds that he thought he did. Though he somehow seems to pass through this experience of sexual knowledge without ever losing his innocence, he demystifies sex—to him it finally takes its place among other human acts in his community, no longer to be feared and guarded against. Not through "Living," exactly, does Strether attain his wise innocence, but through the artist's understanding of "Living," a faunlike combination of engagement and detachment.

In the Preface James suggests complex readings of the garden scene that do not take the advice Strether gives Bilham as "straight." For example, he notes many times the word "mistake" appears in the "Live" passage, "which gives the measure of the signal warning [Strether] feels attached to his case. He has accordingly missed too much, though perhaps after all constitutionally qualified for a better part, and he wakes up to it in conditions that press the spring of a terrible question."[19] James suggests throughout his discussion that the advice "Live" does not represent the epitome of Strether's knowledge and that Strether finds out later that to "Live" might just mean to live like Chad Newsome, at the expense of others' hearts, minds, and purses. Strether also speaks, one recalls, of "moulds of living" in this speech, and these moulds can be designs. The garden scene is not Strether's high point. He later grows in knowledge far beyond his reactions there.

The Ambassadors actually parodies the "Live" speech. In a comic repetition, Strether tells Waymarsh to pursue his lady: " '*Let* yourself go—in all agreeable directions. These are precious hours—at our age they mayn't recur. Don't have it to say to yourself at Milrose, next winter, that you hadn't the courage for them. . . . Live up to Mrs. Pocock!' " (337). Another ironic echo comes from Jim Pocock: " 'And I want to live while I *am* here too. I feel with *you*—oh you've been grand, old man, and I've twigged—that it ain't right to worry Chad. *I* don't mean to persecute him; I couldn't in conscience. It's thanks to you, at any rate, that I'm here; and I'm sure I'm much obliged. You're a lovely pair' " (259). The reader quickly decides that "Living" may have more than one meaning. It may mean simply living at the expense of others, especially if Chad is taken as the supreme "Liver" and Jim as the supreme admirer of "Living" in the book. Not "Living," but something else, perhaps consciousness of having "failed" to "Live," is morally preferable for Strether not because, as at first, it is the only life he knows, but because in the end, when he *knows* what "Living" is, he is able to choose his own life.

Strether has but one piece of advice for Chad at the end, and its origins are to be found both in Strether's traditional New England codes of morality and in his new communal concern: " 'You'll be a brute, you know—you'll be guilty of the last infamy—if you ever forsake her' " (420). For Strether, reality is finally the knowledge of the irreducible heterogeneity of Marie's painful love and Chad's callous indifference. The responsibility Chad refuses to assume would be in Strether's view a superior way of living.

Instead of "Living," then, Strether is left with only his imagination of it in the end. He finds out the strength of his imagination in its social context, that such a personal imagination in such a communal context contributes to, not detracts from, what he believes is a moral life. Strether's imagination teaches him that beauty, freedom, and love are virtues to be sought; that same imagination informs Strether's New England morality with new meaning. Strether thus imaginatively combines the best of Woollett and Paris, creating for himself a new community.

Strether's "revelation" to Woollett of what he has done is to be his victory, his testament to his own kind of living. He wants them to appreciate his imagination—much as James wanted his own family to appreciate his. He goes home to " 'a great difference—no doubt. Yet I shall see what I can make of it.' " Beauty and knowledge will "rule selection" (431). Yet there are muted hints toward the end of the story that Strether knows he is approaching death: "He should soon be going to where such things were not," the narrator says of Strether's conviction that he would never see the beautiful objects of Madame de Vionnet's apartment again. The narrator continues:

> It amused him to say to himself that he might, for all the world, have been going to die—die resignedly; the scene was filled for him with so deep a death-bed hush, so melancholy a charm. That meant the postponement of everything else—which made so for the quiet lapse of life; and the postponement in especial of the reckoning to come—unless indeed the reckoning to come were to be one and the same thing with extinction.

In going home, Strether faces his "final appreciation of what he had done. . . . Wouldn't *that* revelation practically amount to the wind-up of his career?" (397). This ironic question makes the "Live" theme all the more complex. But even if he does approach exile or death, Strether returns to his community with a "difference." He has learned the value of love, and in *The Ambassadors*, love rises above innocence, which can be blindness, and above virtue, which can be merely prudishness. Strether's nobility arises from his acceptance of the complexities involved in living with other people. Indeed, he does learn about the "facts" he originally came to discover by the end of *The Ambassadors*, but he learns that facts—which must be admitted because innocence is no protection from the dangers of personal design—are in themselves not an answer. Facts are replaced by understanding. The reason Strether can have nothing out of the affair for himself at the end of *The Ambassadors* is that for him, morality is a negative mode, a logic of negative capability: "getting all one can" is not a part of his view. Even when Strether is in the act of saying, "live all you can," then, the author's, narrator's, and reader's fuller understanding makes the statement mean something different by the end of the book.

In James's late novels one finds at least three major ways of stepping back from design: Milly Theale dies and gives up all, money, love, life; Strether withdraws and gives up money and love but retains his living imagination; Maggie transforms herself and so wins money, love, and life. But in the end she pays a price the others were not willing or capable of paying: accepting the knowledge of evil, she remains in relation to others both physically and spiritually. The most American of all these protagonists, she continues in the hope of a future that will atone for the past. But Strether's situation is not entirely hopeless or it could not lead to Maggie's compromised victory. Although he will probably be alone in his new world, he leaps into that void willingly. Strether is heading for the territory, as Huck Finn did, and *The Ambassadors*'s conclusion is, as many readers feel Twain's is, a formal failure in the very world of the book to deal with the problems it presents. Like Huck Strether is an innocent abroad, who, because of the shape of the American imagination, is abroad forever: they are both eternally American ambassadors, looking for that world elsewhere.

In these late works problems of knowledge as "seeing" and "Living" are most thoroughly addressed by James's *ficelle*. The *ficelle*, a Jamesian character whose presence brings a protagonist to new knowledge, often finds herself also engaging in a metaconversation with the reader. Maria Gostrey's dialogue with Strether in *The Ambassadors* offers hero and reader a way of knowing that dramatically improves on other ways offered in this novel.

The *ficelle* is an easily misread aspect of James's fiction—she might appear to be merely an expositional device for "drawing out" a main character, a sort of conversational straight woman. But the *ficelle* is much more. From a Bakhtinian standpoint, one may describe the *ficelle* as the very model for a reader's interpretation of the text. Like Hawthorne's Faith Brown and Georgiana Aylmer, she enacts important themes. Indeed, moral questions in James's work are often formed by opposing values of the female *ficelles* to values James seems to define as masculine, those of enjoying financial power, success, and technology at the expense of moral conscience. In *The Ambassadors*, as elsewhere in his fiction, James's remarkable *ficelles* act not only as guides to knowing a text but also as guides to any act of knowing people. With *ficelles* James proposes a certain freedom through conversation, and this freedom is a result of membership in a dialogic community, which, in a novel, a character such as the *ficelle* uniquely makes possible.

In the late works *The Beast in the Jungle*, *The Wings of the Dove*, *The Ambassadors*, and *The Golden Bowl*, *ficelles* move themselves, the hero or heroine, and the reader toward new knowledge of society, of family, and of the self. This last function is particularly important in *The Beast in the Jungle* and *The Ambassadors*, where the *ficelle*, by engaging in dialogue with a hero, demonstrates to her interlocutor and to her reader that knowledge of the self can be achieved only through engagement of the self with others. Rachel Salmon has brilliantly demonstrated this particular role for May Bartram in *The Beast in the Jungle* in her study of hermeneutic knowledge in that story.[20] Many critics have identified other Jamesian female conversational partners, the Maria Gostreys, Susan Stringhams, and Fanny Assinghams in which James delights, as friends of the reader. Yet despite the many critical evaluations of Maria Gostrey's role in *The Ambassadors* (and she is, as James called her, the "most unmitigated, most abandoned of *ficelles*"),[21] perhaps she has not yet received her due: Maria actually moves the story along, for she brings the hero Strether to knowledge of himself, and this is, of course, the subject of *The Ambassadors*. And as Strether learns to be like Maria, to talk like Maria, to think like Maria, so does the reader.

James says in his Preface to *The Ambassadors* that Maria is "the reader's friend." She "acts in that capacity, and *really* in that capacity alone, with exemplary devotion, from beginning to end of the book. She is an enrolled, a direct aid to lucidity." The *ficelle*, "anxiously kept from showing as 'pieced on,'" achieves in this novel the dignity of a prime idea: which circumstance but shows us afresh how many quite incalculable but none the less clear sources of enjoyment for the infatuated artist, how many copious springs of our never-to-be-slighted "fun" for the reader and critic susceptible of contagion, may sound their incidental plash as soon as the artistic process begins to enjoy free development.[22]

The *ficelle* deflects the narrator's design on Strether, as it were, and allows another perspective to emerge; she thus becomes, in the words of Yeazell, "the narrator's verbal collaborator."[23]

Maria's function as *ficelle* becomes clearest when we examine her side by side with the other two primary female roles, Mrs. Newsome and Marie de Vionnet. When these three women, these three potential "madame ambassadors" of knowledge to Strether, are grouped together, Maria emerges as the author's hermeneutical model by exemplifying his rejection of narrow epistemologies as ways of knowing the self and others. I find it helpful to arrange the contrasting attributes of the three women in the following way:

Mrs. Newsome	Marie de Vionnet	Maria Gostrey
Totally Absent	Totally Present	Absent and Present
Totally Controlling	Out of Control	Control Unsought
Overt Designer	Covert Designer	Rejects Design
Caricature	Warning	Model
Mother	Lover	Sister
Threatens to Obliterate Selfhood for Strether	Threatens to Create an Alternate Self for Strether	Allows Self to Grow for Strether

A comparison of these women demonstrates, among other things, the degree to which each female character promotes her own freedom, that of the hero, Strether, and the reader's freedom as well. Mrs. Newsome, through her overseas directives, is a monologic speaker with whom Strether quickly gives up attempts at dialogue. Though she is cruelly designed on, Marie de Vionnet, at first a promoter of freedom for Strether, eventually is revealed to be a designer like Mrs. Newsome, limiting both her own and Strether's development. Only Maria Gostrey demonstrates openness in her dealings with Strether and allows him to *be* Strether in the end.

The Ambassadors is the story of a revolt against Mrs. Newsome and all she stands for, especially her manipulative nature. She is a formidable presence in Strether's mind—stiff lace collars, imposing black satin dresses, firm control of the purse strings—and her looming presence attests to her prominence in her world as benefactress to "culture" in the form of the *Woollett Review*. But her "morality" and "culture"—her versions of community—are not Strether's, and neither are they the author's and reader's. Mrs. Newsome's reductive epistemology, revealed in her attempts to design upon other people, is only heightened by her necessity of working from afar, for despite her absence, she represents the strictest form of control over Strether and her family. All the characters of *The Ambassadors* objectify others, but she sets the tone. Strether even muses early on that he exists because his name is on the cover of the *Woollett Review*, not the other way around (59). Strether changes from a man who tries to make other people fit into his conceptions of them to a man who admits and enjoys the unpredictable two-way connections. He learns that objective distance, manipulation, and a narrow, prejudicial view of others (and this is Mrs. Newsome's failure of imagination) are the way of the world in both Woollett *and* Paris. In rebelling against Mrs. Newsome, Strether becomes the first citizen of his own new world.

Marie de Vionnet presents a strong contrast as well as a comparison to Mrs. Newsome. As Mrs. Newsome is absent, Marie is very much present, especially where she is not supposed to be—at the inn on the river, for example. She is beautiful and charming as Mrs. Newsome is not. Strether falls in love with her as he never could with Mrs. Newsome. He does not seem to mind her playful manipulation of him at first, as when they lunch in Paris on omelettes and straw-colored Chablis. But like Mrs. Newsome, Marie is a designer, and Strether's realization of this follows upon his rejection of Mrs. Newsome. The turning point in his relations with Marie comes after hearing her brittle attempts at conversation at luncheon following their accidental meeting at the country inn—dialogue fails them all in that scene. But all along Marie has used Strether even as she protested otherwise:

> "I don't ask you to raise your little finger for me again, nor do I wish so much as to mention to you what we've talked of before, either my danger or my safety, or his mother, or his sister, or the girl he may marry, or the fortune he may make, or miss, or the right or the wrong, of any kind, he may do. If after

the help one has had from you one can't either take care of one's self or simply hold one's tongue, one must renounce all claim to be an object of interest." (401)

One of Strether's sharpest confrontations with Paris's designs is his discovery that Chad has helped Marie arrange a match between Jeanne de Vionnet and a French nobleman who is a stranger to all of them, a "marriage of pure convenience on Madame de Vionnet's side in more respects than one." Here Strether strongly senses Chad and Marie's personal selfishness as well as the "potential cruelty of custom" (291).[24] Strether has learned, or relearned, about design in Paris; in this foreign language, culture, and environment, he reacts against such designs with a vehemence unthinkable in his native Woollett. By the end of the book, Strether is willing to sacrifice such interests because he has learned what they do to Marie and Jeanne.

In one passage, Marie de Vionnet tells Strether, " 'What I hate is myself—when I think that one has to take so much, to be happy, out of the lives of others, and that one isn't happy even then.' " She continues that the " 'wretched self is always there. . . . What it comes to is that it's not, that it's never, a happiness, any happiness at all, to *take*. The only safe thing is to give. It's what plays you least false' " (401–2). Taking this advice literally, he is able, through his own disinterested "art," to make his devotions to his community. And in large part, Strether's "art" takes its form in his conversations with Maria Gostrey. By contrast, Strether's "conversations" with Marie were not dialogues, for though they led to knowledge for Strether and Marie, that was not their purpose. Maria Gostrey also originally has a design in her mind, but her own balancing disinterestedness, especially in the conclusion, causes her to contrast sharply with Mrs. Newsome and Marie de Vionnet. Strether's failed interactions with Mrs. Newsome, Marie, and Jeanne prepare him for the knowledge of others he is to achieve in dialogue with Maria Gostrey.

Maria is Strether's first and most important community in Paris, for she bridges the Old and the New Worlds, much like James himself, and she is there at the end as she was at the beginning. Strether and Maria make up a tight little community indeed, an "*us*" (86). They become so close that at one point when she is absent he imagines she can hear him speak, "as if, sitting up, a mile away, in the little apartment he knew, she would listen hard enough to catch" (98). When he withdraws temporarily from their community, Maria teaches him how to do this by leaving for awhile herself.

When he leaves for America in the end, she parts with Strether grace-fully, having contributed more than anyone else to his imaginative and moral growth. Through the "negative capability" of her dialogues, she fur-nishes him with opportunities for community and freedom at the same time.

Strether and Maria often complete each other's ideas, but they are not parts of a single self. Maria is there precisely to defeat singleness of mind, to show the reader how to enter the textual community and pursue a version of the story. Maria describes herself and Strether as " 'beaten brothers in arms,' " whose " 'realities have brought us together' " (32). She is "in the current . . . floating by his side" (231). Most of *The Ambassadors* consists of what Bakhtin would call "addressed speech." Indeed, one could actually construct a single text by stringing together Strether's thoughts as they are generated during his conversations with Maria, for her questions and comments provoke him again and again to understanding. Maria's dialogic function is in keeping with her self-appointed role as "a companion at large": in a wonderfully self-revelatory passage, Maria tells him that he must " 'come out' " as she has helped others to do, for " 'of what is our nation composed but of the men and women individually on my shoulders? I don't do it, you know, for any particular advantage. I don't do it, for instance—some people do, you know—for money' " (13). In contrast to Maria's disinterested qualities, the worst thing this pair ever says about Mrs. Newsome is that " 'she imagined meanly' " (372). Maria is quite like the author James, allowing development of a character's personality with-out closing designs, an association she often metafictively reminds us of when she talks of events that " 'suit' " her " 'book' " (300).

Maria's specific techniques are varied: besides completing sentences for Strether (as when, in the conclusion, she completes so many), this *ficelle* most frequently asks Strether questions that prompt both his and the reader's critical apprehension of the events of the book:

> "They're *all* splendid!" he declared with a sudden strange sound of wistful-ness and envy. "They're all at least happy."
> "Happy?"—it appeared, with their various difficulties, to surprise her.
> "Well—I seem to myself, among them, the only one who isn't."
> She demurred. "With your constant tribute to the ideal?"
> He had a laugh at his tribute to the ideal, but he explained, after a moment, his impression. "I mean they're living. They're rushing about. I've already had *my* rushing. I'm waiting."
> "But aren't you," she asked by way of cheer, "waiting with *me*?" (296)

With her questions Maria analyzes Strether's state of mind and his very terms for interpreting it. She frequently argues with him. She asks him what a given situation means to him. She never pretends to have the single answer; she displays instead a remarkable critical mind. Her frequent repetition of Strether's words forces him to reexamine them in a dialogical context, and this role is ironically doubled back on itself in the scene that concludes the novel:

> "There's nothing, you know, I wouldn't do for you."
> "Oh yes—I know."
> "There's nothing," she repeated, "in all the world."
> "I know. I know. But all the same I must go." He had got it at last. "To be right."
> "To be right?"
> She had echoed it in vague deprecation, but he felt it already clear for her. "That, you see, is my only logic. Not, out of the whole affair, to have got anything for myself."
> She thought. "But, with your wonderful impressions, you'll have got a great deal." (432)

Maria's role is indeed to draw Strether out but this does not in any way limit her. She is enacting the same process the reader is experiencing, the attempt to understand Strether, and her allowing Strether his personal freedom to develop his thoughts becomes the reader's hermeneutic model as well. Maria, as a critical point of view, qualifies and thus advances Strether's and the reader's processes of knowledge.

Through the *ficelle* Strether learns by learning about "learning": "The further she went the further he always saw himself able to follow" (129). Indeed Strether and Maria's talk is often about talk itself; as Yeazell comments, Strether's "remorseless analysis" means freedom to him. Strether often questions the meanings of words, and his speech is generally like that of someone thinking out loud, testing meanings and trying new interpretations. As readers, Yeazell finds, we are "witnessing [the] exchange" between Strether and Maria, and we are "left to float in a world seemingly without solid fact—a world in which 'everything's possible,' and discourse does not so much reveal our truths as create them."[25] Dialogue and polyphony generate a creative knowledge that defeats overriding, monologic design such as that of the Newsomes.

And yet as James no doubt realized, some readers might not recognize Strether and Maria's dialogue as "truly" open, for the identity of the *ficelle* sometimes appears threatened with obliteration by the hero's own point of view. The *ficelle* might seem to the reader to be ultimately a design of the hero's and the narrator's, a sacrifice made for the development of the story. One might not usually think of an issue like this in moral terms, but James certainly did. Maria could be cited as a fault in the story, a place where systematic novelistic design overrode the development of fully human characters, free and independent selves. As Yeazell warns, "The late Jamesian novel threatens to engulf its minor chararacters in its major ones, to make much of its dialogue seem a peculiarly solipsistic communing of self with self."[26]

There is also the problem of Maria's dual identity as designer and antidesigner: Maria, despite her role as a model of James's openness in interpretation, also has her own designs in mind. She seems much of the time to be trying to "get" Strether for her own—she is very fond of him indeed, and she clearly recognizes their mental and emotional synchronicity. She slyly lets him in on Marie de Vionnet's slightly questionable past, and her dealings with him in general are often artful. But is Maria a designer like the other characters around Strether, and if so how much does this threaten her status as a model for interpreting?

In spite of these concerns, I think we are to take James's appraisal of Maria's role in his Preface as a "direct aid to lucidity" in a very sophisticated sense: perhaps he means that when Maria is designing the reader is not to take Maria's point of view as an unobstructed view of reality. It is rather a tentative, personal, and even design-ridden point of view, but one that is unusually sensitive to the growth and development of "the other." Maria's role is ambiguous, and this makes her even more an example of narrative freedom for the reader to emulate. Certainly the reader may inquire *as* Maria does, but the reader will not duplicate her version of events. The reader cannot count on her to "clear things up," for Maria imposes interpretations of her own rather than uncovering "facts." When she says, for example, that Strether's talk is " 'magnificent,' " one can only take her statement as an opinion, not as a fact. It is really Maria's self-consciousness about *having* a point of view, about being *in* a dialogic relationship, that distinguishes her as it distinguishes Dostoevsky's characters, for she helps Strether as well as the reader not to "see the truth" but to know that truth is inseparable from hers or anyone else's personal manipulation of it. Understood in this way, the *ficelle* is anything but a one-dimensional device, and she goes beyond "lucidity."

The most important action Maria takes with Strether is simply to talk *with* him instead of to him, and he urgently needs the lessons he learns through dialogue. Strether's earliest desire in his "ambassadorship" is his wanting "to promote intercourse" (120), and throughout the book diversity, variety, and a dropping of inhibitions excite him as he engages in the conversations of Europe. As Crews puts it, for Strether Europe "defies the compartmentalizing mind";[27] one might add that *The Ambassadors*, through its *ficelle*, does likewise. Conversation as a mode of knowledge transcends all others in this novel, both for Strether and for the reader.

At the end Strether is conscious that he is now absolutely "different," that the possibility of Mrs. Newsome wanting to "patch it up" is pointless. He is also different from Marie, who is " 'more than ever the same' " (430). Strether's rejection of both their visions has made him an outcast. Maria tells him: " 'It isn't so much your *being* "right"—it's your horrible sharp eye for what makes you so' " (432–33). Maria is teasing Strether. In his rejection of "visions" in general, it is not his "eye" that has been educated, but his ear, and this has occurred through his dialogues with her. The reader contrasts the sort of knowledge presented in this concluding scene with that of the river scene's "wrong" picture and linguistic cover-up. Maria's role as *ficelle* makes possible this preference for conversation rather than vision as a model for knowledge.

If Strether had gotten everything he wanted, he might very well have turned into Adam Verver of *The Golden Bowl*. Both Strether and Adam abruptly return from Europe to their native America, and the novels in which they appear profoundly address the problems of knowledge and community that lead the heroes to their returns. In *The Ambassadors* and *The Golden Bowl*, one sees in these Americans' repatriation a shift in James's notion of the possibilities of America for his protagonists. Strether's knowledge causes him to withdraw; Adam's leads him directly to action upon his community, his quiet but insistent manipulation of other people—his "success." And James suggests in both men a peculiarly American sense of the dangers of knowledge. Strether fails to reconcile the claims of personal and communal knowledge, of action and imagination, and to avoid becoming a designer, he retreats into an imaginary world, a dream of the New World even he knows is hopeless. As in Faulkner, failure in James is often the victory *not* to have designed on someone else, *not* to have allowed selfish interests to override one's moral sense of communal relatedness. (Strether's rejection of Maria Gostrey is accordingly described by one critic as the creation of a void into which grace might enter.)[28] The strongest contrast between Strether and Adam is, indeed, the nature of their relationships with others, often expressed in dialogues with women. Adam leads a woman, Charlotte, to America on a "silken halter," while Strether departs from a woman he respects tremendously. Adam looks victorious at the end of *The Golden Bowl*, while Strether's victory is only a spoken one. Unlike Adam, Strether has no design at all, no real claims on anyone, by the end of his story.

And he has come a long way. Strether began worried only about himself, and he was willing to do whatever it took to secure for himself a comfortable life. By dialogizing his relationships with Mrs. Newsome and Marie de Vionnet, Maria Gostrey helps Strether to discover himself as someone not merely working for himself. The "real thing" of power or money is replaced by his knowledge that without community, a person is not "Living" or even merely living at all, but just existing. Thus for Strether America must also remain something of a negative, an unknown—an open, endless possibility for freedom of the imagination. In contrast to Adam's taking hold of the New World and profiting by it, Strether will build no American City.

We all learn a great deal about America from that wandering American emissary Maria Gostrey. The answer for James in *The Ambassadors* and *The Golden Bowl* is neither to retreat nor to build American Cities. Strether hopes instead for the successful position between worlds that James accords to his last heroine, Maggie Verver, a *ficelle* fully developed into a protagonist. As women like Maria and Maggie in James's last novels embody a set of values that opposes masculine ones represented by Chad Newsome and Adam Verver and the Prince, throughout *The Ambassadors* the point of view of the "other" argues for a redefinition of community as a value. Maria acts so as to propel, inspire, and draw out Strether's search for self and leads him to locate that self in a hermeneutic moral community. Indeed, if the collective values suggested by Maria, the strongest and most fully developed female character, may be said to oppose the male values of Chad, then one may argue that these female values actually make possible Strether's remarkable understanding of himself and his world. Integrative, communal values as embodied by Maria make knowledge in *The Ambassadors* a complex, dialogic knowledge, and in doing so challenge all our traditionalist assumptions about male and female roles in addition to so many of our other epistemologies. Obviously, in a novel such as *The Ambassadors*, sex roles, like language, are best understood without rigid categories, especially as it seems that choices among values—whether defined as masculine or feminine—are all presented through the three women characters with whom Strether engages. Through dialogue with the *ficelle*, Strether and the reader find that autonomy and intimacy, knowing and not knowing, "Living" and refusing to "Live" are simultaneously possible. Of course, the tendency to make certain female characters representatives of communal values is typical among many male writers, often to the point of cliché. But James is here invoking the raison d'être of his entire narrative undertaking: the knowledge offered by *ficelles* invokes James's most important artistic, epistemological, moral, sexual, and social models of thought.

Strether returns to America in the end with the best of his American values confirmed and the worst of them put away. Europe makes him the ideal American, though it warps most of the other Americans into boors and dullards. Europe seems to have an effect on Bilham and Mamie, however, similar to the one it has on Strether; perhaps they, not the aging Strether, represent for James a hope for the future, the best of American youth. Chad, one need not add, represents the worst. Chad is the man of the modern hour, and the future belongs to him just as much as it does not belong to Strether. *The Ambassadors* is James's warning cry, his testament of another kind of knowledge—something alien to Chad's designing knowledge—that should be available to future citizens of the New World. In *The Ambassadors* James makes Strether an image of himself and proudly offers this alternative consciousness to a mechanical modern world in which it may be impossible ever to understand Strether's hermeneutic knowledge. It is thus no accident that the Newsomes are factory owners interested in new technology (this is why Chad is to come home) or that Chad's idea of a business career should take in as well the manipulative "art" of advertising. Strether's imaginative way may be a flight to the territory, a failure, but it is toward him and his free play of the mind that the reader is drawn in the end, and it is his decision to which the reader responds. Chad's future plans, and the future of the Newsome clan, are Philistinisms of little interest to Henry James or his reader.

4. Community Versus Design in *Absalom, Absalom!*

IT IS A CRITICAL COMMONPLACE that *Absalom, Absalom!* is a story about storytelling, a narrative about narrative, a metafiction. It is the epitome of an exploration of the narrative process Faulkner undertook for most of his career; in it he takes the novel form as far as he can while still retaining an overall unity of style, structure, and theme. *Absalom, Absalom!* strains at its boundaries but structurally does not cross them; as in *The Ambassadors*, the unified structure asserts a resolution its action resists. It thus represents both a resolution and a magnificent "failure" in Faulkner's career: *Absalom, Absalom!* is difficult not because it forbids closure but because it does so while exerting itself so strenuously in that direction.

To achieve what Bakhtin calls a "new integral view of the person," after *Absalom, Absalom!* Faulkner seems to have discovered a "new integral authorial position" vis-à-vis his characters.[1] In *Go Down, Moses*, Faulkner devised structural ways to accomplish this authorial shift in perspective that frees characters and readers—he dismantled the novelistic structure into a series of short stories. But the "failure" of *Absalom, Absalom!* has fascinated critics more than the "victory" of *Go Down, Moses*. The failed structural polyphony in *Absalom, Absalom!* in many ways enacts novelistic freedom as much as does the very different, less strained polyphonic structure of *Go Down, Moses*. Failure becomes a central value in *Absalom, Absalom!*, for where success leaves off, storytelling begins. The storytelling aspects of *Absalom, Absalom!* and the echoing interrelations of narrative voices are its most important hermeneutic narrative techniques, but in addition, Faulkner addresses problems of knowledge through his metaphors and his strategies of negativity, avoidance, and absence.

In *Absalom, Absalom!* the action of storytelling dialogically transforms tellers into hearers and hearers into tellers. The many storytellers—especially Quentin and Shreve—trade roles of speaker and audience. Storytelling is the crucial action in *Absalom, Absalom!* because the telling and retelling of Sutpen's story supply the means for achieving the hermeneutic knowledge necessary to understand and in some sense even counteract Sutpen, slavery, and human pride. This dialogue of telling and hearing drives the transformative alternations in narrative points of view in *Absalom, Absalom!*

Some critics have described *Absalom, Absalom!* as a "progression" of narrators, beginning with Sutpen and "culminating" with Shreve, who is seen as the narrator at the greatest "distance" from Sutpen. Representative of this view is Hyatt Waggoner, who argues that the novel is a search for truth "beyond" narrative distortion, one that presents the past as the real thing the characters' narratives "distort." Waggoner's argument depends on the idea that narrative movement is one of "progressive disengagement, a moving outward from the center." As the character most "removed" from Sutpen, Shreve is thus the one most able to move freely and imaginatively. Although Waggoner does say that neither Shreve nor anyone else in the story offers a "final view," the emphasis on thinking of Shreve as the "freest" of narrators is misleading.[2] No teller in *Absalom, Absalom!* can be called objective because the narrators all simultaneously transform each other as they tell and hear each others' narratives. *Absalom, Absalom!* is a polyphony of storytellers. Indeed, there is no "real" Thomas Sutpen beyond what the narrators say about him; he is not even "in" the book. What is real are all the stories about him—and nothing else.[3]

A strong indication that *Absalom, Absalom!* should not be thought of as a progression of narrators embroidering an objectively true story with their own additions—as opposed to significantly transforming it dialogically—is that the progression is sometimes broken entirely. For example, Quentin reveals to Shreve that *he* has told his father, who is supposedly higher up the chain of authority than Quentin is, that Sutpen chose Charles Bon's name himself (revealing that Sutpen must have known that Bon was his son before Bon ever came to Sutpen's Hundred). " 'Your father,' Shreve said. 'He seems to have got an awful lot of delayed information awful quick, after having waited forty-five years.' " " 'Grandfather didn't tell him all of it either, like Sutpen never told Grandfather quite all of it,' " Quentin explains. " 'Then who did tell him?' " Shreve asks. " 'I did,' " says Quentin (266).

Absalom, Absalom! calls into question usual assumptions about truth in literary telling, or in any telling, for that matter. Narrative progression is not the place to seek truth in *Absalom, Absalom!* One instead juxtaposes the narrative voices, comparing their designs and evaluating their interests without assigning epistemological verity to any one view. No one in *Absalom, Absalom!* tells the truth in ways other characters do not, for the truth of one point of view changes the truth of another point of view. In this context, Quentin and Shreve's fictional creation of the lawyer, for example, is no less true or false in this polyphonic narrative than anything else. Denying the separation of object and subject, *Absalom, Absalom!* offers instead a conversational model for knowing. This dialogic model of tellers and hearers transforming each other better describes what happens in *Absalom, Absalom!* than the progression of narrators because it recognizes the existence of the novel's diversity within community.

Even Joseph Reed, who is so often the best of Faulkner's critics, occasionally makes the mistake of seeing *Absalom, Absalom!* objectively. At times, he seems to assume that there is a hierarchy of narrative truth in the novel through which narrators may be ranked according to the degree to which they tell the truth. Such assumptions slip into Reed's language. He writes that as Rosa Coldfield continues her story, the reader grants her progressively more and more credence, and part of her credibility comes from her status as participant. But being a participant, Reed says, also prevents her from escaping from her own emotionally tortured perspective on the story: "Participation is an entrapment in the long time of continual contact, experience, and memory of every moment of an event, a resultant inability to abstract, to gain distance from moment to moment. To a more objective observer the event could have a beginning and an end and not just a continual curve of increasing and diminishing presence." Reed momentarily misses the point—what character or reader in *Absalom, Absalom!* is objective? Surely no one is; the point of the book is to defeat such expectations. *Absalom, Absalom!* argues throughout for understanding as communal and not objective truth.[+]

Notions of objective truth stymie the reader of *Absalom, Absalom!* The idea that Sutpen is the "real thing" and that as narrators become increasingly removed from him their objectivity grows is misleading, and Rosa's biased, participatory knowledge, as Reed defines it, which allows her personal design to control her view of Sutpen ("the demon"), cannot be, as Waggoner thinks, countered by Shreve's objectivity. Shreve, the most objective narrator, *also* narrates from within his own personal design, particularly his sensationalistic view of the South, and, more significantly, he is the only character other than Rosa to call Sutpen a "demon." All the narrators of *Absalom, Absalom!* are better understood as dialogic characters such as those Bakhtin describes in Dostoevsky. Though he himself would be entirely unconscious of it, even Sutpen could be addressed as one of Bakhtin's "carnivalized" characters because in his tricksterism he embodies in a subverted and yet terribly recognizable form the social ideals of the Old South. All the characters of *Absalom, Absalom!* are dialogized by Faulkner and his many narrators.

By the end of the novel, Rosa's status as participant and her designs for revenge do not make her story any more or less reliable than Shreve's. But she begins things by telling Quentin her story, ameliorating, to some extent, her hatred of Sutpen. Her metaphors help generate the process of storytelling as a communal knowledge that supersedes personal design.

Just as the idiot Benjy Compson is the first narrator in *The Sound and the Fury* and the clairvoyant Darl Bundren is first in *As I Lay Dying*, in *Absalom, Absalom!* Rosa, the "mad" narrator, goes first. What does this suggest about narrators' designs? By placing a questionable point of view first, Faulkner immediately deactivates the reader's desire for an authoritative point of view—one that tells what "really happened." Rosa's excessive, compulsive, hysterical narrative is not accepted as true by her hearer, Quentin, any more than it is accepted as such by the reader—but it is not perceived as false either. It is assimilated and transformed by Quentin's design, by the other narrators' versions, and ultimately by the reader's metadesign. As a way of entering the story, Rosa's tale is immediately involving; it draws the reader into the very difficulties about telling with which the book is concerned, and it introduces the reader to the disorganized, multifaceted nature of the story better than would Quentin's intellectualizing or Mr. Compson's sour stoicism. In particular, Rosa's use of the "demon" metaphor reveals both her design and her desire for a dialogue that will replace personal design with communal knowledge. Indeed, the demon metaphor and its related images are part of a complex storytelling pattern that connects tellers and hearers in *Absalom, Absalom!*

The design of Sutpen as demon is carried through the entire novel by Rosa and Shreve, but before Rosa ever speaks the narrator of the entire novel uses the demon metaphor first while describing what Rosa is telling Quentin: "Out of a quiet thunderclap he would abrupt (man-horse-demon) upon a scene peaceful and decorous as a schoolprize water color, faint sulphur-reek still in hair clothes and beard, with grouped behind him his band of wild niggers like beasts half tamed to walk upright like men" (8). The demon metaphor alone, that is, used by one narrator, is certainly reductive—Sutpen is a man, after all, and not a "demon." Rosa has fallen prey to the design of the metaphor. But because "demon" is a metaphor in a dialogic context, the narrator initiates a process in which several narrators use the word, and the demon metaphor comes to allow characters, narrator, author, and reader to span the divisions between them. In the process of building community, metaphors are handed from Faulkner to his narrator to Rosa to Shreve and then to the reader, and they change in the process. Because in their open-endedness metaphors do not impose restrictive explanations on the process of storytelling, they thus permit tellers and hearers to build freely on their suggestive implications. This "many-voiced" quality of a word like "demon" in *Absalom, Absalom!* is what Bakhtin calls the inherent "heteroglossia" of the shared spoken word. Heteroglossia addresses the ever-expandable multiplicity of meaning in language itself.

Thus the demon metaphor's movement from narrator to narrator significantly transforms it, introducing "ogres," "djinns," and Faustus. Sutpen is the "ogre face of [Rosa's] childhood, seen once and then repeated at intervals and on occasions which she could neither count nor recall, like the mask in Greek tragedy, interchangeable not only from scene to scene, but from actor to actor and behind which the events and occasions took place without chronology or sequence" (62). The ogre face is here consciously identified as a verbal "mask"; its interchangeability suggests both its function as an interpretive design (it slips from scene to scene) and its role as communal narrative device (it slips through dialogue from narrator to narrator not unlike the *"devil's heritage"* [135] that Sutpen's family carries). "Demon" generates two other groups of images, ghosts and tombs.

The South of *Absalom, Absalom!*, "dead since 1865," is "peopled with garrulous outraged baffled ghosts, listening, having to listen, to one of the ghosts which had refused to lie still even longer than most had." Miss Rosa, a "ghost," tells Quentin "about the old-ghost times; and Quentin Compson still too young to deserve to be a ghost, but nevertheless having to be one for all that, since he was born and bred in the deep South the same as she was" (9). Ghosts are related to demons in *Absalom, Absalom!* in that both arise from the evils of the South. The difference between the two is that demons seek to impose their will on people by acting upon them or by forcing them to act in the demons' interests, and ghosts impose a different kind of design, a narrative one. Ghosts tell about demons, and what they tell haunts their listeners. In this sense Quentin becomes more and more "ghostly" during the course of the story; he is described several times in the last chapters as speaking in a dead voice, face cast down, immobile and expressionless. Quentin becomes a ghost by absorbing all the ghostly voices telling about the South: "the mere names were interchangeable and almost myriad. His childhood was full of them; his very body was an empty hall echoing with sonorous defeated names; he was not a being, an entity, he was a commonwealth. He was a barracks filled with stubborn back-looking ghosts still recovering, even forty-three years afterward, from the fever which had cured the disease" (12). Charles Bon is also a ghost; Mr. Compson believes the "living" Charles was "usurped" by the designs of the demon himself. And Quentin becomes more ghostly as he identifies with the dead Henry and Bon.

Quentin and Shreve, fighting Sutpen's "logic and morality" with their own, sit in their room at Harvard "back to back as though at the last ditch, saying No to Quentin's Mississippi shade who in life had acted and reacted to the minimum of logic and morality, who dying had escaped it completely, who dead remained not only indifferent but impervious to it, somehow a thousand times more potent and alive" (280). Quentin becomes *too* ghostly a teller, *too* passive a narrator. He cannot think how he should act in regard to this story; he does not know what to do with the knowledge he has gained. He does not know whether he hates the South or what it means if he does. Though ghosts are tellers, it seems they are sometimes incapable of understanding what they tell, that is, of becoming hearers. Likewise, hearers can remain self-absorbed and never attain the status of tellers when they refuse to join the interpretive community by telling. By the end Quentin, newly a teller, cannot revert to being a hearer and ultimately cannot confront the ways in which what he is telling affects his own life. To be merely a teller is to be a ghost incapable of using the information one tells in one's own life. To be merely a hearer is to be a demon intent *only* on using knowledge for the benefit of one's own designs.

Absalom, Absalom! becomes Quentin's story when he inherits the narrative from Rosa halfway through the book. At the beginning of Chapter VI, Quentin's imagination takes over the story. Rosa's design ignites his own personal design, and he replaces her as the primary subnarrator. But this is according to Rosa's plan: she is a hearer who becomes a teller, and she selects her hearer, Quentin, because she knows he will become a teller, too. His failure later to become a hearer again is his own failure, and not Rosa's, for in the end she comes to terms with Sutpen though Quentin cannot. Her burden becomes his.

Rosa lives in a community of victims, all of "the same folly and mischance" (87). Henry and Judith are a private community of grief: " 'the same two calm inpenetrable faces seen together in the carriage. . . . They didn't talk, tell one another anything, you see— . . . They did not need to talk. They were too much alike'" (121–22). Rosa's community, her family, betrays her; after Sutpen insults her she is "blown back to town on the initial blast of that horror and outrage to eat of gall and wormwood stolen through paling fences at dawn" (177). Her father rejected community, as did her aunt, and now Rosa lives as a town liability, protected by the townspeople but utterly alone. This is the worst thing that happens to her; her loneliness is the thing for which she cannot forgive Sutpen. She fights through her telling to reestablish community, even if only with Quentin, and she succeeds at it where Quentin fails, where Shreve fails, where Sutpen and Henry and Bon fail. But of course, in many senses, including especially the Jamesian, it is all too late.

When the story opens the time is nearly done. "The quaint, stiffly formal request which was actually a summons, out of another world almost," brings Quentin to her home, which is itself an indication of how her time is passing away: "It was of two storeys—unpainted and a little shabby, yet with an air, a quality of grim endurance as though like her it had been created to fit and complement a world in all ways a little smaller than the one in which it found itself" (9–10). An oracle of the past, Miss Rosa speaks to Quentin from behind a "wan triangle of lace at wrists and throat" (11), with "an air Cassandralike and humorless and profoundly and sternly prophetic out of all proportion to the actual years even of a child who had never been young." She employs the "logic- and reason-flouting quality of a dream" (21–22). The elderly Rosa's story—which she began to assemble as a small child—is her obsession for most of her life, " '*equipped*' " as she is " '*with that cunning, that inverted canker-growth of solitude which substitutes the omnivorous and unrational hearing-sense for all the others*' " (145). " '*A child's vacant fairy-tale*' " comes alive in a " '*garden*' " sown with Sutpen's " '*seed,*' " but Rosa's story serves only to torment her year after year until she decides to tell it to Quentin:

> "*I will tell you what he did and let you be the judge. (Or try to tell you, because there are some things for which three words are three too many, and three thousand words that many words too less, and this is one of them. It can be told; I could take that many sentences, repeat the bold blank and outrageous words just as he spoke them, and bequeath you only that same aghast and outraged unbelief I knew when I comprehended what he meant; or take three thousand sentences and leave you only that Why? Why? and Why? that I have asked and listened to for almost fifty years.) But I will let you be the judge and let you tell me if I was not right.*" (166–67)

Only in telling her story to Quentin and in letting him "be the judge" (that is, letting him add his interpretation by hearing and retelling it) does Rosa relieve herself of her obsession with the tale, her "unrational hearing-sense." She returns to Sutpen's Hundred for the first time in decades, daring to do so only in the company of Quentin, her designated hearer who, like her, will become a teller to attempt to assuage *his* burden of knowledge.

But polyphony in telling goes beyond a multiplicity of narrative voices: it explores the internal psychological structure of character itself by questioning the role of that subjectivity in a community of other subjectivities. Quentin is often "the two separate Quentins now talking to one another in the long silence of notpeople, in notlanguage." His psyche is split into hearer and teller, Quentin in the South and Quentin at Harvard, Quentin a ghost and Quentin a young man (9). Polyphony extends outward into the entire community of knowledge in the novel: the doubleness that is so important later (the doubling of Quentin-Henry and Shreve-Bon, as well as of Quentin-Shreve) begins with the doubling of Quentin-Quentin and Quentin-Rosa and takes its form from the hearer-teller relationship.

Quentin's first response to Rosa's invitation is " 'But why tell me about it?' " Mr. Compson first gives Quentin an ironic answer: " 'Years ago we in the South made our women into ladies. Then the War came and made the ladies into ghosts. So what else can we do, being gentlemen, but listen to them being ghosts?' " He follows this, however, with a more somber answer: " 'So maybe she considers you partly responsible through heredity for what happened to her and her family through him' " (12–13). Although Quentin is not responsible through actual kinship, he is responsible in another way, Mr. Compson hints: he is a member of her community. Quentin assumes the responsibility of his communal role (which only begins with his being polite to the old lady), for in listening to Rosa Quentin becomes personally as well as communally attached to her. In becoming a teller he attempts to confront his concerns about both family and community—his home, the South.

Quentin's obsessive subject, that of the entire storytelling community of *Absalom, Absalom!*, is of course Thomas Sutpen. But from the time of his arrival in Jefferson, Sutpen will tell the town next to nothing, for his design will not allow for much communication between him and his community: "He was at this time completely the slave of his secret and furious impatience, his conviction gained from whatever that recent experience had been—that fever mental or physical—of a need for haste, of time fleeing beneath him" (34). Though he eventually confides in General Compson, Sutpen offers only a sketchy and one-sided narrative that merely tries to excuse or explain the failure of his design. Betrayed by the community that made him go around to the back door long ago, Sutpen does not tell his new community his full tale or reveal his designs because that sort of telling is a communal action for which he is unprepared. Sutpen asks for advice (" 'where did I make the mistake?' ") but does not really want it, as General Compson notes (240). But in telling General Compson about himself, Sutpen's need for belonging to a communal group—the need of that little boy with no shoes whom he is always careful not to betray, the little boy seeking admittance into a human community to which he thought he already belonged—seizes him momentarily. Sutpen also talks to Wash Jones, but his actual words are rarely narrated, only Wash's adoring, " 'Sho, Kernel.' " Sutpen talks not to invite participation from a listener but to cover up unpleasant truths about himself. Instead, other characters find themselves participating in Sutpen's telling regardless of his self-imposed isolation. They defeat him not merely in imagining him but in imagining the defeat he failed to imagine.

As a small boy, Sutpen heard tales of Tidewater splendor, but the tales meant nothing to him because he did not live in that community, and he had never

> "even heard of, never imagined, a place, a land divided neatly up and actually owned by men who did nothing but ride over it on fine horses or sit in fine clothes on the galleries of big houses while other people worked for them; he did not even imagine then that there was any such way to live or to want to live, or that there existed all the objects to be wanted which there were, or that the ones who owned the objects not only could look down on the ones that didn't, but could be supported in the down-looking not only by the others who owned objects too but by the very ones that were looked down on that didn't own objects and knew they never would." (221)

Sutpen comes from a place where " 'other people he knew lived in log cabins boiling with children like the one he was born in—men and grown boys who hunted or lay before the fire on the floor while the women and older girls stepped back and forth across them to reach the fire to cook, where the only colored people were Indians and you only looked down at them over your rifle sights.' " In Sutpen's native community

> "the land belonged to anybody and everybody and so the man who would go to the trouble and work to fence off a piece of it and say 'This is mine' was crazy; and as for objects, nobody had any more of them than you did because

everybody had just what he was strong enough or energetic enough to take and keep, and only that crazy man would go to the trouble to take or even want more than he could eat or swap for powder and whiskey." (221)

But Sutpen "'had hardly heard of such a world until he fell into it'" (221–22). In that fall into a new world, Sutpen quickly and painfully learns of his desire for the "objects" of designs, objects incomprehensible at first but later the inspiration for his own grandiose design on society.

Sutpen's desire for objects such as the fine men and women of the Virginia plantations own is related to his desire for objectivity in his design and in his telling. He believes he tells "the truth" to General Compson: "'saying it with his head flung up a little in that attitude that nobody ever knew exactly who he had aped it from or if he did not perhaps learn it too from the same book out of which he taught himself the words, the bombastic phrases with which Grandfather said he even asked you for a match for his cigar or offered you the cigar—'" (240). Sutpen is selfishly unselfconscious; fittingly, he treats people, including himself, as he treats ideas or narratives: as objects.

Sutpen's career in school also suggests interesting things about truth in storytelling. His mountain-born self-reliance and pride make him unable to "condescend to memorize dry sums and such" but allow him "to listen when the teacher read[s] aloud." Sutpen tells General Compson that in school "'I learned little save that most of the deeds, good and bad both, incurring opprobation or plaudits or reward either, within the scope of man's abilities, had already been performed and were to be learned about only from books.'" In spite of his listening to the teacher's telling, Sutpen is suspicious of telling itself; in other words, he believes what he thinks is in the book, but he does not believe the teller. He asks the teacher if what he read about the West Indies was true, that men got rich there, and the teacher answers, "'"Why not,". . . starting back. "didn't you hear me read it from the book?"—'"How do I know that what you read was in the book?" I said.'" But as Sutpen explains, "'I had to know, you see.'" Although his "child's instinct" tells him the teacher is reading what is really in the book—the teacher "lacked that something which is necessary in a man to enable him to fool even a child by lying"—Sutpen demands the "truth." The teacher is frightened. Sutpen grabs his arm, and they struggle:

"and I holding him and saying—I was quite calm, quite calm; I just had to know—saying, 'Suppose I went there and found out that it was not so?' and he shrieking now, shouting, 'Help! Help!' so that I let him go. So when the time came when I realized that to accomplish my design I should need first of all and above all things money in considerable quantities and in the quite immediate future, I remembered what he had read to us and I went to the West Indies." (241–43)

Sutpen's demand for objective truth is here closely tied to some of his worst qualities—his willingness to force other people to do what he wants, to manipulate and hurt them, and of course his all-consuming urge for wealth and power. Faulkner uses Sutpen's monistic, designing way of telling and knowing as a judgment against him.

So it is that Sutpen explains his design to General Compson " 'with that patient amazed recapitulation, not to Grandfather and not to himself because Grandfather said that his very calmness was indication that he had long since given up any hope of ever understanding it.' " According to Quentin, Sutpen tells his story " 'to fate itself, the logical steps by which he had arrived at a result absolutely and forever incredible, repeating the clear and simple synopsis of his history (which he and Grandfather both knew now) as if he were trying to explain it to an intractable and unpredictable child' " (263). The novel indicates the striking similarities between Sutpen's way of thinking and an "objective" way of reading: if one can measure and balance knowledge as Sutpen wants to measure and balance the ingredients of morality like the ingredients of a pie or cake, one can generate a single view of a text, a single interpretation that will defeat all other interpretations. Faulkner warns his readers against such singleness of vision, against designing as ignorantly and innocently as Sutpen does. Instead, by having Sutpen's words—and these are his most important lines—couched in a multivoiced interpretive narration through General Compson, Mr. Compson, Quentin, and Shreve, Faulkner urges us to accept diversity and reinterpretation of Sutpen rather than Sutpen's single view of himself. The single controlling view is the deadly danger to be shunned.

Like Bon, Sutpen does not know where he fits into his community, how he is evaluated by it: "He knew neither where he had come from nor where he was nor why. He was just there, surrounded by the faces" (226–27). Sutpen even at the end "had not only not lost the innocence yet, he had not yet discovered that he possessed it" (228). Sutpen spends his whole life trying to acquire the knowledge he thinks will save him, but because he is a hearer who tries to use only his own "logic and morality," he never addresses his own single point of view—his design—as responsible to the interests of others in his community. Quentin and Shreve approach this more closely. Sutpen, feeling mistreated by his communities, rejects community from his arrival in Jefferson and never finds out the answer to his "mistake."

Although his ideas about "truth" are limited to facts, Sutpen several times in his life acts without full knowledge, out of instinct, and these acts benefit him more than his premeditated ones. Thus when he leaves home and journeys to the West Indies, he does not know what is going to happen to him. When he begins to act out of sheer design, out of a well-planned campaign, his hard work fails resoundingly, his marriages, his divorce, his house, his children's futures. Finally, when he tries to ensure another son for himself with Wash's granddaughter, he is finished. Quentin thinks of Sutpen on the West Indian plantation as "overseeing what he oversaw and not knowing that he was overseeing it" (252). Quentin plays with the meanings of "oversee" and "overlook," and this visual pun is a fitting description of Sutpen's grandiose lack of knowledge throughout.

Sutpen feels he is later "handicapped" in building his domain by "the chance and probability of meddling interference arising out of the disapprobation of all communities of men toward any situation which they do not understand" (274). For this reason he demands objectively verifiable truth that can "understand" *everything*. But paradoxically, though he refuses negativity or ambiguity, he is the most absent of tellers; furthermore, in trying to avoid indeterminacy of identity by siring a child, he is literally cut off from the rest of the community by his only other audience besides General Compson, Wash Jones. Sutpen is not one of the metafictive narrators of *Absalom, Absalom!* He is not in dialogue with the other fictional elements—narrator, characters, readers, author—and he never becomes a fully developed storyteller.

In contrast to Sutpen's "objective" narrative style is Quentin and Shreve's dialogue, which, inspired by Rosa, seeks a community of tellers and hearers, though it too is subject to problems of design. Truth in telling is a narrative problem in every way in *Absalom, Absalom!* and though it is a dialogue, Quentin's and Shreve's conversational search for meaning is troubled all along by objective and personal design. Quentin's story becomes so powerful that Shreve eventually feels he cannot hear it the way Quentin tortuously tells it, and he imposes his own personal designs on it to make it more palatable for him. Shreve's "crass levity," for example, is an "unsentimental sentimentality" that crudely jokes about things it perceives as threatening (" 'He chose. He chose lechery. So do I. But go on.' "). Shreve's reductive mythology of the South is his most limiting narrative design on the story; in distancing the setting and the people there, Shreve's vulgarized, romantic, sensational views of the South ensure that it will retain its thrill and thus its shock value. He also concerns himself rigorously with the story's facts, as when he and Quentin dispute Sutpen's birthplace. When Quentin says he " 'was born in West Virginia, in the mountains———' " Shreve counters, " 'Not in West Virginia. . . .' 'What?' Quentin said. 'Not in West Virginia,' Shreve said. 'Because if he was twenty-five years old in Mississippi in 1833, he was born in 1808. And there wasn't any West Virginia in 1808 because———' 'All right,' Quentin said. '———West Virginia wasn't admitted———' 'All right, all right,' Quentin said. '———into the United States until———' 'All right all right all right,' Quentin said" (220–21). Faulkner demonstrates the failure of such a faith in the "facts." Just as Mr. Compson's trying to understand meaning with a "chemical formula" reminds one of Sutpen's view of morality as a pie with the proper ingredients in it, in this passage Shreve's demand for accuracy is belied by the first sentence of the paragraph in which it occurs: "Sutpen's trouble was his innocence." Like Sutpen, Shreve has a certain innocence and he has a design. But it must be emphasized that through his imaginative participation in the story, Shreve tries to overcome his personal design in narrative.[5]

Shreve performs the crucial function of changing, like Quentin, from a hearer to a teller, and he shares in the difficulties of giving up either role. To a certain extent he overcomes the dangers of relying on one personal design through his involvement in the dialogue, the community of the tale, because he seems to have enough genuine concern for Quentin to tell and retell the story along with his friend, and he unmistakably adds valuable aspects to it, especially as he assists Quentin with his reasoning. Shreve is a subordinate character to Quentin's protagonist, and one of his most important functions is to provoke Quentin to discover new knowledge. Shreve is a *ficelle*.

Shreve finds himself designing more uncontrollably as Quentin rapidly develops problems as a teller, but eventually it is the failure to be simultaneously a teller and a hearer on Quentin's part and not Shreve's that is *Absalom, Absalom!*'s failure, for the dialogue between Quentin and Shreve breaks down completely when Quentin withdraws. Quentin begins to sense that he and Shreve "*have had to listen too long*" when he notices how freely they play with the story, building paradoxes for their own sake, as he does when he thinks of Bon's octoroon mistress at his grave, "*who, not bereaved, did not need to mourn*" (193). From this point in the book, many of

Quentin's best insights into the Sutpen story remain internal and unshared with Shreve, and Shreve's dialogue degenerates into teasing. Quentin peevishly gives up dialogue in favor of personal introspection, and this is the failure, the refusal to speak *and* hear, the refusal to know couched in Quentin's famous " 'I dont hate it!' "[6]

Earlier, Quentin and Shreve's conversation took them to Carolina "forty-six years ago," where "both of them were Henry Sutpen and both of them were Bon, compounded each of both." They suddenly stop talking and "overhear" Henry's visit with his father on the battlefield. Their "transportation" is related by the narrator, and the five voices—Henry, Sutpen, Quentin, Shreve, and the narrator—engage in polyphonic dialogue (351). But by the end of the story, Quentin moves more and more toward ghosthood and away from the community of tellers and hearers. He cannot make another transformation, for in giving up on understanding himself, the South, and the Sutpen story, in refusing to move from hearer to teller to hearer again, he subsides into inaction. Inversely, Rosa moves more and more out of her private obsessions and into the world of the living. At the end, Rosa has one final act left in her, a visit to Sutpen's Hundred to retrieve Henry:

> "she refused at the last to be a ghost. That after almost fifty years she couldn't reconcile herself to letting him lie dead in peace. That even after fifty years she not only could get up and go out there to finish up what she found she hadn't quite completed, but she could find someone to go with her and bust into that locked house because instinct or something told her it was not finished yet." (362)

Fittingly, it was Quentin, the hearer-become-teller, and Rosa, the teller-become-hearer, who earlier made a visit to the house. But it is Rosa alone who acts in the end, journeying again, only to find the house ablaze and the occupants burning within it. Rosa is an instrument of doom to Sutpen's Hundred, an avenging ghost/demon. After her death, Quentin alone is left with the knowledge of what has happened, but as he finishes his role as teller he is personally overwhelmed by the story and unable to hear or tell any more. His telling ends in his repudiation of the entire story. Like Strether in *The Ambassadors*, Quentin retreats in his telling into an isolated world of self; this is an ironic failure for two heroes who try so very hard to know and understand other people. For readers, however, just as it will not allow objective truth, *Absalom, Absalom!* simply will not allow a hearer to remain merely a hearer, or a teller a teller. Quentin and Shreve, like their narrator, go so far as to identify with characters in their story, especially Henry and Bon, much in the way narrators and readers identify with novelistic characters to participate figuratively in their stories. In their process of transforming themselves into tellers and hearers, Quentin and Shreve teach us to enter and sustain a community of voices.

Quentin and Shreve's pairing is paralleled by other sorts of dualities in the communities of *Absalom, Absalom!* The social issues at stake all address "otherness" within community. Learning to address otherness in this book, modeled on dialogue, is the very hope of the Sutpen story, especially when otherness is of race or gender or class. Black characters all along provoke other characters into new knowledge of themselves as members of a failed community. Less obviously, women characters' roles are likewise dialogic. The women of *Absalom, Absalom!* often demonstrate to the reader how to exercise the choice to become involved, not exclusively Quentin or Shreve. Rosa, Judith, and Clytie (and even Shreve in his often-described "femininity") seem to learn to varying degrees that it is fruitless to try to stop time or to conform others to one's own timeless designs. Participation in time is the women's choice, even as it becomes Quentin's failure. Here, the "other" instead of the traditionally conceived male hero demonstrates the author's moral hermeneutics to the reader. As Judith seems to suggest, the world is not a neat design, but rather an uncomfortable juxtaposition of people's doomed efforts to make patterns: " 'Each one wants to weave his own pattern into the rug; and it cant matter, you know that, or the Ones that set up the loom would have arranged things a little better, and yet it must matter because you keep on trying or having to keep on trying' " (127).[7]

The South itself before and after the Civil War is the underlying wrongful cultural community. Quentin and the reader learn that Sutpen was defeated because of his rigid adherence to principles of racial and social inhumanity and that the fatal flaw in his design is the inherent one in the structure of the South. Both the private and the public communities sin through their enslaving designs on "the other." Both Sutpens and southerners at large find they are living in a failed, defeated culture. In a passage that strangely evokes the interrelations among the characters of *The Golden Bowl*, we learn that the sin of Negro slavery drowns the sinners and the sinned-against in mutual suffering:

> "Because the time now approached (it was 1860, even Mr Coldfield probably admitted that war was unavoidable) when the destiny of Sutpen's family which for twenty years now had been like a lake welling from quiet springs

into a quiet valley and spreading, rising almost imperceptibly and in which the four members of it floated in sunny suspension, felt the first subterranean movement toward the outlet, the gorge which would be the land's catastrophe too, the four peaceful swimmers turning suddenly to face one another, not yet with alarm or distrust but just alert, feeling the dark set, none of them yet at that point where man looks about at his companions in disaster and thinks *When will I stop trying to save them and save only myself?* and not even aware that that point was approaching." (73–74)

Denying black people their personhood destroys everyone's personhood, and the social context of the war makes all the other communities in the novel "at war" as well, each person with every other person, except in the act of telling and hearing.

Perhaps Shreve, despite his self-protective stereotypes, really does want to understand the South. Quentin tells him he cannot: " 'You would have to be born there' " (361). But the reader balks at this statement. As I have indicated, knowledge of what something is "really like" breaks down by the end of *Absalom, Absalom!* though Quentin's own solution for the problem of knowledge is no more satisfying than Shreve's demand for "really knowing" or his sensationalistic design of the South. For his own part, the suicidal Quentin is not sure *he* understands the South: " 'I dont know,' Quentin said. 'Yes, of course I understand it.' They breathed in the darkness. After a moment Quentin said: 'I dont know' " (362). Quentin's admission is followed by silence. His refusal to know—or, more exactly, to *learn*—poisons his dialogue with Shreve as well as his own life. Quentin withdraws from conversation into his sensual memories of the South:

He could taste the dust. Even now, with the chill pure weight of the snow-breathed New England air on his face, he could taste and feel the dust of that breathless (rather, furnace-breathed) Mississippi September night. He could even smell the old woman in the buggy beside him, smell the fusty camphor-reeking shawl and even the airless black cotton umbrella in which (he would not discover until they had reached the house) she had concealed a hatchet and a flashlight. He could smell the horse; he could hear the dry plaint of the light wheels in the weightless permeant dust and he seemed to feel the dust itself move sluggish and dry across his sweating flesh just as he seemed to her the single profound suspiration of the parched earth's agony rising toward the imponderable and aloof stars. (362)

Much as a reader "sees" what is not really there, Quentin transcends epistemology by being able to "see" "though he had not been there" the scene in which Rosa goes out to Sutpen's Hundred with the ambulance for

Henry and discovers that Clytie has set fire to the house (374). Quentin's version of reality has changed: like Darl in *As I Lay Dying*, Quentin's imagination places him in a scene in which he is not present, thus rendering his imagination much more important than the "facts." The trip to Carolina to Henry and Bon's fireside forty years ago was a rehearsal for this trip, but though, as before, such imaginative identification is a property of telling, at the same time, ironically, in *not* telling Shreve about it *this* time, Quentin ends the process of telling and hearing and withdraws from his community with Shreve. Quentin's suicide is the ultimate negation of knowledge within a community.

Although "getting at the facts," either in the sense of a search for objective knowledge or in the sense of a withdrawal into strictly personal knowledge, may be a way of starting to understand a story (and one should not forget that these twin manifestations engage most readers and characters of *Absalom, Absalom!* to one degree or another), it obviously does not take one far enough. Another kind of knowing is necessary in trying to understand human beings, a hermeneutic, communal knowledge. Quentin tells us, " 'I am older than a lot of people who have died' " (377), but in not realizing that it is not enough, even imaginatively, to withdraw into one's own mind, informed and guided as it might be by a search for personal freedom, Quentin fails even at his moment of victory. If Quentin's withdrawal were to be understood as a victory, there would be no need for a reader of *Absalom, Absalom!* There is something more than Quentin's exit line—the process of telling and hearing must continue.

Thus the narrative structure of *Absalom, Absalom!* insists on the individuality and irreducibility of its voices, on their freedom and absolute refusal to be "explained," but it also presents them as "public" voices addressing each other in various communities.[8] The voices are discrete and yet inextricably bound together in the telling of the Sutpen story: reading *Absalom, Absalom!* is like reading several books at the same time, or like hearing the Four Gospels' different narrators telling the same story over and over again from diverse points of view. Readers are always struck with the way narrators come in and out, each with a distinctive tone and design, but each also somehow united by a common rhetoric and common memories, as well as by the common narrator. Yet as Bakhtin would expect, there is a moral dynamic at work here: the tension created between the individual voice and the communal context of the novel is precisely what gives rise to an urge to expand context. Faulkner's layering of narratives in a series of narrators speaking through other narrators means that the moment the reader tells anyone else about the book, when he or she even perhaps teaches it in a classroom or writes about it, he or she too continues its communal urge, extending it out even further into the world. How exactly does Faulkner create this effect so important to the storytelling metaphor for knowledge I have been describing? I intend the following outline as a guide for those readers who have gotten a bit lost in piecing together the narrative voices of *Absalom, Absalom!* It also demonstrates further that dialogism rather than hierarchies of knowledge is indicated in reading *Absalom, Absalom!*

Chapter I begins with the narrator of the entire book, unnamed and unidentified, revealing a narrative identity by telling the reader about the characters or about the character narrating at the moment, much as in James's novels. The narrator in *Absalom, Absalom!* is not quite as present as James's narrators are, but this narrator shares the relative anonymity and comprehensive knowledge of the characters.

Rosa speaks for most of the first chapter, focusing on Sutpen's arrival in Jefferson and his early doings there. As is the case in every chapter, interposed between the narrator and the character speaking[9] is Quentin, throughout the book the primary "telling" character. As I have noted, his voice occupies a special position in the novel, similar to that of Lambert Strether in *The Ambassadors*. A good example of the "location" of Quentin's consciousness occurs at the beginning of Chapter IV, where the narrator relates Quentin's thoughts in some detail before Mr. Compson begins to narrate.

The narrator begins most of the chapters and then allows another teller to speak, but the narrator disappears in Chapter V until the very last page, saying, "He (Quentin) couldn't pass that. He was not even listening to her; he said, 'Ma'am? What's that? What did you say?'" (172). This chapter begins with Rosa speaking, and all of the chapter until the last page is hers. Rosa is conscious of her position as a narrator in a community of narrators: "*So they will have told you.*" And yet she has her own special view of events which she feels compelled to tell Quentin: "*But they cannot tell you how.*" Quentin comes in on the last page, imagining what Henry and Judith said to each other after Bon's murder. It is striking how little Quentin has Henry and Judith say ("*Now you cant marry him. Why cant I marry him? Because he's dead. Dead? Yes. I killed him*") in contrast to the verbosity of Rosa's narration. In imagining the brother and sister, Quentin is drawn to their story. From this point on his spoken words and thoughts will take up most of the narrative space of the novel.

The narrator begins Chapter VI. The scene has switched to Cambridge, and the action is momentarily chilled ("There was snow on Shreve's overcoat sleeve" [173]), as is fitting, since the next item in the chapter is the letter from Mr. Compson telling Quentin of Rosa's death. As an example of how the narrator focuses closely on Quentin, Quentin talks (in quotes) in Chapter VI, as does Shreve, but Quentin also thinks (in italics), which Shreve does not. It is not clear to the reader whether Quentin's italicized thoughts are being thought as he is in his room at Harvard or were thought by him earlier and the narrator is recalling them.

In Chapter VI, when Quentin and Mr. Compson visit the Sutpen graves, Mr. Compson tells about Clytie and Jim Bond. The narrator's section occurs in response to Shreve's question to Quentin, " 'How was it?' " This question raises some severe narrative problems. It occurs just after a long passage of Quentin's italicized thoughts and is followed by the narrator's version of Quentin's experience at the graves. In both cases, the reader infers that Quentin is telling or is about to tell all this to Shreve: his thoughts (presumably not identical with the telling but surely the basis of his telling) and the story the narrator tells. Quentin's exact "telling" to Shreve is thus to be supplied by the reader, who, in doing so, joins their little community.

The typology of *Absalom, Absalom!* becomes very complex in Chapter VI. A major typological change occurs when Quentin begins to think in italics *and* addresses himself as "you" (211). At the end of the chapter, Shreve breaks into Quentin's thoughts (or into Quentin's narration to Shreve) and he and Quentin converse in quotes. All of this complicated use of levels of narration, quotes, italics, and roman letters indicates who is speaking and in what relation to the other narrators and manages to indicate interrelationships without placing narrators in a hierarchy of authority. It relates speakers, to be sure, but it merely shows position without saying that a particular position is superior in truth to another, and it is sometimes ambiguous.

The last words are not those of the narrator. Yet the novel does not really end with Quentin's "*I dont. I dont! I dont hate it! I dont hate it!*" (378). Perhaps as part of a desire on Faulkner's part to involve the reader as a participant in the story as much as he could, Faulkner includes at the end three appendixes: a chronology, a genealogy, and a map. It is problematic how the reader is supposed to take these additions, since they appear to be offered by the author himself (as opposed to the narrator), particularly in the case of the map. It declares very clearly, "William Faulkner, Sole Owner

& Proprietor" of Yoknapatawpha County. Here Faulkner replaces the narrator and extends the community of the novel to include himself directly, by name, to reach the reader in yet another way. These appendixes appear to be objective in a sense that the text is not, yet they do not need to be there at all—they are not necessary to the understanding of the novel. Perhaps of all the possible reasons for their inclusion one should probably first examine their very unnecessariness: Faulkner can only here, "outside" the novel, risk imposing his authorial design to the extent of signing his name and declaring the contents of his county his own property, as well as allude to his other books, both of which he does in the map. The appendixes are not formally symmetrical with the very unified text of *Absalom, Absalom!* but they are valuable for that reason. By undercutting the unity of the rest of the book, they also forecast the broken structure of *Go Down, Moses*. The appendixes contribute to the kind of reading Faulkner hoped for from the readers of *Absalom, Absalom!*; they are a suitably unsystematic part of the novel's diverse community of voices.

Such a communal collaboration of voices—including the voice of the appendixes—empowers the narrative structure of *Absalom, Absalom!* The book allows collaboration to have a transforming effect, as we found in the discussions of storytelling and structure above: though the first half (Chapters I–V) seems to focus on Sutpen's story, the second part (VI–IX) introduces Quentin's and Shreve's difficulties as storytellers and the problems of knowledge these difficulties raise. As Reed stresses, in the second half Quentin and Shreve model the function of "becoming" in the book; they become protagonists, "in the stead of their doubles in the first half."[10] They become highly self-conscious protagonists who are more like authors of their stories than objects of someone else's, and their failure occurs within their community but accordingly upholds community at the same time. Everything in *Absalom, Absalom!* is moving either toward community or away from it. The difference between Sutpen's or even Quentin's positions and the reader's understanding is crucial, and it is hard won. The reader of *Absalom, Absalom!* knows he knows within a community of knowledge, for the narrative communities of *Absalom, Absalom!* educate the reader to this position.

In *Absalom, Absalom!* the word "interest" does not make the constant appearances it does in *The Ambassadors*, but when it does it takes on the suggestive double meanings it has in *The Ambassadors*. As in *The Ambassadors*, in *Absalom, Absalom!* one's interest in someone, both emotional and financial, leads to personal design. Sutpen's design is the most important one of the book, but his interests are not those of the other characters, nor are they in the end those of the reader. But interest in this novel only begins with Sutpen; the interests and designs of all the other characters actually tell the Sutpen story and thus generate the novel. Sutpen's interest in the plantation life, one recalls, begins as an innocent, boyish curiosity about that community and later turns into the demonically self-centered interest of a tyrant. But Sutpen's interest never really changes. Sutpen's innocence —the key to the story, as Cleanth Brooks calls it[11]—is the innocence of a man who does not hate and does not love, an abstract innocence that creates his abstract code of honor, his false respectability, his reductive morality. It characterizes everything he does from beginning to end; his warped innocence enacts through his interest a design that becomes a blind agent of destruction. Like many of the blighted male heroes of modernity, in his hollowness and banality, Sutpen personifies reductive epistemology: his failure lies mostly in his poisonous "interest" in others.

Sutpen's design spawns everyone else's. He is the character who actually uses the word "design" to describe his plans: " 'You see, I had a design in my mind' " (263). Rosa immediately falls into designing when confronted with Sutpen—when she describes his arrival and establishment in Jefferson he seems to her larger than life, "creating the Sutpen's Hundred, the *Be Sutpen's Hundred* like the oldtime *Be Light*" (9). And she is right to be afraid: Sutpen's goal upon establishing himself in Jefferson is to get "that prospective bride whose dowry might complete the shape and substance of that respectability Miss Coldfield anyway believed to be his aim" (41) because he wants "the license, the patent" such a marriage will give him (51).

Sutpen's ideas of "respectability" create a false design on community, as false as his model for such values, Virginia plantation society. Once in Jefferson, he builds his "house the size of a courthouse" and calls his land " 'Sutpen's Hundred as if it had been a king's grant in unbroken perpetuity from his great grandfather' " (16). There is nothing between Sutpen and the people of Jefferson at first except "the common civility of two men meeting on the street," but even this is false, Rosa feels, for what common civility could there be between " 'a man who came from nowhere and dared not tell where and our father' " (20). Later when Sutpen returns from the war he does not share community with the assembled women who have guarded and maintained his community for him while he was gone: " *Yes. He wasn't there. Something ate with us; we talked to it and it answered questions; it sat with us before the fire at night and, rousing without any warning from some profound and bemused complete inertia, talked, not to us, the six ears, the three minds capable of listening, to the air, the waiting grim decaying presence, spirit, of the house itself*' "(160). When Sutpen does talk he only rants on and on, with no regard for his audience. He merely berates the women and his dependent, Wash Jones, with accounts of how he did or could have done this or that heroic deed in the war.

When Sutpen returns from the war he may be a "shell" (160), but with his "schedule" (264) he soon sets his designs back in motion. His design for his family has collapsed in the fratricide, and he must start anew. His "spurious delusion of reward" and his "fierce vain illusion" (161) drive him to pursue his shattered design by, among other things, seeking a third marriage. He asks Rosa to marry him, then asks her to provide a son first. Rosa is shocked but not surprised: like Joseph Conrad's Mr. Kurtz, Sutpen's " '*compelling dream [is] insane and not his methods,*' " according to Rosa, who knows that toward her he is coldly practical, as he would be toward " 'any young female no blood kin to him' " (166).

A "current of retribution and fatality" follows Sutpen's design (269), a current that the design itself set in motion. Sutpen cannot address it:

> " 'Either I destroy my design with my own hand, which will happen if I am forced to play my last trump card, or do nothing, let matters take the course which I know they will take and see my design complete itself quite normally and naturally and successfully to the public eye, yet to my own in such fashion as to be a mockery and a betrayal of that little boy who approached that door fifty years ago and was turned away.' " (274)

Sutpen's " '*old impotent logic and morality*' " (279), however, is what betrays him, not Virginia, not the family of Eulalia, not Ellen or Rosa, not his own children, nor even the war by themselves. Sutpen's design just will not work in a world filled with other people, and sooner or later it will destroy itself. His attempt to live the American Dream is a caricature of the Dream itself; his paternalism reflects but never comprehends its chosen society, and Sutpen finds himself defeated by his rigidity—his success—at every turn. His notion of his own individual freedom is paramount, but he denies this freedom to everyone else, most importantly to blacks and women. In repudiating the blackness of his son Charles, he loses two sons, a daughter, and his own life; in repudiating Rosa, he gains for himself a strident eulogy he neither expected nor desired. But because it is voiced by others, in its brokenness and tentativeness, the story of Sutpen counteracts his perfect design with every word.

Wash's touching admiration for Sutpen is surely one of the cruelest effects of Sutpen's design, for Wash is betrayed and killed by Sutpen's selfish abuse of his devotion. Although to Wash the "Kernel" is always "bigger" than Yankees, bigger than *this whole county*," bigger than everyone, and although Wash believes for most of his life that no matter what, the "Kernel will make hit right" (284), Sutpen's seduction and repudiation of Wash's granddaughter explodes Wash's design of the proud man on the fine black horse. All the fine rich white men, "symbol[s] also of admiration and hope, instruments too of despair and grief," become "bragging and evil shadows . . . of a kind throughout all of the earth which he knew," who "set the order and the rule of living" (289–90). In one of Faulkner's most powerful passages, Wash thinks of the men among whom Sutpen walked, men with *"hand wrote ticket[s]"* from General Lee testifying that they were brave: " ' "Brave! Better if narra one of them had ever rid back in '65' thinking *Better if his kind and mine too had never drawn the breath of life on this earth. Better that all who remain of us be blasted from the face of it than that another Wash Jones should see his whole life shredded from him and shrivel away like a dried shuck thrown onto the fire"* ' " (290–91). Sutpen not only mocks but also betrays the little boy who approached the plantation door back in Virginia, for savaging Wash's life causes the final ironic blow to his design. Death, in the form of the Grim Reaper, is a design there to meet Sutpen at this last gasp of his design, fittingly, his attempt to have a son to inherit his design. The act that would have saved Sutpen's design, simply recognizing Charles privately as a human being related to him, is of course the one thing Sutpen will not do. And the "interested" act of Sutpen's that causes his death is just one more in a long series of refusals to recognize others as human—when he jokes about Milly's not having a clean stable to lie in, his crude male domination is consonant with his objectivism toward his family and everyone else. Ironically, as a counter to his design, Wash's referring to Sutpen as the "Kernel," the standard of truth and justice, points to the futility of looking for a "kernel" of truth.[12]

Sutpen's monistic knowledge destroys community, but it is not the only anticommunal design working in *Absalom, Absalom!* I have already examined the designs lurking in Quentin and Shreve's conversations, but many other sorts of knowledge are criticized in this novel. Understanding of them makes Quentin's and Shreve's attempts to understand more admirable if still awkward. For example, university knowledge is severely questioned in *Absalom, Absalom!*: it too is a design. The Harvard dorm room is a "snug monastic coign, this dreamy and heatless alcove of what we call the best of thought" (258), "that best of ratiocination which after all was a good deal like Sutpen's morality and Miss Coldfield's demonizing" (280). And later, the Ole Miss that Bon and Henry attend is compared to Quentin and Shreve's Harvard. As Bon prepares for school, he is

> "watching from behind the smiling while the lawyer did the heavy father even, talking about the scholarship, the culture, the Latin and Greek that would equip and polish him for the position which he would hold in life and how a man to be sure could get that anywhere, in his own library even, who had the will; but how there was something, some quality to culture which only the monastic, the cloistral monotony of a—say obscure and small (though high class, high class) college." (310–11)

Harvard and Ole Miss are both described as male-only "cloisters" where knowledge can (temporarily) do no harm, can have no effect. Though while he is at Harvard Quentin's knowledge of himself grows to its fullest point, and at Ole Miss Bon confronts his brother and eventually his father, colleges in the world of *Absalom, Absalom!* are designed to "equip" a man for a "position," help him succeed in the world through closing designs. The idea of education as expressed by the lawyer is thus analogous to the culture represented by Mrs. Newsome's *Woollett Review* in *The Ambassadors*; conversely, the noninstitutional, subverting knowledge the heroes of these novels acquire despite—and in reaction to—the institutional designs around them attacks institutional design itself. At the end of these novels Quentin's and Strether's interpreted designs challenge such institutional designs, although neither ever breaks from them.

Like Sutpen's, the lawyer's knowledge is purely manipulative. In his design he hopes to capitalize on the situation with Bon and Bon's mother and father, and when he first begins to see Bon as a young man, " 'he was never worried about what Bon would do when he found out; he had probably a long time ago paid Bon that compliment of thinking that even if he was too dull or too indolent to suspect or find out about his father himself, he wasn't fool enough not to be able to take advantage if it once somebody showed him the proper move' " (309). The lawyer, using his "code," rates people according to their monetary value to him:

> "Writing steady and even into the space where the *daughter? daughter? daughter?* never had showed—and with the date here too: *1859. Two children. Say 1860, 20 years. Increase 200% time intrinsic val. yearly plus liquid assets plus credit earned. Approx'te val. 1860, 100,000. Query: bigamy threat, Yes or No.*

Possible No. Incest threat: Credible Yes and the hand going back before it put
down the period, lining out the *Credible,* writing in *Certain,* underlining it."
(310)

The metafictive parallels here, the lawyer trying to figure out his plan and
the author trying to plot his story, are striking, as are those elsewhere
between Bon and the author. But what is most important about the lawyer
is that he is a paradox. He is a subjective creation of Quentin and Shreve,
and yet his purpose is to provide an objective explanation of how Sutpen
and Bon got to know about each other. He is a device for factual knowledge
but he himself is created in a highly imaginative way. The lawyer's knowledge represents a knowledge like Sutpen's own: it is reductive, designing,
selfish, and narrow. But all of this is built into his character by his creators,
which provides yet a twist; he cannot help but be the way he is because of
his necessary role in the story. The lawyer is a good example of a designing character designed upon himself, and his "code" thus points not only
to his own skewed morals and knowledge but also to how Quentin's and
Shreve's narrative interests lead them to create this highly interested character.

Henry's and Bon's ideas of truth are contrasted as designs. Bon's
"barrier of sophistication" makes Henry and Sutpen look like "troglo-
dytes." Bon's knowledge makes him "a mere spectator, passive, a little
sardonic, and completely enigmatic." Bon

> seems to hover, shadowy, almost substanceless, a little behind and above all
> the other straightforward and logical, even though (to him) incomprehensi-
> ble, ultimatums and affirmations and defiances and challenges and repudia-
> tions, with an air of sardonic and indolent detachment like that of a youthful
> Roman consul making the Grand Tour of his day among the barbarian
> hordes which his grandfather conquered, benighted in a brawling and
> childish and quite deadly mud-castle household in a miasmic and spirit-
> ridden forest. (93)

In New Orleans Bon brings Henry to new knowledge. Bon knows the
strange world of his octoroon mistress, the dark, crowded luxury of the
New Orleans apartment, and the lives the men like him lead will shock
Henry and change him: "Henry would have to know now." Bon "develops" Henry's mind as he would a photographic plate: "the calculation,
the surgeon's alertness and cold detachment, the exposures brief, so brief as
to be cryptic, almost staccato, the plate unaware of what the complete

picture would show, scarce-seen yet ineradicable." Bon tries to build a "community" of sorts with Henry, but the community is a false one because it is a personal design on Bon's part, a "cold and catlike inscrutable calculation" to change Henry (107). Sadly, Bon's designing and his urge for community occur simultaneously because he is a victim of the designs of others. Like his chief victimizer, Sutpen, he is prevented from joining the community of family for which he longs.

Despite Bon's manipulating Henry and the rest of the Sutpens to fulfill his wishes, he does not seek to manipulate Sutpen by forcing him to recognize him as a son, and he does not want direct, full acknowledgment. Just a sign from Sutpen would be enough:

> "*So at last I shall see him, whom it seems I was bred up never to expect to see, whom I had even learned to live without,* thinking maybe how he would walk into the house and see the man who made him and then he would know; there would be that flash, that instant of indisputable recognition between them and he would know for sure and forever—thinking maybe *That's all I want. He need not even acknowledge me; I will let him understand just as quickly that he need not do that, that I do not expect that, will not be hurt by that, just as he will let me know that quickly that I am his son.*" (319)

Bon asks almost nothing of Sutpen: " ' "*He will not even have to ask me; I will just touch flesh with him and I will say it myself: You will not need to worry; she shall never see me again*" ' " (327). But Bon realizes that Sutpen will never acknowledge him. He sees only Sutpen's " '*expressionless and rocklike face, at the pale boring eyes in which there was no flicker, nothing, the face in which he saw his own features, in which he saw recognition, and that was all. That was all, there was nothing further now*' " (348). Bon wants a word, but will settle for only a dead look of "recognition." He gets neither.

Although Bon does " '*not seem to know what [he] want[s]*' " (319) and is tortured by his lack of certain knowledge as to who he is, he turns to Judith as revenge on Sutpen for years of enduring Sutpen's refusal to know him. Sutpen's propensity not to share his knowledge again brings disastrous results: " ' "He should have told me. He should have told me, myself, himself. I was fair and honorable with him. I waited. You know now why I waited. I gave him every chance to tell me himself. But he didn't do it. . . . I thought at first it was because he didn't know. Then I knew that he did know, and still I waited. But he didn't tell me." ' " Instead, Bon continues, Sutpen just told Henry: " ' "He just told you, sent me a message like you send a command by a nigger servant to a beggar or tramp to clear out. Dont

you see that?" ' " (341). Like Sutpen turned away from the front door, Bon
is turned away at his front door, denied the knowledge, the *spoken* acknowledgment, that would include him in the community of the Sutpen family
and save him and the family. Indeed, *Absalom, Absalom!* is largely about
community of family: Henry and Bon are brothers; Henry and Judith are
brother and sister; Sutpen and Henry are father and son; Bon and Judith
are incestuous half-brother and sister. There are Sutpen's communities of
his wives, Sutpen and Bon, Sutpen and Judith, Sutpen and his father-in-
law. Quentin's communities make up another group: Quentin and the
Sutpens, particularly Quentin and Henry; Quentin and Mr. Compson;
Quentin and General Compson; Quentin and Shreve; and, of course,
Quentin and his sister Caddy, who is not mentioned by name. But for Bon
the community of family goes unacknowledged to the end.

At the end Shreve summarizes the way design works in the story:

> "So it took Charles Bon and his mother to get rid of old Tom, and Charles
> Bon and the octoroon to get rid of Judith, and Charles Bon and Clytie to get
> rid of Henry; and Charles Bon's mother and Charles Bon's grandmother got
> rid of Charles Bon. So it takes two niggers to get rid of one Sutpen, dont
> it? . . . Which is all right, it's fine; it clears the whole ledger, you can tear all
> the pages out and burn them, except for one thing. And do you know what
> that is?" (378)

Shreve's "one thing" left is Jim Bond: " 'Now I want you to tell me just one
thing more. Why do you hate the South?' " Shreve picks out Bond as the
unknown quantity, the irreducible figure, the loose relation that will not let
the story fall neatly into a design; Bond is still unbound and, though he is
the end result of Sutpen's familial design, both intended and unintended,
he will not be caught, and he will not conform to a design. Shreve is
needling Quentin about his own design of the South: " 'Why do you hate
the South?' " No amount of tying up of loose ends, no amount of rationalization on either Shreve's or Quentin's part will change Jim Bond. Shreve's
question is profound. Quentin can never get past that howling, can never
"clear the ledger." Design following design continues out of the story with
Jim Bond, a truly unknown quantity and a truly negative character.

In *Absalom, Absalom!*, as in *The Ambassadors*, the primary mode
through which interest is sustained and design is foiled is indeed negativity:
as simple "nots," as absence, as avoidance, as empty centers. As has been
widely noted, Faulkner repeatedly uses pronouns whose antecedents are

unstated. The title's biblical reference is carefully left out: according to John Hagopian, this "ironic inversion" (or negativity) is an important clue to loveless Sutpen's lack of compassion—for *he* cries no "O my son Henry, O Henry," as King David cries for his eldest son.[13] But the most obvious example of absence in *Absalom, Absalom!* is, of course, Sutpen himself, and because this central absence prevents the reader from attaching to an interpretation of Sutpen any absolute authority, it furthers *Absalom, Absalom!*'s aspirations toward hermeneutic knowledge—and, as we have noted, it morally repudiates Sutpen and all he stands for.

" '*But they cannot tell you,*' " says Rosa to Quentin, what happened on that day Henry shot Bon when she went out to Sutpen's Hundred, although Faulkner scholars love to try. The paragraph that follows this statement is the most intense use of negativity in the entire novel. After she tells Quentin how she cried, "Judith! Judith!" up the stairs, blocked as she was by Clytie, Rosa says:

> *There was no answer. I had expected none; possibly even then I did not expect Judith to answer, just as a child, before the full instant of comprehended terror, calls on the parent whom it actually knows (this before the terror destroys all judgment whatever) is not even there to hear it. I was crying not to someone, something, but (trying to cry) through something, through that force, that furious yet absolutely rocklike and immobile antagonism which had stopped me—that presence, that familiar coffee-colored face, that body (the bare coffee-colored feet motionless on the bare floor, the curve of the stair rising just beyond her) no larger than my own which, without moving, with no alteration of visual displacement whatever (she did not even remove her gaze from mine for the reason that she was not looking at me but through me, apparently still musing upon the open door's serene rectangle which I had broken) seemed to elongate and project upward something—not soul, not spirit, but something rather of a profoundly attentive and distracted listening to or for something which I myself could not hear and was not intended to hear—a brooding awareness and acceptance of the inexplicable unseen, inherited from an older and a purer race than mine, which created postulated and shaped in the empty air between us that which I believed I had come to find (nay, which I must find, else breathing and standing there, I would have denied that I was ever born)—that bedroom long-closed and musty, that sheetless bed (that nuptial couch of love and grief) with the pale and bloody corpse in its patched and weathered gray crimsoning the bare mattress, the bowed and unwived widow kneeling beside it—and I (my body) not stopping yet (yes, it needed the hand, the touch, for that)—I, self-mesmered fool who still believed that what must be would be, could not but be, else I must deny sanity as well as breath, running, hurling myself into that inscrutable coffee-colored face, that cold implacable mindless (no, not mindless: anything but mindless: his own clairvoyant will tempered to amoral evil's undeviating absolute by*

the black willing blood with which he had crossed it) replica of his own which he had created and decreed to preside upon his absence, as you might watch a wild distracted nightbound bird flutter into the brazen and fatal lamp. "Wait," she said. "Dont you go up there." Still I did not stop; it would require the hand; and I still running on, accomplishing those last few feet across which we seemed to glare at one another not as two faces but as the two abstract contradictions which we actually were, neither of our voices raised, as though we spoke to one another free of the limitations and restrictions of speech and hearing "What?" I said. (137–38)

I count at least thirty-four negative constructions in this paragraph. Why is Faulkner's prose so heavily negative? In concealing Henry, Faulkner follows the Jamesian technique of forcing the reader to imagine. But the answer mainly concerns Clytie, who wishes to protect Henry from further designs were he captured and punished for Bon's murder. Clytie's preventing Rosa from knowledge at this point—from seeing Henry upstairs—makes her a negated Cassandra who will not allow the truth to be "seen." Clytie acts against design, instead of allowing knowledge like Sutpen's " 'but I had to know.' "

Although this amazing paragraph is an extreme of negativity, it is accompanied by many other examples, of which the following are only representative:

"His fierce provincial's pride in his sister's virginity was a false quantity which must incorporate in itself an inability to endure in order to be precious, to exist, and so must depend upon its loss, absence, to have existed at all." (96)

Because I asked nothing of him, you see. And more than that: I gave him nothing, which is the sum of loving. (147)

Only they would miss this now and then without knowing what it was that they missed but not often; serene, pleasant, unmarked by time or change of weather, only just now and then something, a wind, a shadow, and the demon would stop talking and Jones would stop guffawing and they would look at one another, groping, grave, intent, and the demon would say, "What was it, Wash? Something happened. What was it?" (186)

"And [Bon] never learned if Sutpen had been there or not. He never knew. He believed it, but he never knew—. . . . So he told the lawyer nothing and the lawyer told him nothing." (331–32)

Quentin didn't answer. He lay still and rigid on his back with the cold New England night on his face and the blood running warm in his rigid body and limbs, breathing hard but slow, his eyes wide open upon the window, thinking "Nevermore of peace. Nevermore of peace. Nevermore Nevermore Nevermore." (373)

At the end of *Absalom, Absalom!* one is left with something like Quentin's feeling of emptiness. The collapse of the Sutpen design, though a positive movement away from design and a statement against all designs, leaves an emptiness filled only by the meaningless cries of Jim Bond, questioning the story's capacity to mean anything.

Quentin's despair is partly the result of a mistaken assumption on his part that his telling of the story will somehow finally purge him of his confusions about the South and about himself. What he has not adequately taken into account—and this seems almost unbelievable in the context of his awareness of the many narrative voices of the story—is the saving effect of the story's having been told by so many tellers. In the end, although he has been part of a community of tellers, Quentin finds himself unable to fit into his community. Quentin Compson is alone. His only community is with his tortured self, and his progressively interior telling does not save him. But he is not the only hero/interpreter of *Absalom, Absalom!*, for the story addresses many voices. If the conclusion finds Quentin despairing and alone in his new knowledge, then is the entire narrative to be construed as a negative—that is, is it to be called a failure? Hope for understanding lies with the reader, who has been taught, to a much greater extent than Quentin, to value the multiple interpretations of the story more than what the story "really" means. The reader and author thus find themselves in a community of knowledge in which they communicate through two terrific failures, Thomas Sutpen and Quentin Compson.

5. The Negative Design of *The Golden Bowl*

THE SUBJECT OF James's last great novel is the exquisite authority of creative power. More than any other of James's works, *The Golden Bowl* reflects in all its parts the author's intense concern with problems of knowledge. In this novel, James's characterization of power as interest and design—the "fascination as well as [the] fear"[1]—explores as far as seems possible scruples about the "reality" of characters and the degree of power an author has over them. Knowledge as power is confronted by James's characters as sexual power, financial power, social power, intellectual power, aesthetic power. The narrator teaches us how to understand what happens to these characters by teaching us how to know them without closed designs. Such a narrator must accordingly give, James notes in his Preface, criticism and interpretation "not as my own impersonal account of the affair in hand, but as my account of somebody's impression of it—the terms of this person's access to it and estimate of it contributing thus by some fine little law to intensification of interest." But perhaps the narrator's personality is invoked not so much to guard against a too "impersonal account of the affair in hand on the part of the author," but rather a too personal one, in the sense that the narrator's power prevents the author from forcing his own authoritative, explanatory design on the novel. The narrator's sensibility is "a convenient substitute or apologist for the creative power otherwise so veiled and disembodied," providing as it does enrichment "by the way." What James calls "the idea of the particular attaching case *plus* some near individual view of it" thus protects the subject from the "mere muffled majesty of irresponsible 'authorship.'" Structurally, presenting first the Prince and then the Princess in Books First and Second also furthers the appeal of "endless interest" and "the appeal of incalculability."[2] To heighten interest, then, as well as to protect readers and characters from interest that leads to closed designs, James creates a narrator and a structure that serve the reader as hermeneutic models for responding to characters and their designs. At the end, Maggie Verver transcends designing. As James and his narrator treat characters, so Maggie learns to treat other people: as "incalculable."

In *The American Scene*, James speaks of the attempt to "gouge an interest *out* of . . . vacancy, gouge it with tools of price, even as copper and gold and diamonds are extracted, by elaborate processes, from earth-sections of small superficial expression."[3] "Gouging out an interest" is what the designing characters of *The Golden Bowl* do for themselves throughout the novel. As in *The Ambassadors*, the key word "interest" seems to occur on every page:

Half the interest of the thing at least would be that she shouldn't suspect. (91)

He might have even felt a trifle annoyed—if it hadn't been, on this spot, for his being, even more, interested. (95)

Interest certainly now was what he had kindled in her face. (178)

Well, Charlotte's answer to this inquiry visibly shaped itself in the interest of the highest considerations. (198)

The main interest of these hours for us, however, will have been in the way the Prince continued to know . . . a certain persistent aftertaste. (246)

"I always pay for it, sooner or later, my sociable, my damnable, my unnecessary interest." (289)

To make the comparison at all was, for Maggie, to return to it often, to brood upon it, to extract from it the last dregs of its interest—to play with it, in short, nervously, vaguely, incessantly. (323)

"Your husband, whom *you* see as viciously occupied with your stepmother, is interested, is tenderly interested, in his admirable, adorable wife." (377–78)

"He did it for you—largely at least for you. And it was for you that I did, in my smaller, interested way—well, what I could do." (415)

The Golden Bowl plays with this word in some subtle ways, always invoking the economic metaphor along with the personal meaning in such a way as to make everyone's "interest" in everyone else's "case" an opportunity for designing.

Metaphors of gold and money illustrate the complexity of connections between the economic and personal or "human" senses of "interest" in this novel. The flawed golden bowl is the most obvious symbol for knowledge in the book. The narrator tells us it comes from "a lost time," a time when Charlotte and the Prince were intimate, but its eerie quality in the scene in the shop when Charlotte and the Prince see the bowl charges it with future meaning. An ironic allusion to Adam's art collecting—it is gilt, not gold, flawed, not perfect, split, not whole—the bowl speaks against the emptiness of perfect designs such as Adam loves. Maggie tells Fanny that she wants " 'a happiness without a hole in it big enough for you to poke in your finger.' 'A brilliant, perfect surface—to begin with at least. I see.' 'The golden bowl as it *was* to have been.' And Maggie dwelt musingly on this obscured figure. 'The bowl with all the happiness in it. The bowl without the crack' " (445). But Maggie's great lesson is that human life is more like the bowl with the crack than it is like a "brilliant, perfect surface"—and that she must go on living in an imperfect world with the knowledge of its imperfection.

All the gold metaphors in *The Golden Bowl* are strongly conditioned by their association with the designs of money. Gold generally serves to connect the mysterious symbolism of the bowl with economic interests of the characters: for example, between Charlotte and the Prince, a "mystic golden bridge" exists, but when they get away at last for a weekend at Lady Castledean's, he thinks of their good fortune as "the chink of gold in his ear" (260) and "a bottomless bag of solid shining British sovereigns" (251). Before his marriage the Prince thinks of how he will inhabit "the Golden Isles" (46), and, later, Adam's art collecting in Europe is described as rifling "the Golden Isles" (122). The Prince thinks of Maggie as a "gold-topped phial" pouring "exquisite drops" into his bath of luxury (34), but he thinks of Charlotte as an empty purse. There are "golden mists" and "silver mists" (320, 322) around Maggie, but Charlotte's "golden flame" ends in "a handful of black ashes" (521).

The Prince is always accompanied by money metaphors, for his need of a comfortable living is his absorbing design. Everyone in the novel is a victim of his desire for money. To him Maggie is more than anything else "a young woman who has a million a year" (80). In Bond Street, he stops before windows "in which objects massive and lumpish, in silver and gold," are tumbled together with precious stones, leather, brass, and steel, objects of "the insolence of Empire," the "loot" of "far-off victories" (29). Like Gilbert Osmond, the Prince himself is described as an old embossed coin

(43). The Prince sees everything in terms of money; he even wonders if Fanny was paid for her matchmaking (41). In the last two pages, the Prince thinks of himself as "paying" Maggie with himself, and Maggie knows it: "[She] had an instant of the terror, that, when there has been suspense, always precedes, on the part of the creature to be paid, the certification of the amount" (546). To Maggie he "might have been holding out the money-bag for her to come and take it. . . . His acknowledgement hung there, too monstrously, at the expense of Charlotte, before whose mastery of the greater style she had just been standing dazzled" (547). One admires Maggie for not wanting to hear a confession at the "expense" of Charlotte, but it is also strongly suggested that Maggie wishes to suppress knowledge of the "values" of herself and her rival. The Prince, who had earlier been "bought" by Adam for Maggie, is now the one holding the "money bag" that represents himself.

Charlotte thinks of Maggie's love of Adam as something " 'to count with' " (199), but Adam is the supreme calculator of the book. He looks at people as though they are "cheque[s] received in the course of business," and he "[makes] sure of the amount . . . from time to time" (245). As with Amerigo's greed, without Adam's wealth the events of the novel would not have occurred. His eye for "calculability" is what Maggie must overcome; she must learn not to reduce other people to "figures" in her interests.

The two meanings of interest are powerfully yoked together early in the novel when the Prince recalls a conversation with Maggie. She tells him then that his history is what originally interested her:

> "It wasn't—as I should suppose you must have seen—what you call your unknown quantity, your particular self. It was the generations behind you, the follies and the crimes, the plunder and the waste—the wicked Pope, the monster most of all, whom so many of the volumes in your family library are all about. . . .Where, therefore"—and she had put it to him again—"without your archives, annals, infamies, would you have been?" (33)

But the Prince answers her interest in kind, for he senses the jab; he teases her, " 'I might have been in a somewhat better pecuniary situation.' " Despite his resentment, Amerigo is "deep" in "the sense of his advantage" and keeps "no impression of the girl's rejoinder" to his remark. He congratulates himself on his new situation:

> What was it but history, and of *their* kind so very much, to have the assurance of the enjoyment of more money than the palace-builder himself could have

dreamed of? This was the element that bore him up and into which Maggie scattered, on occasion, her exquisite colouring drops. They were of the colour—of what on earth? of what but the extraordinary American good faith? They were the colour of her innocence, and yet at the same time of her imagination. (34)

Here the Prince and Maggie are similar in their possession, but there are deep differences. The Prince does not share Maggie's "American" innocence or good faith, and this is a simple but important Jamesian contrast. Like Strether's, her "colouring drops" are transformative, at least for her. Maggie's passionate interest in the Prince does at first partake of ownership of a "fine thing" and becomes stronger than even her obsessive interest in her father, but later her innocence of possession is transformed by her "imagination."

Still, interest, even when tempered by heroic sacrifice, is the controlling motive for most of *The Golden Bowl*. Characters attempt to reconcile their interests, but of course power in their world is largely the ability to ensure that one's interests will come before other people's. Maggie's interests from beginning to end come first, though they are not identical from beginning to end because her entire notion of interest and design changes. Early in the novel, after her own storybook marriage is performed, her father marries to please her: "It all came from her not having been able not to mind—not to mind what became of him; not having been able, without anxiety, to let him go his way and take his risk and lead his life" (355). Similarly the pliable Prince quickly learns to follow Maggie's cues. Maggie's relationship with Charlotte is one of Charlotte's consciously deferring to Maggie in public, "throwing over their intercourse a silver tissue of decorum" that "hung there above them like a canopy of state, a reminder that though the lady-in-waiting was an established favorite, safe in her position, a little queen, however good-natured, was always a little queen and might, with small warning, remember it" (325). (The tragedy of Charlotte's being sent to America at the end is partly that she has no interests there: " 'It's the country for interests,' said Charlotte. 'If I had only a few I doubtless wouldn't have left it' " [66].) Fanny calls Maggie "divine" and is determined to "see her through," although Maggie "would verily, at this crisis, have seen Mrs Assingham's personal life or liberty sacrificed without a pang" (369). When Maggie thinks she is acting in Adam's interests, not telling him about Charlotte and the Prince, she is really, of course, acting in her own (355). Thus in contrast to many other Jamesian heroes and heroines, Maggie wants very much to get something for herself out of the whole affair.[+] She must learn what that means by allowing her imagination to revise what interests mean in a community.

Keywords most closely associated with design in *The Golden Bowl* include "possession," "separation," and "equilibrium." Maggie begins to fear her "sweet . . . sense of possession" after her encounter with Amerigo upon his return from Matcham (313). In contrast, Charlotte struggles throughout the novel to stay "visibly in possession of her part" (511). Fine objects, social positions, and husbands are possessions to be fought for. Charlotte tells Maggie: " 'I want, strange as it may seem to you,'—and she gave it all its weight—'to *keep* the man I've married. And to do so, I see, I must act' " (512–13). Recalling Sutpen of *Absalom, Absalom!* Charlotte and the others suggest most especially his design to possess objects, human or otherwise. It is not so much what Sutpen and Charlotte or Amerigo or Adam do that relates them, but rather how they do it, why they do it, and how they justify it.

"Separation" is Maggie's greatest fear, and separation is the father and daughter's eventual fate, the price of her newly understood "possession" of Amerigo. As Adam pointedly asks her, " 'How can the one separation take place without the other?' " (350). This is one of the ironies of Maggie's situation: if she wishes to separate the Prince and Charlotte, she must also separate herself from her father. In the last few pages of the novel, separation becomes the dominant action: Maggie knows Charlotte is "doomed, doomed to a separation that was like a knife in her heart" (510). Maggie imagines Charlotte in a glass cage, "frantically tapping, from within, by way of supreme, irrepressible entreaty." Charlotte's ignorance and her doom move Maggie to pity her, and this is why the heroine is Maggie, not Charlotte: we cannot imagine Charlotte trying to put herself in Maggie's place. Maggie and Adam are " 'lost to each other—father and I' " (523), but despite her loss Maggie's design is "equilibrium": "*That* was at the bottom of her mind, that their equilibrium was everything, and that it was practically precarious, a matter of a hair's breadth for the loss of the balance" (311).

Indeed, a good part of the reader's activity in reading *The Golden Bowl* is to watch the two couples go through their various permutations of attachment and identification: Maggie and Adam, Maggie and Amerigo, Amerigo and Adam, Charlotte and Amerigo, Charlotte and Maggie, Charlotte and Adam. In their pairing off of themselves and others, they all try to maintain equilibrium, but they try to do so by making their own interests the controlling weight in the balance.

Everyone in *The Golden Bowl* spends most of the time pursuing designs: Adam makes himself a little Princess and buys her a Prince; Fanny Assingham plays matchmaker and then confidante; Charlotte plans her one short hour with the Prince to be a lasting one, and it is; the Prince designs himself the comfortable existence he feels he deserves, sacrificing his lover and his pride to keep it. But Maggie, the "little American heroine," is the chief designer of the novel. For the last half of *The Golden Bowl* the plot consists of a succession of events she desires to occur, culminating in her sacrifice of her father for Amerigo and her getting Charlotte to think that going to America is her idea. But in becoming fully aware of the dangers of design, she manages to act by not acting, receive by giving up, win by appearing to lose, and prevail (in the Faulknerian sense) though she sees her reward is imperfect. Her development to this point is the plot of the novel, just as Strether's development of knowledge was the plot of *The Ambassadors*.

Early in the story the Prince asks Fanny whether Charlotte " 'has come with designs upon me?' " (54). Some readers would blame Charlotte's impossible design of regaining her lover as the starting point for all the designs of the book, or perhaps hers and the Prince's design. But the Ververs' strange design is already there. The Ververs buy, sell, arrange, and rearrange *objets*, whether inanimate or animate, and the Prince and Charlotte are both "gotten" to fill the Ververs' needs. But Maggie in the end introduces a new design no other character has managed to develop. Her victory is not beating Charlotte as much as it is beating her own design. She gives up the design, embodied in large part by the father she sacrifices, which has controlled her all her life.

Maggie gives up the Verver design of seeing people as things, however precious, to be manipulated for a father and daughter's enjoyment. She learns a new design that treats the other person, friend or enemy, as a free individual, a human being who is a member of her community and hence as worthy of fair play as she is. Maggie overcomes the designs of her past, and, although she may have to regard the future with "pity and dread" (547), she has been thrust into reality past her previous narrow designs. Perhaps her marriage will continue to be happy. She may end it later, or perhaps Amerigo may learn from her how to help improve it. What is important is that knowledge for her has become knowledge of "the other" as a subjective reality, irreducible and nonobjective, with which she has to contend and which she cannot design away. The Prince is weak and shallow, and he has betrayed her, but she is able to reconcile her knowledge of his shortcomings with her need of him, and she will live ever after, if not happily, at least with the knowledge she has fought for and the chance to live with that knowledge in her own way. She is a Lambert Strether clearly located in the conclusion in a real community. Frederick Crews finds that the entire idea of community in *The Golden Bowl* is redeemed by Maggie's interpretation of it, especially her acceptance of her husband for who he is. This raises society itself as a positive value; Maggie establishes social harmony as a worthy goal "for the full American identity of soul." A corrupted social world has been in place for characters until now, a "harmony of social deception." Eventually, "instead of paying lip service to idealistic standards of impossible purity, the characters are encouraged to work for the saving of their human situation. People, not ideas, become the things worth preserving." In the end Maggie "has come to love people for what they are," he says, "good and bad qualities together, rather than for what they should ideally be. She has learned to accommodate evil. In other words, she has learned to *live*."[5] Maggie's changing *relationships* with the other characters provide the major action of the second half of the novel.

Among the other characters, achieving a designed equilibrium is a matter of clumsily arranging people according only to personal design with little concern for their own knowledge. Much of Charlotte's design, for example, involves blindly "placing" people. The most extended discussion of this occurs when Charlotte corners Fanny at the party for the ambassador. Charlotte proves to be more correct than she knows when she tells Fanny, " 'It belongs to my situation that I'm, by no merit of my own, just fixed—fixed as fast as a pin stuck, up to its head, in a cushion. I'm placed— I can't imagine anyone *more* placed. There I *am*!' " She goes on to recognize Maggie's facility for "placing" people, which " 'peculiarly suits her.' " Charlotte concludes that " 'The great thing is, as they say, to "know" one's place. Doesn't it all strike you . . . as rather placing the Prince too?' " Fanny's response is pointed: " 'So placed that *you* have to arrange?' " (200) The Prince thinks that it is Charlotte's and not Maggie's "doom . . . to arrange appearances," and he regards her efforts as "the thing that gave her away" (61). Charlotte, who passionately values her freedom, from the beginning is setting traps and being entrapped, and the designing she does catches her most surely of all in the end.

Charlotte makes a great point of the lovers' correctly "understanding" their situation, for "it appeared thus that they might enjoy together extraordinary freedom, the two friends, from the moment they should understand their position aright" (220). Charlotte tells the Prince, " 'It's not that you haven't my courage, . . . but that you haven't, I rather think, my imagination' " (229). But later the Prince says Charlotte is "stupid," and his reason for saying so is that Charlotte never "knows" Maggie. It is Charlotte who is finally held " 'by her ignorance' " (525); *really* not knowing is a punishment, it seems, but pretending not to know is a powerful design. Fanny describes the lovers' ignorance: " 'They'll be mystified, confounded, tormented. But they won't *know*—and all their possible putting their heads together won't make them. That,' said Fanny Assingham, 'will be their punishment.' " Fanny ruefully observes that it will probably be hers as well (392). Charlotte's warning to Adam when he asks her to marry him, " 'Do you think you "know" me?' " (176), could serve as a motto for all the characters.

Maggie's education in the dangers of design comes first through her feeling herself "arranged" or "known": "The word for it, the word that flashed in the light, was that they were *treating* her" (328). Maggie feels herself drowning in the "baths of benevolence," the "submarine depths" of the Prince's and Charlotte's design, "preventing her freedom of movement." But she also sees that "of course they were arranged—all four arranged; but what had the basis of their life been, precisely, but that they were arranged together?" (330). Arrangement seemed all right as long as it was Maggie and Adam who were doing the arranging, but now that "Charlotte had designs upon her of a nature best known to herself, and was only waiting for the better opportunity of their finding themselves less companioned" (452), Maggie is alarmed into inventing a new, different design. It is Charlotte who says, " 'I've dreamed another dream,' " but it is Maggie who must do that: "Ah! Amerigo and Charlotte were arranged together, but she—to confine the matter only to herself—was arranged apart" (330). Later, "that they were in the fact of it rearranging, that they *had* to rearrange, was all before her again: yet to do so as they would like they must enjoy a snatch, longer or shorter, of recovered independence" (341). Giving the Prince and Charlotte the chance to "rearrange" is part of Maggie's plan, but a greater part of it is that Maggie, while she attempts to rearrange the Prince and Charlotte, must also rearrange herself. Maggie wins in all of her "rearrangements" (349) because she redefines what it means to "arrange."

Unlike Amerigo's "place" in "history," Maggie sees her place as "that improvised 'post'—a post of the kind spoken of as advanced—with which she was to have found herself connected in the fashion of a settler or a trader in a new country" (516–17). Maggie's "post" is "advanced" into the uncharted territory of the "fundamental passions" instead of "examples, tradition, habits," but it is the sophisticated Charlotte and Adam who actually set off into the wilds of the New World at the end of the story. Maggie instead reconciles her husband's history to her "post." In *The Golden Bowl*, the usual directions of consciousness one tends to take for granted are reversed: the unconscious, emotional side of personality, not the civilized and well-documented, is the new world that Maggie Verver will enter. This is an ironic inversion of the movement of the innocent, untutored American toward the complex world of Europe. Maggie's "place" will be a completely new one, even newer than Strether's.

Maggie's knowledge in the end of what evils "placing" and "arranging" can cause is not shared. Amerigo does not comprehend Maggie's quality of knowledge. Instead, his "cool, high refuge" of the "shade of the official" (539) is precisely his willingness in the end to *be* so arranged by his wife. The Prince's designing and his presenting himself as a design are substitutes for community, and alone these cannot hold a community together, even if all the members of the community are engaged in similar designs.

In the beginning of the novel, to make himself a "new history," the Prince realizes that he does not mind "allying himself to science, for what was science but the absence of prejudice backed by the presence of money? His life would be full of machinery, which was the antidote to superstition, which was in its turn, too much, the consequence, or at least the exhalation, of archives." There is "machinery . . . all about him," there is money and power, "the power of the rich peoples. Well, he was *of* them now, of the rich peoples; he was on their side—if it wasn't rather the pleasanter way of putting it that they were on his" (39). Thus he feels at the beginning of the book "as if his papers were in order, as if his accounts so balanced as they had never done in his life before and he might close the portfolio with a snap" (40). James here conflates the designs of money, machinery, and personal advancement, but he also describes the Prince as a work of art.

The Prince represents the success of personal design, especially when one accounts for the appeal to taste and history he constitutes. He is an admirable acquisition for Mr. Verver's daughter's delight, surprisingly malleable and pleasing to Adam: " 'You're round, my boy,' he had said— 'you're *all*, you're variously and inexhaustibly round, when you might, by all the chances, have been abominably square.' " The Prince's "crystalline" surface is perfect for the Ververs' "golden drops": "They caught in no interstice, they gathered in no concavity; the uniform smoothness betrayed the dew but by showing for the moment a richer tone" (120). He is smooth, wholly complete, desirable, accommodating. But like the golden bowl, his pleasing surface conceals abysses. They are works of art that leave no surface empty, that explain all, and pleasantly conceal the depths of meaning they might contain. The Prince is dangerous and dishonest, acquisitive and selfish. He is sexually potent but cold and calculating about love. Maggie sees his agile grace as "one of those intentions of high impertinence by the aid of which great people, *les grands seigneurs*, persons of her husband's class and type, always know how to re-establish a violated order" (448). The Prince is absorbed by a society that values money above all else, and some readers accordingly judge him a victim. If so, his is a Sutpen-like innocence, a Chad Newsome-like innocence, a desire *only* to be safe and secure in the order of "the rich peoples" rather than a movement to develop a new world himself.

Like Sutpen, the Prince is quite conventional. He likes "explanations, liking them almost as if he collected them, in the manner of book-plates or postage-stamps, for themselves, his requisition of this luxury had to be met." Indeed, he has an "appetite for the explanatory" for which he turns to Fanny Assingham (135). Fanny feels that the Prince is "saving up, for some very mysterious but very fine eventual purpose, all the wisdom, all the answers to his questions, all the impressions and generalizations, he gathered; putting them away and packing them down because he wanted his great gun to be loaded to the brim on the day he should decide to let it off. . . . He knew what he was about" (137). In the Prince James thus warns against perfection: a monadic system such as the Prince's works, but only for its own ends and without any of the communities. The Prince's perfection contrasts strongly with Maggie's doubt, confusion, hesitation, inaction, and release. Despite Amerigo's New World name, Maggie embodies that Jamesian "good faith" attributed to America, or rather to James's own position as a "dispossessed" American.

Just as Charlotte's conversations with Fanny reveal her designs, so do the Prince's. The Prince tells Fanny that he has no moral sense (48), and his talks with her bear this out. Similarly, he acknowledges Maggie's interest in his "archives, annals, infamies," his "old history," but he warns her: " 'There's another part, very much smaller doubtless, which, such as it is, represents my single self, the unknown, unimportant—unimportant save to *you*—personal quantity. About this you've found out nothing' " (33). The Prince has "a certain inward critical life" (247), but what this means is that his moral feelings are split from his intellect; his public is split from his private life; and his facade is split from his "inner self." In asserting that the unknowable, private self is the true one, he says he finds "public" or written things "abominable." Again, like Sutpen, the Prince does not see anything wrong with satisfying his single, private self at the expense of everyone around him.

Maggie, on the other hand, in developing her identity feels drawn *outward* through the novel. She learns to be "public," as her metaphors of dancers, actresses, and playwrights attest. Paradoxically, she discovers much about the "inner selves" of herself and everyone around her through her contact with other selves, while throughout the novel the Prince always pursues knowledge of others by looking for an outward sign, the "straight tip," and he consistently models his behavior on what he thinks is called for by those around him. The Prince lacks any sense of inner or outer lives besides his own inner one, and he tries to develop and inner life by responding only to other people's surfaces, not by engaging with them. Maggie successfully develops her inner life by acknowledging other people's inner lives, finding that she cannot learn about the self by knowing only the self. The Prince says he lives by his instinct (109), but since his instinct is based strictly on reading appearances and responding to cues from others more powerful than he, his knowledge is serviceable but passive, amoral, and manipulative. The Prince and Charlotte are beautiful, powerful, admirable celebrities, but because they act only for themselves they are always alone—and alone they are no match for each other's designs or those of others.

At first Maggie tries to be the daughter of her father by keeping her knowledge to herself, and when she is with him, she does. But this is ultimately not enough for her, and she confides in the *ficelle* Fanny; after the golden bowl is shattered and Maggie has admitted her knowledge, she then has the courage to talk to her father, to come into genuine contact with him. Here she delicately refrains from telling him what she knows directly, just as she did with the Prince. It is clear, however, when Adam leaves for America that Maggie's new community has won out. These crucial changes occur through dialogues, especially those in which the reader has to listen between the lines.

Early on Adam feels the strain of the design of an overly private father-daughter relationship, especially when asking Charlotte to marry him: " 'Can't a man be, all his life then,' he almost fiercely asked, 'anything but a father?' But he went on before she could answer. 'You talk about differences, but they've been already made—as no one knows better than Maggie. She feels the one she made herself by her own marriage—made, I mean, for me' " (177–78). Maggie has tried to marry without giving up her former status as daughter:

> "Why did he, why did he?" rushed back, inevitably, the confounding, the over-whelming wave of the knowledge of his reason "He did it for *me*, he did it for me," she moaned, "he did it, exactly, that our freedom—meaning, beloved man, simply and solely mine—should be greater instead of less; he did it, divinely, to liberate me so far as possible from caring what became of him." . . . It all came from her not having been able to mind—not to mind what became of him; not having been able, without anxiety, to let him go his way and take his risk and lead his life. (354–55)

At this point, Adam and Maggie are trapped in mutually exploitive designs, and they are in not dialogue with each other. But it is not Adam who is not direct—it is Maggie.

When Maggie at last manages to accept Adam on a shared plane of discourse, a plane that includes her as an equal, she never admires him more than then: "The 'successful,' beneficent person, the beautiful, bountiful, original, dauntlessly wilful great citizen, the consummate collector and infallible high authority he had been and still was—these things struck her, on the spot, as making up for him, in a wonderful way, a character she must take into account in dealing with him either for pity or for envy" (484). Adam's qualities thus "placed him in her eyes as no precious work of art probably had ever been placed in his own" (484). But as Maggie hints to Adam that he and Charlotte should go to America, Maggie at last sees Adam as a person, instead of as a "precious work of art," and "sees" things in him she had not before, including the limitations of their type of seeing itself. In learning to see and not see her father, Maggie has learned how to see and not see everyone, and part of what she sees in Adam is an alternative to him. His silence in several conversational scenes is Maggie's call to grow up; his reticence is her spur to action. Her revision of what "seeing" means occurs in the context of conversations that get progressively more serious. For one thing, Maggie finally has to admit that she shares Adam's affections. When she tells him, " 'I believe in you more than anyone,' " he asks, " 'Than anyone at all?' ":

> She hesitated, for all it might mean; but there was—oh a thousand times!—no doubt of it. "Than anyone at all." She kept nothing back now, met his eyes over it, let him have the whole of it; after which she went on: "And that's the way, I think, you believe in me." He looked at her a minute longer, but his

tone at last was right. "About the way—yes." "Well then—?" She spoke as for the end and for other matters—for anything, everything, else there might be. They would never return to it. (485)

Maggie's open preference for her father at this point is obviously not matched by his preference for her over his wife.

Maggie has thought of herself and her father as "'positively stage-pirates, the sort who wink at each other and say "Ha-ha!" when they come to where their treasure is buried.'" They visit their treasures all over the world and travel with the "'smaller pieces, . . . the things we take out and arrange as we can, to make the hotels we stay at and the houses we hire a little less ugly,'" and this is the class in which she placed not only the Prince (36) but also Charlotte, whom the Ververs originally "got" to "do the worldly" for them with her "perfect, her brilliant efficiency" in the "duties of a remunerated office" (241). Maggie eventually moves away from these designs, but Adam is in the end still the acquisitive designer and collector of people. Surveying Maggie's drawing room on the morning of Adam and Charlotte's departure, Adam takes in the *objets* there, particularly "the two noble persons" of Charlotte and Amerigo, and he comments to Maggie: "'*Le compte y est*. You've got some good things'" (541). The Ververs find out just how high the price of these objects, Charlotte and Amerigo, really is; they are forced to come up with what Charles Thomas Samuels calls "the necessary spiritual capital to possess what they had only procured."[6] In this Maggie surpasses her father.

Although the characters of *The Golden Bowl* avoid knowledge as long as possible, acts of knowing form the plot of the novel. Not only does James constantly warn of the difficulties of any act of knowing through the reductive economic metaphors of knowledge his characters and narrators employ, but he also rejects epistemologies by causing us to suspect the ocular metaphor. To ocular certainty he opposes knowledge as communal and conversational, as demonstrated especially by Fanny and Maggie. This was hinted at in the visual nature of the characters' "arranging" each other, but it occurs in various other forms as well. For example, when the Prince sees Charlotte again for the first time, his impressions of her features make up "a cluster of possessions of his own . . . items in a full list, items recognized, each of them as if, for the long interval, they had been 'stored' —wrapped up, numbered, put away in a cabinet. While she faced Mrs Assingham the door of the cabinet had opened of itself; he took the relics out, one by one" (58–59). He goes on to remember her as a "case" like none other he has known. The Prince recognizes her "narrow hands," "long fingers," "special beauty of movement and line when she turned her back." Above all,

> he knew . . . the extraordinary fineness of her flexible waist, the stem of an expanded flower which gave her a likeness also to some long, loose silk purse, well filled with gold pieces, but having been passed, empty, through a finger-ring that held it together. It was as if, before she turned to him, he had weighed the whole thing in his open palm and even heard a little the chink of the metal. (59)

We learn in this scene that the Prince's "knowing" Charlotte in the past and his "knowing" her in the present are different. She may have a beautiful waist, his thoughts imply, but she is after all an empty purse—the Prince's unconscious transformation of the lovely flower image into the purse shows where his heart lies now. He appreciates her only as an object, and he knows her only insofar as she can give him pleasure. He even interprets *her* hesitation and uncertainty upon entering the room as an act deliberately giving him "more time" to compose himself. His "knowledge" of her thus reveals him most of all.

When Charlotte and the Prince spend their afternoon together shopping, Charlotte says she just wants him to "know" the truth about her. She wants the wedding present to " 'always be with you—so that you'll never be able quite to get rid of it.' " But the Prince is not as astute as Charlotte wants him to be; her finer points are lost on him. As he "clutched, however, at what he could best clutch at—the fact that she let him off, definitely let him off" even from merely answering, he is mute. When she continues, " 'You may want to know what I get by it. But that's my own affair,' " the uncurious Prince "really didn't want to know even this—or continued, for the safest plan, quite to behave as if he didn't. . . . He was glad when, finally—the point she had wished to make seeming established to her satisfaction—they brought to what might pass for a close the moment of his life at which he had had least to say" (94). That the Prince has little "to say" turns out to be a serious error on his part, as the shocking visual evidence of the bowl later declares. Charlotte's bait has been taken, however, and the "one little thing" she wants from him turns out to be like some half-overlooked action in a fairy tale that reappears to haunt everyone. The golden bowl that finally convinces Maggie to confront her husband, the gift of Charlotte's little hour, eventually eclipses every other object in the book. Charlotte's positive pretense of "wanting nothing" is in direct contrast to Maggie's negativity expressive of an honest willingness to "want all." The action Charlotte takes for her "nothing" fails miserably, but Maggie's inaction succeeds.

Maggie must earn her extraordinary sensitivity to the complexities of others by understanding her own complexity. To the Assinghams, she is a "'creature of pure virtue'" who suffers her "'sympathy, her disinterestedness, her exquisite sense for the lives of others to carry her too far'" (388). But that is more a description of Fanny herself than of Maggie, and Maggie later sheds others' designs of her. Indeed, Maggie learns from Fanny what it is to have "gone too far" with her knowledge, with her "visions" of others. Her intelligence allows her to know without seeing—as when she imagines Charlotte's speech to Adam. Maggie's disinterest continues to attempt to preserve everyone from pain; in the end she is hardly the innocent, spoiled little girl she seems to have been before.

The title of *The Golden Bowl* comes from Ecclesiastes 12:5 and from Blake's "Thel's Motto" in his "Invocation" to *Milton* ("Does the Eagle know what is in the pit? / Or wilt thou ask the mole; / Can Wisdom be put in a silver rod? / Or Love in a golden bowl?"). It asks the question, What form does knowledge take? Wisdom and love cannot be contained by physical vessels of silver and gold. When they are so contained, the "bowl" will not stand the strain. The Princess's wisdom consists in her seeing the crack in her golden bowl; her love consists in her learning what the crack means. The Princess learns that there is a flaw in her life, but, more important, she learns that it was she who helped put it there and that it is she who must be responsible for it. She must look into "the pit," and furthermore she must live there, along with everyone else. Maggie finds out that no amount of "doing" or "magnificence" of person or plan will in the end make its possessor happy: all designs founded on personal desire without regard to community will fail because their knowledge is incomplete and distorted. Maggie finds out that imperfection, like the crack in the bowl, is morally preferable to the slippery smooth, elegant "curves" the Prince possesses. She realizes that "the infirmity of art was the candour of affection, the grossness of pedigree the refinement of sympathy; the ugliest objects, in fact, as a general thing, were the bravest, the tenderest mementoes, and, as such, figured in glass cases apart, worthy doubtless of the home, but not worthy of the temple—dedicated to the grimacing, not to the clear-faced, gods" (406). Maggie's awakening starts when she begins, in Fanny's words, "'to doubt, for the first time . . . of her wonderful little judgment of her wonderful little world'" (283). She begins to *address* instead of merely "see" her world.

In their comic commentary from the sidelines, Fanny and Bob Assingham provide a warm, humorous element in a book that would otherwise be somewhat cold and remote. Fanny is as imperfect, implicated, and interested a friend as Maggie could find, and it is important that it is this imperfect woman who takes the action of smashing the golden bowl on the floor. Indeed Fanny's human presence is as powerful in its infirmity as the imperfect works of art Maggie often thinks of. The value of "imperfection" generated through dialogues with Fanny becomes Maggie's special strength. As Ruth Bernard Yeazell tells us, "Only by granting others the power to invent their own saving fictions can Maggie herself genuinely triumph. If her verbal coercion is finally more effective than that of her manipulative predecessors, then, it is precisely because she does not always control the terms of the discourse. The Princess conquers by affirming the imaginative autonomy of her victims." Maggie's dialogic role is unique in her family. Amerigo for one has little conception of Maggie's allowing Charlotte to think " 'what she likes.' " His "distressing arrogance," according to Yeazell, is betrayed in his language when he speaks of his "right" to "correct" Charlotte. Maggie asks him, " 'Aren't you rather forgetting who she is?' " Charlotte's rival, not her former lover, here proves her champion. In the second half of the novel, Maggie alone keeps the memory of Charlotte's "splendor" alive. In fact, Yeazell notes, the most poignant images of Charlotte—the "wine of consciousness," "the golden flame," "a mere handful of black ashes"—find expression in Maggie's mind. Maggie's intersubjectivity is what distinguishes her knowledge: her dialogic imagination allows her to feel the pain she has caused. Yet her self-abasement, like Fanny's, does not lead her to sacrifice her self, and her compassion does not change things for Charlotte. Yeazell concludes, "Maggie weeps, but Maggie wins"; I would add to this that Maggie "wins" *because* she "weeps."[7]

Fanny suggests to Maggie and the reader how to step back from design by doing so herself. Fanny does not abandon her friends, but helps Maggie by changing her tactics. Instead of active designing, like Maria Gostrey Fanny retreats to the sidelines to allow Maggie freedom, providing her friendship and support but ceasing to design with her knowledge. The only exception to her new design, her only major act in the last half of the book, is her smashing the golden bowl, but she leaves the room immediately thereafter and in doing so leaves Maggie with Amerigo. Fanny has learned that "helping" people can be dangerous. She is guilty of "helping" many people, but she is not the only "helper": the Prince and Charlotte believe they are helping Adam and Maggie; Maggie believes she is helping

Adam; Adam helps Maggie; Bob helps Fanny. Fanny ruefully admits to Bob that her " 'knowledge was my reason for what I did.' " In bringing in Charlotte in the beginning Fanny " 'had fallen in love with the beautiful symmetry of [her] plan' " (289). Such symmetries, as interested designs or as "help," make knowledge the painful process it is in this novel. Fanny's many difficulties in "helping" forecast Maggie's own.

Fanny may be understood as a highly developed *ficelle*. Like most *ficelles*, Fanny's interest often takes the form of pretended ignorance, which she believes is what Maggie wants from her—and which turns out later to be Maggie's mode of knowledge as well. Like Strether and Maggie, past a certain point Fanny does not want to seem to understand what she cannot accept (203). Fanny's "seeing for them all" (277) eventually takes the new form of refusing to see: " 'Whatever they've done I shall never know. Never, never—because I don't want to, and because nothing will induce me. So they may do as they like. But I've worked for them *all!*' " (281). Fanny and Bob say they will help Maggie " 'by looking like fools,' " like " 'absolute idiots' " (297–98). Fanny's greatest fear is being held responsible for the suffering of others (389). Her new-found knowledge, which consists in pretending not to see, is the opposite of her real ignorance earlier in not seeing what would happen as a result of Charlotte's reappearance on the scene. She has learned the dangers of "seeing" at all—and she has learned this through her dialogues with Bob and others. Accordingly, when the Prince enters the room just in time to see Fanny destroy the evidence, Maggie, following Fanny, wants to let the Prince see that "she *knew*, and her broken bowl was proof that she knew" (424), and that is all. She gives him no guidance as to what he should do. She wishes merely " 'to see what difference it would make for myself.' " To Maggie's assertion, " 'I've ceased to be as I was. *Not* to know,' " the Prince says, " 'I know nothing but what you tell me.' " Maggie replies, so like Fanny, " 'Then I've told you all I intended. Find out the rest!' " (436–37). Much as Maria encourages Strether in *The Ambassadors*, Fanny's action has freed Maggie for her final stage of development in the novel.

Maggie later watches her family and friends play a bridge game, and, because of her new knowledge, she feels responsible for their safety. Their "personal intensity and their rare complexity of relation" become "freshly importunate to her":

> The fact of her father's wife's lover facing his mistress; the fact of her father sitting, all unsounded and unblinking, between them; the fact of Charlotte's keeping it up, keeping up everything across the table, with her husband

beside her; the fact of Fanny Assingham, wonderful creature, placed opposite to the three and knowing more about each, probably, when one came to think, than either of them knew of either. (455)

But "erect above all for her was the sharp-edged fact of the relation of the whole group, individually and collectively, to herself—herself so speciously eliminated for the hour, but presumably more present to the attention of each than the next card to be played." Maggie feels the surging power of her knowledge, "the sense that if she were but different—oh, ever so different! —all this high decorum would hang by a hair." Maggie once again keenly senses the temptation in such a power of "seeing," "that fascination of the monstrous, that temptation of the horribly possible" (456). The card-playing scene ironically points to the gamble Maggie takes in allowing the others to pursue their games; her slow circuit around the table indicates her status as a mistress of the game both in and out of the game, rather like the author himself. In this scene she decisively chooses not to act on what can be seen.

As in *The Ambassadors*, sexual knowledge is a motive for all the characters' designs, but it is almost nowhere to be seen. Adam is sexually attracted to Charlotte; Charlotte and Maggie both desire the Prince; and even Fanny and Bob accuse each other of being attracted to Amerigo and Maggie. Maggie's intense sexual passion for the Prince is for her the knowledge most to be delayed. Charlotte and the Prince underestimate Maggie's sexual possessiveness and power. Many readers feel that Maggie is afraid of Amerigo's sexuality, especially in the scene in which he returns from Matcham, in the carriage scene, and in the final scene. Maggie is reticent in these scenes not because of disaffection or prudishness but rather of her awareness that sexual knowledge will obliterate the other types of knowledge with which she is working, and she must delay it. Maggie does not fear sex, but she does fear Amerigo's sexual *designs* on her. And in the final scene, Maggie dreads the Prince's "explanation" more than she fears succumbing to sexual knowledge (535–37).

Unlike Maggie, and despite his "dark blue eyes . . . of the finest [color], and, [which,] on occasion, precisely resembled nothing so much as the high windows of a Roman palace, of an historic front by one of the great old designers, thrown open on a feast-day to the golden air" (55–56), the Prince's vision is extremely limited. Charlotte thinks in the shop how the Prince "below a certain social plane, . . . never *saw*," for her interest in the shopman as a " 'type' " is not met by the Prince's. She says the shopkeeper knows "we, clearly, were right people—he knows them when he sees them" (99). Ironically, as they find out later, the shopkeeper would have cheated them with the cup, but he has a change of heart when he talks to Maggie. Maggie unknowingly predicts what she will see in Charlotte when she announces to Adam, " 'Yes, I'm going to see in Charlotte,' said the Princess—and speaking now as with high and free expression—'more than I've ever seen' " (150). And Maggie sees guilt and uncertainty in the Prince's face, "and back and back it kept coming to her that the blankness he showed her before he was able to *see* might, should she choose to insist upon it, have a meaning" (310). She sees the same mask on Charlotte's face the next morning: "the blankness in her blandness, assuredly, and very nearly an extravagance in her generalizing gaiety," reminding Maggie "of other looks in other faces" (370). Maggie decides to educate the Prince's vision with a new perspective on their situation: "What it would most come to, after all, she said to herself, was a renewal for him of the privilege of watching that lady watch *her*." Maggie wonders "how long would he go on enjoying mere spectatorship of that act? . . . Wouldn't he get tired—to put it only at that—of seeing her always on the rampart, erect and elegant, with her lace-flounced parasol now folded and now shouldered, march to and fro against a gold-colored east or west?" (397). Maggie has indeed seen much in Charlotte and has made the Prince see her anew as well. But she has also become aware of to what ends all this seeing can lead. By Chapter XXXV, Maggie realizes that as her "telescope" has "gained in range," so "her danger lay in her exposing herself to the observation by the more charmed, and therefore the more reckless, use of this optical instrument" (449).

The narrator calls Charlotte's pursuit of Maggie one night on the terrace a "perceptive pursuit" (499), and Maggie also pursues Charlotte later in the garden scene of Chapter XXXIX: "The relation, today, had turned itself round; Charlotte was seeing her come, through patches of lingering noon, quite as she had watched Charlotte menace her through the starless dark" (499). Maggie eventually redefines "seeing" altogether, and knowledge becomes, through dialogue, something much more tentative and complex than simply "seeing" another person. She struggles for this new knowledge. Near the conclusion, she must overcome the insistent sight of Adam, in his straw hat and white waistcoat, "the so remarkably distinct figure that, at Fawns, for the previous weeks, was constantly crossing, in its regular revolution, the further end of any watched perspective." Knowing that she is designed to "see" him, however, Maggie is on the road to repudiating "seeing" and being "seen." By the end, Maggie's "picture" of her father includes the "gleam of the silken noose," which "never failed now as an item in the picture . . . so marked to Maggie's sense during her last month in the country" (521–22). "Not seeing" is now her mode: "She felt once more how impossible such a passage would have been to them, how it would have torn them to pieces, if they had so much as suffered its suppressed relations to peep out of their eyes" (543). It is the dread of seeing that causes Maggie to bury her eyes in Amerigo's breast in the last scene; she has learned to see in new ways, even though what she sees is not very picturesque. No wonder she rejects seeing in favor of something else.

Community in *The Golden Bowl* means dialogue. Knowing within the context of the community defines both the quality and the moral direction of knowledge: communality evaporates when knowledge is restricted to the personal or when someone prevents someone else from knowing something. *The Golden Bowl* suggests that those with whom we share ideas are those we count in our community; whoever does not "know what's going on" is not in the community. If Maggie prevents others from knowing, she also does not force knowledge upon them and she allows them to act on their own. This is as far as James can go. The qualifications about Maggie's status he could not eliminate are his most profound expression of metadesign. Just as she is not completely happy at the end, Maggie is never "all good," but she more than any other character is aware of the dangers of knowledge in building community. Her position contrasts with the isolation of others in her community. Charlotte hatches plans and dreams dreams, glows in success and burns in defeat—always on her own. The Prince would like to "get off with nothing," ignoring dire problems in life's most important relationships. Fanny, so sure of her knowledge at first, finds that in talking out what she "knows" and agonizing over her mistakes she develops a better knowledge—though she never goes as far as Maggie.

Despite his roles as the founder of American City and the patriarch of the troubled family in the novel, Adam is against community as Maggie is for it. Adam's American City is false because it was created as a receptacle of history, and it has no history. It is an absent monument to Adam's pride. There is something unsavory about the game of looting Europe for *objets d'art* by wealthy Americans—something crudely grasping—and James certainly was one to notice it. Adam's "aesthetic flame" does not justify his collecting because the motives are faulty. Adam's sense of artistic beauty does not lend itself to connection with other people's senses of beauty. He longs for "the blessed impersonal whiteness for which his vision sometimes ached"; the "many-colored human appeal" has no interest for him. He plays a "game" of withdrawing to be alone, for he is "inscrutably monotonous behind an iridescent cloud" (111–13). By contrast, Maggie is always "there" among the others in her community, and she is willing to sacrifice Adam to save herself and the others, while helping Adam to sacrifice her. Although Adam and Maggie are both responsible for what happens to Charlotte and the Prince, unlike her father Maggie can tolerate admitting their guilt. In contrast, Charlotte tells Maggie, " 'We're all nice together—as why shouldn't we be? If we hadn't been we wouldn't have gotten very far—and I consider we've gone very far indeed' " (327). Being "nice together," though, is not being a community.

As a failure of community, at Matcham the illicit relationship between Charlotte and the Prince is like the too exclusive relationship between Maggie and her father: "Both our friends felt afresh, as they had felt before, the convenience of a society so placed that it had only its own sensibility to consider—looking as it did well over the heads of all lower growth" (249–50). Amerigo grasps at the false "community of passion" (260), but when the pair returns Maggie offers "the flower of participation, and as that, then and there, she held it out to him, putting straightaway the idea, so needlessly, so absurdly obscured, of her *sharing* with him, whatever the enjoyment, the interest, the experience might be—and sharing also, for that matter, with Charlotte" (317). Maggie not only appears to be eagerly interested in the couple's trip to Gloucester but later makes a point of entertaining the entire house party from Matcham, including the infamous Lady Castledean. Maggie's invoking community here is her first warning; she is setting up the grounds of her defense and the terms of her eventual victory.

Maggie's communal role expands dramatically. She wryly evaluates her role as "the little Princess" of her society: "She couldn't definitely have said how it happened, but she felt herself, for the first time in her career, living up to the public and popular notion of such a personage, as it pressed upon her from all round." Maggie thinks of Fanny as her assistant at a three-ring circus, there "to keep up the pace of the sleek revolving animal on whose back the lady in short spangled skirts should brilliantly caper and posture," and this ironic version of herself as princess marks Maggie's growth in self-awareness. But her "expected role" clashes with her role as daughter to Adam, and she sacrifices Adam for community's sake. She must "charge herself with it as the scapegoat of old" (457–58), yet not succumb even to that design. This theme of sacrifice for the good of the community contrasts with and balances her role as Princess and challenges all designs of power. Maggie begins to act with everyone's interests in mind, and because of this she is more than ever conscious of those interested designs on her. At luncheon at Fawns near the ⸢ ⸣d of the story, despite the "viands artfully iced" and the "slow circulation of precious tinkling jugs," a pall hangs over the table. Charlotte is upstairs with a headache, and when Maggie is seated she finds "marked reserves of references in many directions—poor Fanny Assingham herself scarce thrusting her nose out of the padded hollow into which she had withdrawn. A consensus of langour, which might almost have been taken for a community of dread, ruled the scene" (500). Maggie works to prevent the "community of dread" from becoming their final community.

In some sense, America is everyone's community in *The Golden Bowl*, even the Prince's. But although it is Adam who returns to American City at the end, Maggie is the "little American heroine" because she, more than the founder of American City, has explored new territory and found a new life for herself. Unlike Adam, who buys the Old World to decorate the New, Maggie must develop a new community in which worlds can exist alongside each other without an imposed synthesis of either America's or Europe's expectations. She has declined to make her individual will the measure of all things like the American Adam, but she has not become a European wife either. In her new community Maggie combines an "American" belief in freedom and a willingness to set off in new directions with a "European" willingness to work within received forms, a sophisticated but not cynical idea of human relations that accepts human limitations and vague moral victories and attempts to live within them. Indeed, rather than defining an idea of Love—a theory of Love—Maggie merely loves. Through her loving rather than through her design of what Love should be Maggie takes on the "responsibility of freedom" (426) within her community.

James's techniques of ambiguity and negativity help him with Maggie's transition from monologic to dialogic character. Her "lucid little plan" (318) evolves into her learning instead to be a "mistress of shades" (396), and the usual light/dark good/evil dichotomy is entirely replaced in the novel with degrees of exposure and shade. Ambiguity in *The Golden Bowl* is best described as the narrative expression of the duality of human experience. Dorothea Krook calls this "the sense of the grimness and bitterness of human life . . . inseparably fused with the sense of its beauty and blessedness."[8] And though Maggie makes errors in "doing good," Samuels notes, she does not withdraw from life but decides to use evil, "relinquishing her status as innocent victim to take up her rightful place in the world." The significance of this ambiguity is "its transformation of social forms into means of resisting the very evil they embody."[9]

Tzvetan Todorov characterizes the ambiguous narrative as one that tends to locate the solution within the "quest itself" rather than in the "truth" the quest is supposed to yield: "L'essential est absent, l'absence est essentielle." Following Todorov, Shlomith Rimmon defines ambiguity in two ways: mimetic ambiguity "considers the phenomenon as a device used to reflect, express, represent a parallel phenomenon beyond itself—out there, in the world of 'reality' "; but nonmimetic ambiguity "concentrates on the role of the given phenomenon in relation to the process of reading and on the manner in which it draws the reader's attention to itself, becoming a self-reflexive mediation on the medium of art, rather than a mirroring of a reality outside art." The nonmimetic ambiguity Todorov and Rimmon describe strongly suggests *The Golden Bowl*'s conflicts of knowledge, especially when it presents ocular metaphors in conflict with conversational ones. Such ambiguity, Rimmon says, encourages the reader to "search for clues, group evidences, and weigh them against each other" as part of a dynamic, conversational reading process that "prevents the reader from being merely a passive consumer." It turns the reader "into an active producer of the text"; indeed, as James remarks in the Preface to *The Aspern Papers*, his highest values "are positively all blanks." Rimmon concludes that in becoming aware of "the movements and fluctuations of his own mind, the reader actively lives James's conception of consciousness as a constant flux, forever receptive, forever modified. Such a conception of reading requires a reader who is willing to collaborate in the enterprise."[10]

Adam Verver's ambiguity allows Maggie to develop her own interpretations, and, at the same time his seeming benevolence conceals the tenacity and cunning it has surely taken this postlapsarian Adam to succeed as a robber baron. James hints at Adam's concealed power when he uses the image of Satan on the mountain showing Christ the kingdoms of the earth: "He had come out; quite at the top of his hill of difficulty, the tall sharp spiral round which he had begun to wind his ascent at the age of twenty, and the apex of which was a platform looking down, if one would, on the kingdoms of the earth and with standing-room but for half a dozen others" (115). Is Adam Verver Christlike or Satanic as he views the earth before him? Adam is an adult who sacrifices his adult life for his child's happiness; he is a ruthless financier but a good, generous father; he is independent and unpredictable but sensitive and responsive.

Adam's mind is almost completely unexplored. It is revealed (as is Charlotte's) only in the Prince's Book, yet what is disclosed there adds to the mystery surrounding him instead of clarifying it. For example, there are two hints that he may have confided in Fanny, but the reader never sees him do so and never hears about it from Fanny: "The right person" for Mr. Verver's "confidence" and "his notion of the history of the matter . . . had not, for this illumination, been wanting, but had been encountered in the form of Fanny Assingham, not for the first time indeed admitted to his counsels" (118–19). And later: "Mrs Assingham would be, by so much as this, concerned. . . . It amounted to an intimation, off his guard, that he should be thankful for someone to turn to. If she had wished covertly to sound him he had now, in short, quite given himself away" (366). But Adam *never* "gives himself away," for he refers everything to his own designs, people and objects of art. The narrator is likewise reluctant to reveal the "true" Adam; in describing Adam, the narrator often mentions intriguing qualities but then avoids looking too closely: "Nothing perhaps might affect us as queerer, had we time to look into it, than this application of the same measure of value to such different pieces of property as old Persian carpets, say, and new human acquisitions; all the more indeed that the amiable man was not without an inkling, on his own side, that he was, as a taster of life, economically constructed" (159–60). In the last scenes a strange combination of Adam's character traits seems paralleled by Maggie and Charlotte. As Charlotte wants to become acquisitive, so Maggie has learned the more valuable lesson of "giving up."

Whether or not Adam loves Charlotte makes all the difference for interpreting his character. On the one hand, Adam says that he married to please Maggie and to relieve her of the guilt of having "abandoned" him by her marriage. But on the other hand, there are indications that he really loves and desires Charlotte. For example, his initial decision to ask her to marry him is so presented as to sound like a rationalization on his part. His saying he is doing it for Maggie seems only a pretext he invokes to overcome in his mind the age difference, the indelicacy of marrying a daughter's friend, and his guilt toward Maggie about marrying at all. Yet Adam seems sterile despite his vitality, and this casts doubt on Charlotte's saying she cannot give him any children.[11] Perhaps he refuses to love, and perhaps Maggie helped cause this. This ambiguous knowledge complicates Maggie's thoughts and actions.

Adam's " 'unfathomable heart,' " as Yeazell calls it, "may stand as a sign of all that the Princess—and perhaps James himself—ultimately chooses not to confront." We never know what Adam knows "of the adultery and betrayal, of the radically flawed structure of his life, of his daughter's own painful awakening." Yeazell suggests that perhaps we are baffled "because Maggie wills herself to be." Maggie "prefers to leave the enigma of Adam Verver undisturbed, to worship, but not to question him too closely," for Adam's "inscrutable energy" is "the necessary ground of her faith in herself."[12] Samuels adds that whereas most Jamesian innocents, "even at the cost of life, seek a glittering moral clarity, Maggie agrees not to know or judge [and] labors to keep things fuzzy" especially in regard to her father. Maggie's reason for doing so is, fittingly, ambiguous. Is she still in a sense protecting her father, or is she afraid of finding out what he knows? Is she afraid to confront his "inscrutable energy" because she may discover she shares it? Qualification instead of outright statement becomes Maggie's mode, but Maggie refines upon Adam's own ambiguity just as she refines upon what she learns from Fanny's dialogicity. According to Samuels, James is "supremely interesting not, as decades of criticism have argued, because he shows what is right, but because he shows how difficult it is to show it."[13] Adam's mystery involves not revealing the self, but Maggie's consists of a complex recognition of how very dangerous both withholding and revealing the self can be. In this she is very close to James himself.

James uses negativity much as he uses ambiguity. It does not really negate, but rather provides another view; like ambiguity, negativity presents knowledge as constant oscillation between interpretations. The negative tone is set by Maggie, of course, who does not act and yet has "done all." But throughout the story many reticences indicate the author's desire for freedom of interpretation, and these are often couched in dialogic contexts. For example, "Some such words as those were what *didn't* ring out, yet it was as if even the unuttered sound had been quenched here in its own quaver. It was where utterance would have broken down by its very weight if he had let it get so far" (312). Like Fanny, many characters seem to feel "the horror of the thing hideously *behind*, behind so much trusted, so much pretended, nobleness, cleverness, tenderness" (459), but in the end it is Maggie who is "left in the breach" by the other characters, "essentially there to bear the burden, in the last resort, of surrounding omissions and evasions" (503).

In an important scene, Maggie imagines herself not telling the Prince all she knows and feels upon his return from Matcham. Maggie's presence in the drawing room waiting for her husband to arrive becomes a "complication" and a statement when it should not be anything unusual at all (310). This element of surprise is the secret of Maggie's "negative" knowledge. She is a "timid tigress" (306), not elegant and showy like Charlotte, but subtle and wise. Here, as with everyone, Maggie feels "the note of the felt need of not working harm!" (343), "her constant check and second-thought" (348). In contrast, Charlotte's facade of proud splendor covers up her emptiness: toward the end, her "high quavering voice" is stretched over a "silent scream." The Prince's outward ease even more successfully guards his inner self. The metaphor of the facade could be said to suggest the form of the novel itself, wherein resolution in the end points to terrible difficulties beneath.

Opposed to negativity in *The Golden Bowl* is "doing," and "doing" can work for good or evil. In the sense that Charlotte "does" and plans, and in the way Adam manipulates, doing is dangerous, but it is also a positive value—the performing of one's duties—as Colonel Bob means when he says the Prince has nothing to "do." Maggie asks her father: "'Do you consider that we're languid? . . . Do you consider that we are careless of mankind?'" (361–62). Adam agrees that they do not have enough of "'the sense of difficulty,'" that they are "'selfish together.'" He believes "'we're tremendously moral for ourselves—that is, for each other; and I won't pretend that I know exactly at whose particular expense you and I, for instance, are happy.'" He finds "'something haunting'" and "'uncanny'" in "'such a consciousness of our general comfort and privilege,'" as though they are "'sitting about on divans, with pigtails, smoking opium and seeing visions.'" He quotes Longfellow's "Let us then be up and doing," which rings out like "'the police breaking in—into our opium den—to give us a shake.'" He continues, "'But the beauty of it is, at the same time, that we *are* doing; we're doing, that is, after all, what we went in for. We're working it, our life, our chance, whatever you may call it, as we saw it, as we felt it, from the first. We have worked it and what more can you do than that? It's a good deal for me,' he had wound up, 'to have made Charlotte so happy.'" The irony gets even stronger when he reassures Maggie that her being all right was "'a matter of course'" so that his interest since then has been "'making sure of the same success, very much to your advantage as well, for Charlotte'" (362–63). Like helping, doing can be a coercive design, Maggie learns.

The Prince's unstated question at the beginning of Chapter XVII, "What are we to do?" is answered by Charlotte's "'Do?'":

"Isn't the immense, the really quite matchless beauty of our position that we have to 'do' nothing in life at all?—nothing except the usual, necessary, everyday thing which consists in one's not being more of a fool than one can help. That's all—but that's as true for one time as for another. There has been plenty of 'doing,' and there will doubtless be plenty still; but it's all theirs, every inch of it; it's all a matter of what they've done *to* us."

In Charlotte's mind, she and the Prince have only "taken everything as everything came, and all as quietly as might be" (221). Yet Charlotte also differentiates between herself and Amerigo: " 'Oh, what should people in our case do anything for? But you're wonderful, all of *you*—you know how to live. We're clumsy brutes, we others, beside you—we must always be "doing" something' " (230). Charlotte's last remark points to some telling distinctions among all the characters, as is also suggested by Adam's comments quoted above. While Adam "works it" as he "saw it from the start," the Prince has "taken everything as it came." Adam is speaking for Maggie and Charlotte is speaking for the Prince (" 'But you're wonderful, all of you' "). This has the effect of making Maggie and Amerigo passive receivers of Charlotte's and Adam's doing and seeing. Maggie escapes this role by learning to act by not acting, to win by sacrificing, and neither the passive Prince nor the active Adam and Charlotte ever match her moral development. In contrast, Charlotte loses out to Adam in doing and seeing—he proves the stronger of the two doers and in the end leads her offstage as another of his possessions. As Daniel J. Schneider notes, though the "overwhelming evil" in James's fiction is to "be passive, to surrender to the world as it is, to allow oneself to be caged or trapped," there is a paradox: the most "active" people are, in truth, the most passive. People like Charlotte Stant may do and do, but for all their ferocious energy, they remain essentially inert and fixed; for they "do" only within the world of necessity, the "enslaved world of time and extension." Such doers as Charlotte "never act spontaneously." They are puppets "always being driven—with all the pounding passivity of machinery." Schneider contrasts Maggie's growing activity in the novel with Amerigo's passivity, pointing out that in *The Golden Bowl*, inauthentic versions of freedom "are the products of men who lack imagination." Schneider makes a metafictive connection when he suggests that James found active participation in the world impossible, and thus he developed "the alternative of 'living' indirectly—living by writing." The artist thus lives by "letting himself go." In dialogically reaching out to his audience, in assimilating as much of life as possible, in refusing to allow his imagination to be confined or intimidated, an artist like James may enjoy unprecedented freedom. Maggie's freedom thus parallels what Schneider calls the artist's own "indirect 'living'" in activity qualified by inactivity.[14]

Negativity means letting go because, as Maggie finds, "it doesn't always meet *all* contingencies to be right" (140). Charlotte's mode is confrontation as Maggie's is silence, and in this novel of negatives, silence speaks louder. Many crucial speeches go unnarrated, and at times in this novel the characters almost seem to hold entire conversations telepathically. But silence raises ambiguity and tends to isolate the characters in their own uncertainties; what is unknown is precisely who knows what and how. This is the price Maggie is willing to pay even as she "wins": not to "know all." Her burying her head in Amerigo's breast at the end has often been cited as her refusal to acknowledge what they both know, but the novel's negativity can help us read this scene in a more complex fashion. Critics agree that Maggie's victory is qualified by her painful knowledge. But there is another aspect of the conclusion's ambiguity. It actually is a "happy" ending if one recognizes Maggie as someone about to embark on an adult life, cognizant of disappointment and imperfection but willing to live with that knowledge in her community. Negativity in *The Golden Bowl* is thus anything but simple denial. Through its many turns of meaning it leads protagonist and reader to fuller understanding of the complexities involved in accepting knowledge—and living with it.[15]

In *The Golden Bowl*, because so much goes unsaid—one contrasts it, for example, with the constant conversation in *The Ambassadors*—James's always rich metaphorical imagination is expressed in an astonishing poetic range. This befits the mystery or "negativity" of Maggie's victory in the end. The images he develops in *The Golden Bowl*, like the silent conversations, offer an alternative to our everyday, reductive epistemologies of "seeing." Images replace editorial abstraction, and thus as in other works, through figurative language James's characters and narrator *create* their reality.[16]

But like *The Ambassadors*, *The Golden Bowl* goes beyond description to demonstrate metafictively that the kind of knowledge used in writing a novel has application within the moral world of the novel itself. The images of fiction address all the others. Characters in this novel are always "reading" people, interpreting "signs," and guessing at others' knowledge (50). Bob thinks of Fanny as a text: "He edited, for their general economy, the play of her mind, just as he edited, savingly, with the stump of a pencil, her redundant telegrams" (73). But he is also "a little the artless child who hears his favourite story told for the twentieth time and enjoys it exactly because he knows what is next to happen" (387). The emphasis on "reading" occurs within the novel's overall dialogic structure.

Rachel Salmon finds metafictive "reading" and "interpreting" by characters to be an essential aspect of hermeneutic fiction. She contends that *The Beast in the Jungle,* for example, "is a hermeneutical exercise about a hermeneutical exercise which seeks to induce in the reader a further, identical hermeneutical exercise."[17] Although I would qualify this statement by pointing out that the nature of these exercises is not "identical," this amazing sentence of Salmon's is an excellent description of similar processes in *The Golden Bowl* as well as *The Ambassadors.* In James's novels, as in Faulkner's, we all become storytellers, and we all join in the suffering and the rewards of dialogic knowledge in fiction.

Until the conclusion of *The Beast in the Jungle,* Salmon argues, John Marcher tries to "name" in order to "know" his premonition of "the Beast." Similarly, the reader is absorbed in problems of reading the story in order to illuminate Marcher's understanding of the "text" of his life. Salmon argues that a distinction can be made between two fundamental formal structures in fiction—the sacred and the profane. A profane text already interprets itself and invites ever more definitive interpretations; it is oriented, she says, toward *naming.* The reader of such a text carries on the cognitive activity of its internal reader: one formulates a conceptual analogy to the text. By contrast, the reader of a sacred text is constrained by language that refuses to interpret itself by analogies. Demanding that its reader simply repeat it, the sacred text denies that it can be known through naming. *Knowing* a sacred text, in Salmon's terms, merely involves the acknowledgment of a relationship, the "discovery of the story of the Self within the story of the Other." In *The Beast in the Jungle* James superimposes a sacred text upon a profane one, asking the reader to reiterate "the progression from naming to knowing experienced by the hero of the tale."[18]

The "peculiar" authority of language in a Henry James piece is such that the work simply "*is* what it is *about,*" Salmon urges. Marcher's education in "reading" is also the reader's; his search for his special fate is like looking for a single view of a text—Marcher "talks *about,* looks *for,* thinks *of* the Beast." For him, naming and knowing are identical, "and they remain so until his apocalyptic vision at the end." In trying to find external verification for his life, Marcher "becomes oblivious to *how* he is living it." May Bartram furnishes an ironic point of view on Marcher's desperate struggle with himself, and the reader shares her awareness that his search is misguided. The reader learns slowly what Marcher learns in a flash: Marcher has wanted the power to name the essence of life, but when he finally does experience knowing his Beast, naming it becomes irrelevant. There is nothing to be said finally about *what* he knows so he shows us *how* he knows, "how he reads his life anew," by narrating his story. When we discover that he is the narrator, we experience a similar hermeneutic awakening—we must revise our own views of Marcher. The process of knowing (loving), rather than the essence of knowledge (Love), becomes the most important value for Marcher and for us.[19]

Salmon's reading of this tale's conclusion immediately suggests the conclusions of *The Ambassadors* and *The Golden Bowl*, for there too the knowledge offered by hermeneutic metafictive devices depends upon a community of knowledge among character, narrator, author, and reader. The ironic view of Marcher offered by May is mostly present in *The Golden Bowl* in Maggie herself, for Maggie learns to read herself in a process of critical awareness, allowing her to educate and cooperate with the reader much sooner than Marcher does in his conclusion. At one point Maggie reads the Prince and Charlotte as "high Wagnerian lovers . . . interlocked in their wood of enchantment, a green glade as romantic as one's dream of an old German forest" (488–89). But this European romanticism changes into a broader American mythology when Maggie approaches Charlotte with her hands held high, like some character out of a Wild West story (509). All the characters of *The Golden Bowl* think in metafictive terms, and they all transform themselves and each other when they do. They offer multiple readings of themselves, just as Salmon argues in regard to Marcher, but Maggie is the most adaptable "reader" and "writer." Through such metafictive devices James allows Maggie to teach the reader how to know, not name her story. By addressing herself as well as others dialogically, she teaches us to do the same.

Maggie rapidly becomes more skilled at forms and fictions than Charlotte. When Charlotte "shows" Maggie the bridge players through the terrace window, Maggie sees that "the full significance" is "a matter of interpretation" (464). In return for this vision, at the moment when Maggie lets Charlotte see she has a design, Maggie pursues Charlotte to give her the correct volume of a novel she is reading, as though to suggest that she is writing the "correct" version of their story. She does not allow Charlotte to substitute her version of events but leaves the question open all the same. Maggie imagines Charlotte's thoughts: "At first, clearly, she had been frightened; she had not been pursued, it had quickly struck her, without some design on the part of her pursuer, and what might she not be thinking of in addition but the way she had, when herself the pursuer, made her stepdaughter take in her spirit and her purpose" (509). This is an important moment. The relationship between the author's design and the designs of the characters is slyly asserted in Charlotte's "wrong" volume. "Balancing" designs is very much like writing a story, this scene suggests, and just as risky: in the end Maggie and the Prince have "so shuffled away every link between consequence and cause that the intention remained, like some famous poetic line in a dead language, subject to varieties of interpretation" (531). The overheated, intense multiplicity of all the characters' "interpretations" generates words and more words open to further interpretation.

In their interpretations of each other the characters of this novel mimic authors and critics—perhaps this is why critics themselves cannot resist endless interpretations of the characters' moral qualities. Several characters evoke James as author. Adam, for example, wonders what Amerigo and Charlotte "so resembled each other in treating him *like* . . . but the difficulty here was of course that one could never really know—couldn't know without having *been* one's self a personage; whether a Pope, a King, a President, a General, or just a beautiful Author" (165–66). Adam is also the "little meditative man in the straw hat" who "kept coming into view with his indescribable air of weaving his spell, weaving it off there by himself" (491). Bob's role as a parody of the Jamesian critic is matched by Fanny's parody of the artist himself; Adam, however, is a direr warning to artists about the nature of design.

Fanny has "made" the marriages and is responsible for them, and marriage, of course, is the basis of the plot: Fanny has "invented combinations" (52). Fanny is a "fairy godmother" to the "little Princess," the heroine, and to her, the Prince is "profoundly, a Prince" (296). Fanny's "divergent discussion" and her interest from the sidelines make her, like James, an absent but omnipresent artist. But unlike the author, Fanny is " 'doomed to consistency; she's doomed, poor thing, to a genial optimism' " (257); her desire for the happy ending often distorts her thinking. "Getting through" is all that is important. As the voice of society, Fanny wants to make things look right, even though she sees for herself that they are not. Her guilt also makes her want things to be harmonious. James's sense of the dangers of knowledge, so much greater than Fanny's, makes his more ambiguous approach to the conclusion of the novel more appropriate to the tone of the book than Fanny's hope for a happy ending. In fact, as Maggie matures, Fanny becomes merely an "artist's helper," as Yeazell puts it.[20] And as Fanny becomes less like the author, she is more closely connected to the reader. Like Shreve in *Absalom, Absalom!* as a *ficelle* Fanny is a deputy narrator but also a representative of the reader in the novel. Fanny dramatizes the reader's epistemological difficulties, for her curiosity is always mixed with her concern at what this struggle might mean.

Bob is a critical adjunct to Fanny and in his way another narrator, another author-figure. It was an inspired choice to have Bob as the narrator and introducer of the BBC version of *The Golden Bowl*—he took on this role naturally. The Colonel dislikes "statements" and "theories" (218), and he is always undercutting Fanny's exalted view of her role. Despite his "eternal observances," Bob, in spite of himself, craves Fanny's conversation (502). Bob and Fanny love each other very much. Indeed, the Assinghams' marriage is the only happy one in the book and one of the only happy ones in all James's works. The image of their staying up late in their bedroom, talking about their friends' problems, has less design to it than genuine concern; their cozy colloquy is comforting in contrast to Charlotte's dramas and Maggie's needs. Bob listens because he loves, and he seems to the reader an engaging and reliable, though detached, witness of the actions of others. He and Fanny are in dialogue, and they furnish an important action for Maggie and the reader to emulate.

Yet another metafictive model is *The Golden Bowl*'s characterization of itself as a "drama." Adam is the "financial 'backer'" of the play, "watching his interests from the wing, but in rather confessed ignorance of the mysteries of mimicry" (141). Amerigo "almost resembled an actor who, between his moments on the stage, revisits his dressing-room and, before the glass, pressed by his need of effect, retouches his make-up" (193). Charlotte is certainly a good actress, especially in her parting scene with Maggie in the garden. Much of the plot is presented as a series of dramatic moments. In talking to Adam, for example, Maggie, who earlier felt like the circus princess, sometimes feels like "an actress who had been studying a part and rehearsing it, but who suddenly, on the stage, before the footlights, had begun to improvise, to speak lines not in the text. It was this very sense of the stage and the footlights that kept her up, made her rise higher" (322). The drama metaphor is often accompanied by a card-playing metaphor, as Maggie keeps the others from "as much as suspect[ing] her hand." She knows "there was a card she could play, but there was only one, and to play it would be to end the game. She felt herself—as at the small square green table, between the tall old silver candlesticks and the neatly arranged counters—her father's playmate and partner" (322–23). The light of the footlights is connected to that of the candles, and these symbolize Maggie's roles in life. The footlights are her "public," adult, social career while the silver candlesticks represent her father's wealth and his overprotective care of her. To get on the stage and stay there, Maggie will have to avoid revealing her "hand." In other words, she must make her "play" (her speaking "lines not in the text") without ending the "play" by overtly revealing her damning knowledge of the other players. Maggie feels like "some young woman of the theatre who, engaged for a minor part in the play and having mastered her cues without anxious effort, should find herself suddenly promoted to leading lady and expected to appear in every act of the five" (439). The Princess is able to "show something of . . . the creative hand" (399). She experiences "extensions of view." She plays for Amerigo not the "small strained wife of the moments in question" but "some panting dancer of a difficult step who had capered, before the footlights of an empty theatre, to a spectator lounging in a box" (449). But Maggie is promoted to a higher status than leading lady.

Throughout the book her role progresses from actress, to dancer, to circus performer, until finally she is the playwright. The bridge players "might have been figures rehearsing some play of which she herself was the author" (458). In the last chapter, "play" takes on yet another meaning, a meaning related to the idea of freedom in the novel. Maggie feels "the note of possession and control" that they were "parting, in the light of it, absolutely on Charlotte's *value*—the value that was filling the room out of which they had stepped as if to give it play" (545). Like James, Maggie connects her own form of authorship of the "play" to the dialogic "play" of freedom of knowledge or "value" itself.

Maggie, like Maria Gostrey and Fanny Assingham, takes on the *ficelle* role and transforms it; in a manner of speaking she becomes her own *ficelle*. Indeed, she might be called the *ficelle* apotheosized, achieving the role of heroine by contextualizing her drive for truth within the needs of others. Although she loses her innocence in response to her need for truth, Maggie knows she cannot save her marriage and at the same time master all the pain, cruelty, and deceit that have transpired. Despite her intense desire to know, she must suppress knowledge for others and herself. As Yeazell beautifully says, "If Charlotte Stant and Kate Croy are liars who virtually become artists, Maggie Verver is an artist who is thus also a liar."[21] This is the secret of the strained ending of *The Golden Bowl*. To survive in her community, Maggie must choose her own fictions. Maggie is an ambiguous heroine because she is a statement of the author's own uncertainties about the epistemological status of his work. His duty is to convey the private language of self to the world and to connect self with community, and this is the search for knowledge everyone involved in *The Golden Bowl*—readers, author, narrator, and characters—undertakes. Those who are successful are those who follow Maggie's steps toward what Bakhtin calls "dialogic" knowledge and Rorty "hermeneutic" knowledge. This novel is James's greatest attempt at embodying knowledge with power as well as freedom from its own power.

Maggie Verver is simultaneously a traditional and a radically new Jamesian heroine. It is true that she combines the best aspects of James's previous heroes and heroines—Isabel, Maisie, Milly, Strether—but she infuses their delicacy with a new power emanating from her new knowledge. Maggie is also the best of America, as James saw it. She is a Daisy Miller with James's own sense of human relations—she has a toughness mingled with compassion that James rarely gave his characters. Like Hilda of Hawthorne's *The Marble Faun*, Maggie is virtuous, but there is more of Miriam in her, a sense of relativity in human interactions that is, in a profound sense, her art. Maggie is James's ultimate American heroine.

6. *Go Down, Moses*: Dissolution of Design

LIKE ALL OF FAULKNER'S SINNERS, the characters of *Go Down, Moses* carry out designs on other people. The problem of knowledge in this last great novel by Faulkner is a problem of identity and freedom for the characters, but it becomes a problem of interpretation for the reader. *Go Down, Moses* challenges the characters' designs on each other and the design of the novel itself. This community of tales finds Gavin Stevens's victory in the final story able to challenge the McCaslin design created by L. Q. C. McCaslin and unwittingly continued by his grandson Isaac McCaslin, in spite of Isaac's noble intentions to repudiate it. Knowledge as personal design is surmounted by the communal knowledge for which Gavin struggles, but the novel upholds both forms of knowledge—Isaac's negativity as well as Gavin's positive action. It is a constantly transformative book, strangely satisfying in offering resolution and yet refusing to be resolved.[1] *Go Down, Moses'* hermeneutics represents Faulkner's continuing search for a metadesign that might counteract the closed designs of Yoknapatawpha's social realities.

Design and antidesign occur on all the levels of knowledge in *Go Down, Moses*. The most desirable form of knowledge for the author, the characters, the narrator, and the reader is an open, communal, unforced knowledge; to know in this novel one must accept multiple interpretations and reject consuming designs in favor of communal ones. This Isaac cannot do, but the reader must keep admitting contradictions all the way through. Such metafictive concentration marks a shift toward hope in the author's work. *Go Down, Moses* was written in the period of Faulkner's *The Unvanquished*, *The Wild Palms*, and *The Hamlet*, all novels that are, in different ways, made up of short stories. It is the most optimistic of these late works, as well as the most complex in its stories' interrelatedness. *Go Down, Moses* fulfills the aims of the artist Faulkner cites in his 1950 Nobel Prize Award Speech: the act of addressing the "human heart in conflict with itself" becomes a way of enduring and prevailing for artist and reader. We *all* become members of its community.[2]

The strongest moral argument in *Go Down, Moses* is made through its attack on racism. The great novels of Faulkner's later career, including *Light in August* as well as *Absalom, Absalom!* and *Go Down, Moses*, reflect his most significant development of this theme, which addresses, in the words of Eric J. Sundquist, "the definitive crisis of twentieth-century American social history." Sundquist, however, prefers the two earlier novels to *Go Down, Moses* because it reveals "the extraordinary strain his moral vision and fictional design came under as he drove to the heart of the South's experience." Faulkner's best work, he argues, "reflects a turbulent search for fictional forms in which to contain and express the ambivalent feelings and projected passions that were his as an author and as an American in the South," but *Go Down, Moses'* process of analogy and juxtaposition seems to him a regression from *Absalom, Absalom!*, a failure by the author "to hold his design of tragic involvement in place." The last story of *Go Down, Moses* is a "hasty flight from a tragedy that . . . would admit of no actual or dramatic solution." He calls characters such as Ike and Lucas "failed visions"; the novel itself he says is always "poised on the brink of *dis*integration."[3] But *Go Down, Moses'* seeming structural "disintegration," along with its accompanying repudiation of "vision," is its most successful feature: how better to make the point that the designs of racism are evil than to repudiate closed design altogether in the entire structure of the novel? *The Sound and the Fury*, *Light in August*, and *Absalom, Absalom!* all tried to tell it just one more time to get it right, but *Go Down, Moses*, despite its repeated unifying motifs, moves beyond this urge to something qualitatively different. Its moral argument is only strengthened in the process. If the last story offers no ironclad solutions to the complex personal and social dilemmas of the characters, if it moves us toward a "realistic" universe away from the first story's wilted romanticism, then so much the better for Faulkner's moral arguments, for they become even more immediate as the reader's own interpretive role expands.[4]

As in all of Faulkner's novels, the characters of *Go Down, Moses* find themselves cruelly caught in many designs that contain and are contained by racism: personal design, which is L. Q. C.'s and Isaac's design; historical design, the designs of the past on the present; and genealogical design. As with Thomas Sutpen's personal design in *Absalom, Absalom!*, in *Go Down, Moses* the designs of the past on the present are crucial to the story, as is simultaneously the sense of a vanishing world. The land is as much a tie to the past as it is to a diminishing future. Yet though most of the characters seem trapped in the landscape of the past, *Go Down, Moses* calls for new beginnings.

Genealogical design is a combination of personal and historical design; the single most important mental activity one performs as a reader of *Go Down, Moses* is to construct the genealogy. There is no genealogical chart in the book itself, but Faulkner carefully constructed one.[5] Genealogy represents the formal and not so formal relationships among people: "the human heart in conflict" with other human hearts, as well as "with itself." Interrelationships of blood form a metaphor for relationships among all people. Genealogy is also a design on time, a way of ordering it, and all these characters, especially Isaac, are obsessed with their relationships to time. The genealogical chart closes up at the bottom, bringing the white and black families together, but the descendants of L. Q. C. McCaslin tragically repeat his sins, particularly Roth Edmonds. And the design of community and family relationships is asserted negatively as well. The missing link (named only in Faulkner's chart) between the McCaslin and the Edmonds families, Mary McCaslin Edmonds, daughter of L. Q. C. McCaslin, is never mentioned in the novel. Her absence is only one of many significant omissions.

The author's hopes for demonstrating a hermeneutics are worked out in the constant but always tentative connecting and juxtaposing of the diverse elements of narrative design the reader performs. In addition to the new structure and the present/absent narrator, Faulkner achieves polyphony through echoes between the openings and closings of the stories, the metaphors, and the nature of the hero, Isaac. Through its endless combinations, comparisons, and resonances created by its juxtapositions and its subtle pattern of negativity—its suspense by omission, its carefully timed revelations, and the total absence of certain crucial pieces of knowledge—*Go Down, Moses* achieves coherence but maintains freedom from the design of a novel. This structure allows the conclusion to be optimistic but not forced, positive but not positivistic.

The five "middle" stories begin with "first," "this time"—indicating a new dawn or beginning. These words signify what is about to happen—a new episode in Isaac's life:

First, in order to take care of George Wilkins once and for all, he had to hide his own still. ("The Fire and the Hearth")[6]

He stood in the worn, faded overalls which Mannie herself had washed only a week ago, and heard the first clod strike the pine box. ("Pantaloon in Black," 135)

At first there was nothing. ("The Old People," 163)

There was a man and a dog too this time. ("The Bear," 191)

Soon now they would enter the Delta. ("Delta Autumn," 335)

But there are two stories, the first and the last, that do not begin this way; these end in a similar fashion:

"Damn the fox," Uncle Buck said. "Go on and start breakfast. It seems to me I've been away from home a whole damn month." ("Was," 30)

"Come on," he said. "Let's get back to town. I haven't seen my desk in two days." ("Go Down, Moses," 383)

These two endings also signify future events, for the parallel here is the idea of getting back to daily life. Furthermore, along with the glancing repetitions of the openings, the change of parallelism from openings to closings helps generate a dynamic, hermeneutic structure.

The most important metaphors of the book are those of the hunt, marriage, and gambling and, to a lesser extent, animals, eating, names, the supernatural, and enclosures. Marriage and hunting appear in all the stories. The literary convention of venery comes to mind, especially as one realizes that hunting and marriage in *Go Down, Moses* are always accompanied by gambling, defining them as games, or designs.[7] Faulkner's metaphors, like James's, arise from day-to-day life but are transformed by being opened to an ever-expanding imaginative field of reference in their complex echoing among the voices of the novel.

Isaac, though he is replaced in the end, comes closest to tying the novel together because it is, for the most part, the story of his life. Though Isaac is a decent man who tries to do what he believes is right, he is a failure. He always has the "high and selfless innocence" of a child (106), yet by the end, he is an old man who has forgotten about love. Like Roth, Isaac has no love, only responsibility. Gavin can live within the community because through the context of community Gavin can put his knowledge (his "Heidelberg Ph.D.") to use. Isaac's knowledge only tortures him at the worst and renders him passive and impotent at the best. Unlike Gavin, most Faulkner heroes do not know what to do with their knowledge—

including Darl Bundren, Quentin Compson, the Rev. Hightower (and even other versions of Gavin himself). Yet ideals make pragmatic acts meaningful in *Go Down, Moses*: Isaac is crucial to the meaning of the story, as one realizes when one imagines reading the last story without Isaac there in the background to give resonance to Gavin's deeds. Although by the end of the book Gavin comes to stand for the form of knowledge the author seems to believe is desirable, the reader does not forget Isaac's "negative" moral system of not forcing designs, for it informs the structure of knowledge in the book and contextualizes Gavin's moral imperative. Gavin also seems to echo Lucas's accommodation in "The Fire and the Hearth," as well as Mollie's constant wisdom. And, of course, Gavin is by no means a perfect hero, as Maggie Verver was not a perfect or a perfectly happy heroine. But he is presented on the reader's "dialogic plane." He lives in time, our time. In contrast, frozen in time, Isaac wants to stop and hold onto the "old times" all his life, like the couple on the Grecian urn. Even as he thinks he escapes time in the wilderness, time holds him to his genealogy. Indeed, one of the reasons Gavin is able to act freely is that he is not related by blood to anyone involved. These opposed heroes thus place the idea of relationship foremost in the reader's knowledge. Isaac's fatalism is a sharp contrast to Gavin's getting back to his desk at the end of the novel, but both are necessary to an understanding of the novel.

"Out of the old time, the old days": "Was"

The tales in the fictional community of *Go Down, Moses* all begin in "Was" with several narrative levels. We first briefly hear the narrator of the entire book. Next we meet "he," McCaslin Edmonds as a little boy, the main character of "Was." Third comes the implied listener, presumably a young Isaac McCaslin. "Was" immediately asks the reader to participate by addressing these narrative levels. Although it is not told in the first person and there is no direct mention of a listener, the reader must assume that at some future point Cass tells Isaac this story. And the first three paragraphs that mention Isaac are not part of that story but part of the whole novel, an oblique introduction. "Was" is thus a deliberately confusing beginning, with its references to characters the reader has not yet met, and its negatives: "this was not something." The story works best in retrospect, as a background to all the action of the novel, and it becomes most meaningful as an anticonclusion, for the suggestiveness of "Was" for the novel is not apparent until the entire novel is completed. Cleanth Brooks has noted that "Go Down, Moses," the final story, works best as a "coda" to all the others,[8] but it seems to me that this role is better assigned to "Was." "Go Down, Moses" takes one a long way from "Was"—from slavery times to the eve of the civil rights movement—but to appreciate the fragility of "Go Down, Moses"' depiction of movement toward racial harmony, one needs to return to the memory of the grotesque world of "Was."

The knowledge the reader begins with is sparse, for the narrator, focusing on the mind of young Cass, is accordingly self-limited. For example, the boy does not understand Miss Sophonsiba's banter:

> Then Miss Sophonsiba said something about a bumblebee, but he couldn't remember that. It was too fast and there was too much of it, the earrings and beads clashing and jingling like little trace chains on a toy mule trotting and the perfume stronger too, like the earrings and beads sprayed it out each time they moved and he watched the roan-colored tooth flick and glint between her lips; something about Uncle Buck was a bee sipping from flower to flower and not staying long anywhere and all that stored sweetness to be wasted on Uncle Buddy's desert air . . . , or maybe the honey was being stored up against the advent of a queen and who was the lucky queen and when? "Ma'am?" Uncle Buck said. (11)

The narrator and reader are in on the joke, but Cass is not. This will continue to be a pattern of knowledge throughout the novel—something that is not known is central; readers *and* characters have to figure it out for themselves. A more significant example is the role of Tomey's Turl, easily overlooked in a first reading. It is he whom Isaac finds out about later in the ledgers, the son of L. Q. C. McCaslin and L. Q. C.'s own daughter, and he who engineers the two marriages of the story and thus the continuance of the black and white family lines of the book, as well as, of course, the eventual birth of Isaac himself. In league with Miss Sophonsiba, Turl deals the cards in the final poker game with his "saddle colored hands." Hubert asks,

> "Who dealt these cards, Amodeus?" Only he didn't wait to be answered. He reached out and tilted the lamp-shade, the light moving up Tomey's Turl's arms that were supposed to be black but were not quite white, up his Sunday shirt that was supposed to be white but wasn't quite either, that he put on every time he ran away just as Uncle Buck put on the necktie each time he went to bring him back, and on to his face; and Mr. Hubert sat there, holding the lamp-shade and looking at Tomey's Turl. Then he tilted the shade back

down and took up his cards and turned them face-down and pushed them toward the middle of the table. "I pass, Amodeus," he said. (29)

Hubert sees Tomey's Turl and suspects a plot, but this visual evidence means something more to the reader than just such evidence: the description of shades of light and dark reminds us that Buck and Buddy are wagering with a half-brother and a sister. These characters' limited "knowledge" of blacks is expressed visually in the image of "saddle colored hands" in the lamplight, and the ocularity, as is often the case in Faulkner, symbolizes the reductive. The saddle suggests both Turl's servitude and the coming chase. In the end Gavin manages to replace the McCaslin and Beauchamp legacies of design with understanding achieved through his attempts at dialogue, but the novel has a long way to go before this can take place, and the reader too must learn the lessons of voice over vision. In a very important sense "Was" will be a "chase" or journey for knowledge by the reader.

In "Was," a young boy gives us from his relatively ignorant point of view a story of marriage and of slavery in which hunting and gambling supply the action that upholds and sometimes challenges these institutions. Though its eventual outcome points to the birth of the novel's major character (as the reader already knows from the first paragraph of the story), it does not really seem to end with Buck and Sophonsiba having to marry because Hubert "passes" and Buddy thus wins Buck's freedom. The mystery of why Buck eventually does marry Sibby is contained in the passage quoted above. As Buck's fate is being determined by the cards, we are reminded that "Uncle Buck put on the necktie each time he went to bring [Turl] back." For whom does he put the tie on, if not for Miss Sophonsiba? He later marries her even though he does not have to because he has secretly fancied her all along.

Why does what is supposed to happen not happen? And why are the wagers so complicated? The final act of "Was" hinges on deceit and passing up a bet. Hubert does not know if Buddy has a trey, but he does know who the dealer is. Furthermore, Hubert has reversed the stakes: the loser "wins" Sibby! The confusion of the story is designed to reinforce the idea of marriage and slavery as games played with people, designs on their freedom. As Hubert says to Buck,

"Hah. . . . This is the most serious foolishness you ever took part in in your life. No. You said you wanted your chance, and now you've got it. Here it is,

right here on this table, waiting on you. . . . Reasonable is just what I'm
being," Mr. Hubert said. "You come into bear-country of your own free will
and accord. All right; you were a grown man and you knew it was bear-
country and you knew the way back out like you knew the way in and you had
your chance to take it. But no. You had to crawl into the den and lay down by
the bear. And whether you did or didn't know the bear was in it dont make
any difference. So if you got back out of that den without even a claw-mark
on you, I would not only be unreasonable, I'd be a damned fool. After all, I'd
like a little peace and quiet and freedom for myself, now I got a chance for it.
Yes, sir. She's got you, 'Filus, and you know it. You run a hard race and you
run a good one, but you skun the hen-house one time too many." (23–24)

From being the prey (intriguingly, in this passage, a bear), Miss Sibby is
now the hunter, and Buck is the fox. Like Turl, she is turned into an
animal—the language of the hunt, applied to human beings, appears at
every turn. The men treat everyone as objects of interest and design: Turl
and Tennie, Sophonsiba and themselves. They are wagering with people,
and the extremely disturbing nature of this "serious foolishness" dictates
the ambiguities and contradictions of the story.

One of the story's chief mysteries lies in its humor, and there is a lot of
comedy in "Was." The elderly lovers are treated humorously: Miss
Sophonsiba makes silly entrances and exits; she sends a knight a lady's
token; the bedroom scene is farce. Miss Sophonsiba's romantic design of
her "Warwick" is certainly narrated for its humor. When people did not call
her land that, "she wouldn't even seem to know what they were talking
about and it would sound as if she and Mr. Hubert owned two separate
plantations covering the same area of ground, one on top of the other" (9).
What is all this comedy and more doing in a story about catching slaves? Is
humor supposed to help overcome the evil in this story? The discrepancy
between the humor and the evil in "Was" cannot be synthesized away but
rather is held unresolved by the reader. This uncomfortable, even grotesque, juxtaposition of humor and horror throws the reader off balance
until the final story, when there is a comic balancing, if still no synthesis, of
the tensions between black and white, between generations in a family,
between neighbors, between fable and tragedy.

The tone of comic burlesque in "Was" has made some readers question
Faulkner's attitude toward racism and ask about its relation to other events
in the book. Later in the novel, "Was" could seem like a golden age of sorts,
a strong contrast to the bleakness of "Delta Autumn." Buck and Buddy
seem to be lenient masters, allowing Turl to escape, letting their slaves out

at night, and eventually manumitting all of them. They are not pretentious like Hubert or Sophonsiba or (more darkly) L. Q. C. They are somewhat nontraditional as well—it would be hard to picture L. Q. C. contentedly cooking in his apron like Buddy. But the question of "Was" is best answered by characterizing its comedy as irony, recognizing that Buck and Buddy *are* morally outrageous. Faulkner parodies the "golden age" tradition in "Was" by giving us a story that *almost* makes slave times funny. And as a background to "Delta Autumn" and "Pantaloon in Black," "Was" does much more. It becomes for the reader a terribly painful exercise, a grotesque in the most traditional sense of that term, describing something that evokes simultaneous, uncontrollable laughter and fear. And the reader's laughter and fear may be directed toward one's own susceptibility to the humorous design of "Was." As Bakhtin would describe it, "Was" is a very carnivalized beginning to a carnivalistic novel. It forces us to question our myth-making and fictionalizing tendencies even when we have barely entered the fiction. It is a highly critical introduction indeed.

The comedy of "Was" thus performs a double function: it creates a tension for the reader, who wonders what such comedy will lead to, and it functions in retrospect as an ironic or parodic design on the past. Because the moonlight-and-magnolia tradition is invoked self-consciously, even metafictively, by Faulkner, one may thus read the story and respond to its comedy, feeling troubled about its relation to the subject of slavery, and then read the rest of the book with this unanswered question in mind. The reader comes to realize that the humor of "Was" is a design among designs. Despite its apparently innocent and farcical nature, cruelty lives in its humor. The comedy reveals the design in what "was," and design explains all the behavior in the book, including slavery, Warwick, fox hunting, gambling with people, love and marriage, and even clothes (Miss Sophonsiba's get-up, Buck's tie, and Buddy's apron). The main design is slavery, and it addresses Isaac's later rejection of his land and his future. Isaac's iron cot precedes this humorous wedding story, and though the story points to his birth, instead his sterility—he is "uncle to half a county and father to no one"—is the eventual outcome. Slavery and marriage in "Was" lead both to Isaac's lonely cot in "Delta Autumn" and to Rider's prison cot in "Pantaloon in Black." This tension between comedy and tragedy in "Was" thus supplies a hermeneutic context for the rest of the novel's simultaneous narrative openness and complexity.

"One long course of outrageous trouble and conflict": "The Fire and the Hearth"

The new main character, Lucas, does not at first seem connected to the characters of "Was," and when he becomes obsessed with his designs, he is replaced as hero by his wife, Mollie. As the narrator moves beyond Cass and Isaac to share their consciousnesses and consciences, we are eventually led to sympathy with all the characters of the story. This structural migration of dialogicity from that between Cass and Isaac to that between Mollie and Lucas is an important forecast of later relocations, as the novel progressively addresses more and more related "others." "The Fire and the Hearth" opens up *Go Down, Moses* to compassion in its handling of relationships; it is empowered by this compassion to inspire moral strength.

The focus of "The Fire and the Hearth" is community, the lack of it and the discovery of it. Roth's development of racial awareness, his knowledge of the old "curse of his fathers" (111), takes up much of the story: "Then one day the old curse of his fathers, the old haughty ancestral pride based not on any value but on an accident of geography, stemmed not from courage and honor but from wrong and shame, descended to him." The story of Roth refusing to let Henry share his bed is followed by Roth's lonely dinner in Mollie's kitchen, the first he has had alone there. This meal forms a metaphor for Roth's later emptiness. One recalls the importance of the sustaining kitchen in *The Sound and the Fury*. Roth always eats alone and never enjoys it, ever since that fatal dinner (113–14). It is his "bitter fruit," this "one long and unbroken course of outrageous trouble and conflict" of the last twenty years of his life, trouble mostly "with the old negro who in his case did not even bother to remember not to call him mister, who called him Mr Edmonds and Mister Carothers or Carothers or Roth or son or spoke to him in a group of younger negroes, lumping them all together, as 'you boys.'" Roth thinks that Lucas will outlast them all, outlive the "very ledgers which held the account," for Lucas is "impervious to time" (116–17). For Lucas, community eventually rises above the ledger mentality, but for Roth it never does.

Though it will later be Roth who commits L. Q. C.'s sin, Lucas says he is more like L. Q. C. than is Roth or Isaac. Roth himself realizes this, "and he thought with amazement and something very like horror: *He's more like old Carothers than all the rest of us put together, including old Carothers*" (118). Lucas is obsessed with his role as a McCaslin. As he enters Zack Edmonds's house with the intent of killing him for stealing his wife, Lucas thinks of "the old days, the old time, and better men than these; Lucas himself made one, himself and old Cass coevals in more than spirit even" (44). Cass was one of the "better men," though a McCaslin "only by the distaff." Cass had "enough of old Carothers McCaslin in his veins to take the land from the true heir simply because he wanted it and knew he could use it better and was strong enough, ruthless enough, old Carothers McCaslin enough." Lucas thinks Isaac gave Cass the land because he was weak, in that he was being gallant to Cass because Cass was descended from the female side of the family, and that Isaac accordingly could not resist such an appeal. To Lucas, Isaac, "say what a man would, had turned apostate to his name and lineage by weakly relinquishing the land which was rightfully his to live in town on the charity of his great-nephew" (39–40). By raising the question of what Isaac will do as a descendant of L. Q. C., Lucas's ambivalence about Isaac early on suggests the author's as well. Though Lucas's contempt for Isaac is strong, one also notes Isaac's generosity as well as Lucas's eventual capitulation to a woman, Mollie. Isaac gives Lucas his inheritance money on his twenty-first birthday, and he tracks down the other black descendants of L. Q. C. and pays them too (107ff.). This is Isaac's only community with Lucas, and limited though it is, Isaac believes he is doing right to pay the descendants, even though it is only with money.

More like Isaac than he thinks, Lucas operates with stereotypes about family and especially women firmly in mind. Lucas always struggles with Mollie: "*Women*, he thought. *Women. I wont ever know. I dont want to. I ruther never to know than to find out later I have been fooled*" (59). He tells Roth, " 'I'm a man,' Lucas said. 'I'm the man here. I'm the one to say in my house, like you and your paw and his paw were the ones to say in his' " (120). Lucas lets his struggle over mastery in his house nearly break up his marriage. He believes that he has old L. Q. C. on his side, but L. Q. C. is an evil influence—Lucas is a better man when he is on his own at the end, when he saves his marriage. Lucas's delusions are another legacy of the design of L. Q. C.; Mollie escapes them here, and she escapes them in the final story. The genealogical design of the past is nearly the undoing, not the making, of Lucas Beauchamp. He must remain "not only impervious to that blood" he inherited from L. Q. C. but become "indifferent to it." Instead of being at once the "battleground and victim" of the two strains, he becomes "a vessel, durable, ancestryless, nonconductive, in which the toxin and its anti-toxin stalemated one another, seetheless, unrumored in the outside air" (104).

Like "Was," "The Fire and the Hearth" is another marriage story, relating details about Mollie and Lucas, Zack and his wife and Mollie, Nat and George, and Isaac and his wife. Manipulation of identity by husbands and wives severely tests marriage as community in "The Fire and the Hearth." Identities become confused: Lucas muses that Zack's wife "never existed" (52). Mollie for a time is Zack's wife and Roth's mother. Lucas meddles in Nat and George's marriage, then he not only causes Mollie to want a divorce but he also attempts to have George arrested. Lucas has much to learn about the community of family. The fire and the hearth is the symbol of home, and it provides a transition to the next story, "Pantaloon in Black," which is a tragic marriage story. The fire in the hearth returns again in "Go Down, Moses" as a symbol of threatened harmony, but the image is there in the campfires of the hunting stories as well.

This is also a hunting story, but the hunt is not for animals. Why does Lucas hunt for buried treasure when he has a sizable bank account? He refuses to spend his own money to finance his hunt. Perhaps he hunts to irritate Roth, but he goes too far—he becomes entranced by the game, the design of it. Lucas hunts for respect by hunting for a way to beat everyone else at their games. But Lucas has to learn something more than beating everyone. "The Fire and the Hearth" becomes a story about accommodation, compromise, and resignation. Lucas thinks that "maybe when he got old he would become resigned" to Zack and Mollie. At the end of the story, he does get old and he does resign himself to his life, marriage, and bank account. The story of Lucas's victory over the white community results in a victory not over Roth—finding the treasure—but in a victory for Lucas over himself—giving up the treasure hunt. This is the opposite of what Isaac later does: Lucas admits he is wrong. At the end, when Roth says he will let him use the metal detector machine every now and then, Lucas says,

> "No. . . . Get rid of it. I dont want to never see it again. Man has got three score and ten years on this earth, the Book says. He can want a heap in that time and a heap of what he can want is due to come to him, if he just starts in soon enough. I done waited too late to start. That money's there. Them two white men that slipped in here that night three years ago and dug up twenty-two thousand dollars and got clean away with it before anybody saw them. I know. I saw the hole where they filled it up again, and the churn it was buried in. But I am near to the end of my three score and ten, and I reckon to find that money aint for me." (131)

Lucas's noble renunciation invokes several different types of knowledge.

The empirical knowledge he cites—he *saw* the hole and the churn—is almost certainly false. The certainty of ocular evidence is rejected in "The Fire and the Hearth"; it is replaced by something heard and told about:

> "Hah," Edmonds said. "And . . . you know damn well that there aint any money buried around here. You've been here sixty-seven years. Did you ever hear of anybody in this country with enough money to bury? Can you imagine anybody in this country burying anything worth as much as two bits that some of his kinfolks or his friends or his neighbors aint dug up and spent before he could even get back home and put his shovel away?" (79)

Lucas turns his back on the tall tale he believes to be true—the ideal he cherishes—and chooses instead the traditional ties of family, of the fire and the hearth. Lucas's most positive action in "The Fire and the Hearth" is thus a negative one, giving up his design for the good of his family. He surmounts the influence of L. Q. C. instead of fulfilling it, and his reconciliation with Mollie forecasts the antidote to Isaac's rigid epistemologies before Isaac has even entered the story. As we will find, Lucas's and Gavin's accommodations frame Isaac's epistemological "heroism" with their small victories for community. Lucas could be said to embody both Isaac's repudiation of blood and Gavin's communal embrace of strangers—he is accordingly another critical introduction to the novel. And Mollie, of course, will return as the catalyst for communal action in the last story.

" 'And what do you think of that?' ": "Pantaloon in Black"

"Pantaloon in Black" sharply departs from the tone of "The Fire and the Hearth," splitting into the nondialogic consciousnesses of Rider and the deputy sheriff. The hermeneutic distance in the story occurs between Rider's agonized, hopeless knowledge of his wife's death and the deputy's facile knowledge of blacks as "animals." Although the deputy feels uncomfortable enough about his knowledge to ask his interlocutor, " 'And what do you think of that?' " he does not know how to know blacks any other way than as animals. The irony is that Rider's grief *is* somewhat "animal-like," for it comes straight from his heart and he cannot control it. The all-important moral difference is between the narrator's seeing Rider's grief through the fictional metaphor of animal grief and the deputy's stereotypical, prejudicial design. The title's clown dressed in mourning, related as he is to Faulkner's other marionettes, especially the marble faun, quietly carnivalizes these opposed aspects of knowledge, tragedy and stereotype.

The story turns on such contrasts. Rider's distance from the whites contrasts with Lucas's manipulations. Rider both forecasts and contrasts Butch Beauchamp of "Go Down, Moses"; he is as innocent as Butch is guilty, though he and Butch are both victims. Although each is killed, Rider is lynched and Butch has a public funeral. Rider's ineffectual aunt contrasts with Butch's grandmother Mollie, who will be more successful in getting her grandson home, though the women are alike in their grief. Gavin and the deputy sheriff form an important contrast, as do the community of the last story and "Pantaloon in Black" 's lynch mob. Further contrasts occur in the chase motif and the image of the marriage hearth. Joseph Reed characterizes "Pantaloon in Black" as a story of nearly total "negation"—Rider, wife, family, possessions, blood, and heritage are all negated, things that supplied context for Lucas's eventual compromise with the whites. The title "Pantaloon in Black" suggests for Reed that this will be a drama or a comedy, distanced by artificiality, and it is, but not, he emphasizes, in the way one might suspect. Alternation between apparent intimacy and objective drama is its mode, but it also operates in cancellation of these elements. Its negation causes many critics to say it does not fit in with the rest of the book (of the main characters of the novel, only Roth Edmonds and Lucas Beauchamp are in this story, and they are merely mentioned once and do not appear in person), but "Pantaloon in Black" must be read in terms of what it lacks and what its protagonist does not do. What is not there, Reed finds, points to what *is* in the other stories, a dramatic case of emphasis by contrast.[9]

"Pantaloon in Black" follows two burlesques about slave-catching, trickery, and marriage. This story is the only one whose title suggests burlesque, yet it is hardly slapstick. Can the horrors of "Pantaloon in Black" ever be overcome? Only perhaps. Like "Was," only more so, the story painfully strains the optimism of the concluding "Go Down, Moses." Uncomfortably embedded in the book, mysterious and strange, it is also all too familiar. "Pantaloon in Black" is a warning against any easy hope for the future of humankind.

Besides its negative allusions to the other stories, "Pantaloon in Black" offers ironic parallels as well. Here the two themes of racial cruelty and personal loss are interwoven, as they will be in "The Bear." Rider's passion for his wife and the passion of the white men against the blacks is the common thread of the story, the opposed forms of knowledge about people that distance Rider from the deputy and the other white men. It contains the gambling, hunting, and marriage themes of the other stories. It connects with the supernatural of "The Old People" and the funeral of "Go Down, Moses." Even the moonshine Rider drinks has a parallel in "The Fire and the Hearth" 's still.

But "Pantaloon in Black," even in its parallelisms, always transforms *Go Down, Moses'* images to suit its own purposes. Gambling in "Pantaloon in Black" recalls the card game of "Was," but this time the black man is cheated and speaks out against it—and he is lynched. It is another story of the hunt, but this hunt consists of two brutal murders. Such viciousness changes the tone of the book to that point and continues to transform it. "Pantaloon in Black" makes one realize, for example, that the death of Old Ben is caused by a lynch mob of sorts, and that he too is innocent. The murder of Rider, who is hanged at the Negro schoolhouse, is the worst hunting "game" in the book, but like most of the others, it is predicated upon ignorance, and no one involved in it ever seems to understand what it was all about.

All Rider knows is that he loves so much that he cannot live; his death comes about because he cannot stop thinking about Mannie. The contrast is Isaac, who loves too little. In contrast to both is Mollie, who in her love is willing to let go—even to get divorced. Rider's passion obliterates his hard work, happy home, and marital comfort. His devotion to work and to his home relate him to other hard workers in the book, including Sam Fathers, Mollie, and Gavin. But as Rider's designs for life are destroyed by uncontrollable grief, the white men's stereotypes are driven by mindless, hateful passion: when they look at him they know nothing of his love for his dead wife, and this of course is their failure of knowledge, their moral lapse. They kill Rider for the very thing they never know, for it is Rider's passion that incites him to murder. Love is Rider's undoing because there is no place for his passionate grief in the world in which he lives. There is no community between the white men and Rider, no common knowledge. Knowledge in "Pantaloon in Black" gets only as far as the unreadable surface of Mannie's grave, which, "save for its rawness, resembled any other marked off without order about the barren plot by shards of pottery and broken bottles and old brick and other objects insignificant to sight but actually of a profound meaning and fatal to touch, which no white man could have read" (135). As is the case with Isaac's later learning to read signs in the wilderness and in the ledgers, here knowledge is deep, hidden, and dangerous.

Rider cries, " 'Ah'm snakebit now and pizen cant hawm me' " (148), and " 'Ah'm snakebit and bound to die' " (152). Rider is very strong but becomes weaker and weaker as this story goes on. He is grieved, exploited, helpless. He tries to fill himself with moonshine to block out his thoughts, but the metaphors make his thoughts like the moonshine: both "fill" him, as the house fills as his mind fills, and just as he "can't quit thinking," he drinks the moonshine until it comes back up his throat. Though knowledge is hidden, Rider cannot stop thinking.

In Part 2 of "Pantaloon in Black" Rider's story is narrated by the deputy to his wife, who is cooking dinner. He tells of Rider's capture, jailing and near escape, and of his death. He tells what we have not heard—but also retells from a different point of view what we have our-selves learned. His point of view is determined by his prejudice against blacks and by his loyalty to a corrupt sheriff courting votes. The addition of the deputy's monologue furnishes what Wesley Morris calls a "crucial countervoice, . . . another failed interpretation." The deputy is clearly limited as a narrator by his stereotyped abstractions—he never experiences Rider's "unique experiential being" as readers have. Rider's suffering re-mains silent for the deputy because the deputy lacks "a dramatic participa-tion, a hermeneutic engagement," an unavoidable lack for someone whose knowledge is strictly conceptual.[10] Gavin is the deputy's obverse because he is the character in the novel who in the end is most aware of the limitations of his knowing. This is important because they are the two public officials in the book, and we may measure a great distance between them.

When the deputy focuses on Rider's inexplicable behavior (" 'And what do you think of that?' " [159]) his wife's reaction is ambiguous. Why does she refuse him comment? It may be that she does not care about what happened to Rider or that she cannot allow herself to know. But perhaps she does know but cannot speak of her knowledge—for her own good she must keep to herself her opinions about what the swaggering men of her town are doing. In refusing to hear her husband's story, the deputy's wife is refusing to know in the way he knows. She does hear him out—it is dialogue she will not give him, reaction as an audience. Women and blacks throughout *Go Down, Moses* are listeners and understanders and endurers, but though the wife knows about the men's petty corruptions (the Birdsong vote) and their opinions about blacks, she cannot allow herself to name publicly what she knows all too well privately. What good would it do? she seems to ask herself. This failure of dialogue is a very low point in *Go Down, Moses*. The picture show with its numbing ocularity seems a welcome escape, for in this story, it is wiser to "stop thinking," which Rider cannot. The story ends in despair and continues to call into question the knowledge of hope in all the later stories.

"And Sam Fathers' voice the mouthpiece of the host": "The Old People"

Narration in "The Old People" offers the voice of a child again, and young Isaac becomes the character who, present or absent, dominates the remainder of the book. "The Old People" moves toward "The Bear" 's intense telling and retelling of Isaac's encounter with the wilderness. Indeed, the two stories' first paragraphs make clear their sequential connection: "The Old People" begins, "At first there was nothing" (163), and "The Bear" follows this with "There was a man and a dog too this time" (191). In this way the hunt of the buck in "The Old People" is a prelude to the climax of Old Ben's death in "The Bear," for Old Ben himself is one of the Old People—he is their god.

Besides its theme of hunting, "The Old People" is connected to the other stories through the marriage theme, this time addressing Sam's parents. His father, Ikkemotubbe, was a Chickasaw chief who called himself "Doom" and who became "The Man." The day after he murdered to seize power, he pronounced marriage between his pregnant quadroon mistress and one of the slave men he had inherited—"(that was how Sam Fathers got his name, which in Chickasaw had been Had-Two-Fathers)"—and two years later sold the man and woman and child "who was his own son to his white neighbor, Carothers McCaslin" (166). Sam is the most solitary figure in the book. Though several families and races mingle in his blood, he is betrayed by his blood, bequeathed "not only the blood of slaves but even a little of the very blood which had enslaved it; himself his own battleground, the scene of his own vanquishment and the mausoleum of his defeat" (168). Sam lives by the code of his warrior-chief ancestors and by the code of their wilderness, and he maintains nearly total isolation.

Sam shares aspects of many characters in the book, including Lucas, Isaac, Boon Hogganbeck, the dog Lion, and of course Old Ben himself. Like Lucas, Sam is independent; as Cass asks Isaac, " 'Did you ever know anybody yet, even your father and Uncle Buddy, that ever told him to do or not do anything that he ever paid any attention to?' " (168). In bequeathing

Isaac his love for the wilderness, Sam also bequeaths the boy his isolation.
The paradox of Sam's mingling of bloods and his simultaneous virtual
alienation from everyone, an obverse of Lucas's eventual reinstatement in
community, offers an unsettling legacy for young Isaac.

The wilderness provides yet another way this story is tied to the others.
The poignancy of the disappearing wilderness in Part 5 of "The Bear" and in
"Delta Autumn" is made more telling if one recalls the haunting, mysterious beauty of "The Old People." As with "Was," knowledge of "The Old
People" becomes meaningful to the reader later; all the stories of *Go Down,
Moses* are similarly connected, not directly and systematically, but allusively,
metaphorically, and reflexively. The movement of the story of Isaac's initiation is like the movement through the woods of the mysterious buck Isaac
and Sam follow. As in "The Bear," the topography of the woods provides a
model for narrative direction: paths are not straight, one finds oneself
circling back to suddenly familiar and yet simultaneously strange locales,
things appear and disappear in the heavy foliage, footprints fill with water,
and reflections sink into deep, muddy pools. In "The Old People," it is the
ghost buck who determines movement:

> So he tried to go slower. He tried deliberately to decelerate the dizzy rushing
> of time in which the buck which he had not even seen was moving, which it
> seemed to him must be carrying the buck farther and farther and more and
> more irretrievably away from them even though there were no dogs behind
> him now to make him run, even though, according to Sam, he must have
> completed his circle now and was heading back toward them. (180)

Sam, the buck, and the wilderness are Isaac's teachers here as elsewhere.
The buck is mysterious yet near at hand, and to "see" it one must be ready to
know—equipped for what one will learn, through a mental circling and
doubling back, through entertaining the kind of knowledge that demands
such simultaneous doubt and belief. There are no straight lines on a forest
floor and no direct "lines of sight."

"The Old People" 's initiation prepares us for the deeper mysteries of
"The Bear"—hunting the ghost buck in this story transforms Isaac's hopes
for a successful deer kill into a lifelong obsession. Isaac learns from Sam the
Indians' belief that in hunting an animal the hunter respects and loves it and
offers thanks to its spirit when the hunt is done. The love of the wilderness
is the value on which Isaac bases all his decisions from this moment
forward, but the story is about a dying wilderness, and his religion upholds
a defeated god. Ironically, though Isaac here is able to ask his victim for

forgiveness for his "sin," he is unable later to forgive his own family's sins. What Isaac learns about love in the wilderness, his ostensible reason for turning his back on the tamed land, utterly fails him in his responsibilities to others.

The circling back in "The Old People" and "The Bear" is never a single-minded attempt to hunt knowledge down—the "visions" Isaac experiences of the ghost buck and bear are given to him for him to interpret as best he can. He learns, and he refuses to learn. In "The Old People," Isaac moves from grieving over the missed opportunity in not being the one to shoot the buck to a deep awareness of its mysterious life force. On that morning something happens to him: covered in the blood of his first kill, Isaac sees the buck he cannot kill, the spirit of the woods that Old Ben later represents. Two kinds of knowledge are inextricably intertwined—hunting skill and spiritual knowledge—but Isaac later forgets that there could be coexistence between them.

In "The Bear," when Sam, Old Ben, and Lion die, Isaac feels he should have died with them, for their deaths presage the destruction of the wilderness, hinted at in "The Old People," the lumber mills, railroads, and cultivation that gain momentum as the book progresses. To Isaac, Sam's "old times would cease to be old times and would become a part of the boy's present, not only as if they had happened yesterday but as if they were still happening" (171). Isaac can never be happy in the present, in which men own land and yet "their hold upon it actually was as trivial and without reality as the now faded and archaic script in the chancery book in Jefferson which allocated it to them and that it was he, the boy, who was the guest here and Sam Fathers voice the mouthpiece of the host" (171). The play on "host" and "guest" here continues the duality of knowledge presented in this story. The host of the wilderness, Sam, will also be its communion offering. Sam dies as Old Ben dies, as a doomed god. He will continue to live on in Isaac's memory but ultimately will not sustain Isaac, for to live in a doomed past is not enough, despite the allure of the wilderness. Isaac's tragedy is not that he renounces the tamed land, preferring the wild forest, but that he does not understand the lofty standards he learns in the woods. Isaac commits the same sin as Doom, as L. Q. C., as Sutpen: he renounces the community of family and neighbors to pursue an obsessive dream, his own design. Thus Isaac sees Sam's sacrifice in its nobility but not in its tragedy. Sam is "impervious to time" and to the knowledge of white society; to Isaac, he offers something different from what the other men around him offer, a past before the white men created the South and created the war that destroyed the cultivated land and created the recon-struction that still later destroyed the forests. Isaac accordingly thinks that Sam "consecrated him and absolved him from weakness and regret too" (182). As host, however, that is, owner of the plantation, Isaac is not only unconsecrated but absent from the others for whom he is a potential "mouthpiece." Isaac is partly led to failure by Sam, as he also fails even Sam.

Sam salutes the ghost buck, " 'Oleh, Chief,' Sam said. 'Grandfather' " (184), as Isaac will later salute the snake in Part 5 of "The Bear." In these salutes is a recognition and a letting go. Sam reveres the spirit of the Old People; Isaac recognizes their spirit as well as the spirit opposed to it, the snake, his evil grandfather L. Q. C. McCaslin. Isaac learns from Sam the knowledge of beauty and suffering by learning of an Eden threatened with destruction. To "know" the snake for Isaac becomes an admission of sin and grace, a recognition of being human. But because Part 5 occurs before the events of Part 4 but after the hunt of Part 3, Isaac's salute provides an ultimately defeated hope that he will face the evil in his family he has found in the ledgers and will not renounce his responsibilities. As Sam salutes the proud buck in recognition of his own status as hunter and as suppliant in the cathedral of the woods, so Isaac's later salute provides an ironic con-trast. Isaac's salute in Part 5 of "The Bear" *seems* to be a recognition of good and evil, but, oddly, a recognition that for him eventually comes to nought, as "Delta Autumn" painfully indicates.

The contradictions and complexities of Isaac's initiation into the wil-derness in "The Old People" are beautifully expressed through opposed metaphors of seeing and hearing. Sam stands over the boy when they see the ghost deer,

> and the boy knew that Sam did not even see him, that Sam knew he was still there beside him but he did not see the boy. Then the boy saw the buck. It was coming down the ridge, as if it were walking out of the very sound of the horn which related its death. . . . Then it saw them. And still it did not begin to run, . . . just moving with that winged and effortless ease with which deer move, passing within twenty feet of them, its head high and the eye not proud and not haughty but just full and wild and unafraid. (184)

Later, Isaac is engaged in a heated dialogue with Cass, who says the deer is a ghost. Isaac insists, " 'But I saw it!' the boy cried. 'I saw him!' " Cass replies, " 'Steady. I know you did. So did I. Sam took me in there once after I killed my first deer' " (187). Isaac refuses to share his vision or question it in dialogue, much like Quentin in the conclusion of *Absalom, Absalom!* Cass is saying that he shared Isaac's revelation, but Isaac will have none of what he sees as Cass's fictionalizing. As of now, he thinks, " 'there is plenty of room for us and them too' " (187) but later he knows he will have to choose.

Isaac chooses the wilderness over his community, vision over dialogue, isolation instead of involvement. He wants to live as wild and untamed and unthinking as the animals in the woods, like Sam, but his life is spent chasing a dream that is gone forever, like the buck disappearing into the trees. Isaac does not "see" the extent to which he is giving up his responsibility in the wilderness as he forsakes the tamed land. Like Sam, Isaac "smells the cage" (167) but thinks he is out of it when he is not, just as he thinks he can renounce the sin in his family and not be a part of it. Sam is a prisoner:

> "Like an old lion or bear in a cage," McCaslin said. "He was born in the cage and has been in it all his life; he knows nothing else. Then he smells something. It might be anything, any breeze blowing past anything and then into his nostrils. But there for a second was the hot sand or the cane-brake that he never even saw himself, might not even know if he did see it and probably does know he couldn't hold his own with it if he got back to it. But that's not what he smells then. It was the cage he smelled. He hadn't smelled the cage until that minute. Then the hot sand or the brake blew into his nostrils and blew away, and all he could smell was the cage. That's what makes his eyes look like that." (167)

Isaac's agonized response, " 'Then let him go! . . . Let him go!' " is what Isaac fruitlessly tries to do for himself his whole life, since he could not do it for Sam. In not heeding the lesson of Cass's seeing the buck too, Isaac also cannot "see" the community with its slavery and its repression, the fractured community of white and black and Indian. Despite his ideals, Isaac's knowledge of the wilderness cannot be communal knowledge, as it would perhaps be if he accepted Cass's attempt to share the knowledge of the spirit they have both "seen."

Isaac's only community is the ancient one of the Old People. He does not share his relationship with the woods with anyone but Sam, and he leaves his other responsibilities behind him. Cass can see the ghost deer and still go about his daily work—by contrast, Isaac cannot reconcile the two types of knowledge, and so he chooses solitary, passive knowledge over a communal knowledge that allows for action. Isaac seems to inherit Buck's and Buddy's sloth and Sophonsiba's silly fantasies instead of the much-talked-about strength of L. Q. C. McCaslin. Isaac chooses not "to bear"

(186), and "The Old People" is the genesis of his decision to reject his present-day community in favor of an idealized world of the past.

"The Old People" makes clear that the hunters were a community, for they later degenerate into drunkenness, shooting squirrels, and hunting does after the death of Old Ben. One of the most troubling messages of "The Old People" is the sense of a lost community, of Sam's Old People gone forever. Isaac tries to find them again and after Ben's death openly prefers his dreams of the past. But "The Old People," with its rendering of one of the high points of Isaac's life, is also the beginning of his tragedy. Its shades and blurred distinctions between the realms of reality and of the spirit of the woods is the pattern of Isaac's greatest joys and the omen of his defeat. The "gray and unmarked afternoon" of "The Old People" becomes darkness "without any gradation between" (179) by the time of "Delta Autumn."

"Yr stars fell": "The Bear"

In "The Bear," the longest and most complex story of *Go Down, Moses*, Isaac witnesses the death of Old Ben and gives up his plantation to his cousin Cass, thus losing his responsibilities on both tamed and untamed land. "The Bear" completes Isaac's initiation into both the moral imperative of the wilderness and the unwanted knowledge of his family's sins, but it is followed by the grim "Delta Autumn." In "The Bear" Isaac becomes Isaac unsacrificed on the family altar, but he seems addressed as Moses, too: "And the Lord said to Moses . . . because you broke faith with me in the wilderness of Zin . . . you shall see the land before you; but you shall not go there, into the land which I give to the people of Israel" (Deut. 32:48–52). Like Moses, Isaac wanders in the wilderness but falters when he must lead his people into the Promised Land. Like Moses, the prophet who begged not to be called, the leader who at certain crucial moments seemingly lost his faith, Isaac prevents himself from entering the community of the settled land because he cannot admit his knowledge of the evil he sees there.

Part 1 of "The Bear" begins with another "this time" and "he," recalling the beginning of the book. Isaac goes from ten to twenty-one years of age in "The Bear," yet he seems to be "witnessing his own birth" (195) in Ben's death, attending as he does the "yearly pageant rite of the old bear's furious immortality" (194). When he is allowed to go on the bear hunt at the age of ten, he is reborn into what he believes is a knowledge superior to the knowledge of civilization. The problem is ownership. How can one be said to own the land? In rejecting his patrimony, Isaac refuses to acknowledge the design of ownership as much as he refuses to acknowledge his grandfather's sins. Two kinds of knowledge are opposed—the knowledge of the land as skill at hunting and surviving in the wilderness and the knowledge of the land involved in saying that one owns it. Isaac's knowledge through the ledgers of his grandfather's immorality becomes fused with his knowledge of the woods and amounts to a rejection of home, family, and community in favor of a visionary knowledge of the wilderness, and a self-sacrificing but passive morality.

Again there is a negative opening, "this too to be completed later" (195), and negativity recurs throughout the story. The hunting party's wagons move through a sunless afternoon, "following no path, no trail that he could discern, into a section of country he had never seen before" (200). Though Isaac has never been to the big bottom before, Ben "already" knows him (201). When Ben first comes, Isaac does not even see him. " 'I know it,' Sam said. 'He done the looking. You didn't hear him neither, did you?' " (203). Yet in a sense Isaac already knows Ben, too, for Ben "ran in his knowledge before he ever saw it" (193).

Old Ben is " 'the head bear. He's the man,' " according to Sam (198). Old Ben is the mystery Isaac seeks to know in the world of *Go Down, Moses*, and from the beginning of the story Old Ben is a giant of ambiguity, negativity, and contradiction. The metaphors used to describe Ben are designedly contradictory: the "shaggy and tremendous shape" of the old bear speeds with the "ruthless and irresistible determination of a locomotive" through Isaac's dreams. The irony is that even as Old Ben is compared to a locomotive, the actual locomotives are the agents of destruction in the woods, "constricting" the future of the whole country. The old bear is "a phantom, epitome and apotheosis of the old wild life which the little puny humans swarmed and hack at in a fury of abhorrence and fear like pygmies about the ankles of a drowsing elephant;—the old bear, solitary, indomitable, and alone; widowered childless and absolved of mortality—old Priam reft of his old wife and outlived all his sons" (193–94). Ben is a locomotive, that ubiquitous, ambivalent symbol of modern America in so many works of literature, and a "phantom" of "the old wild life," a "drowsing elephant," and even the Trojan King Priam. There are echoes not only of Doom, but of L. Q. C. and of Isaac himself in this design of Ben. Isaac's knowledge of Ben as the god of the wilderness does not take in all these meanings, however. Just as Isaac would not allow Cass to share his knowledge of the ghost buck in "The Old People," here not he but the narrator and reader are capable of thinking of Ben in several contexts.

One tends to forget that most of "The Bear" is not Isaac's thoughts but the narrator's. The narrator teaches us that to *know* a self-contradictory image is to admit its irreducibility and thus to recognize the limits of one's own knowledge. To accept alternate interpretations is to participate in a hermeneutic, communal knowledge. This is what Isaac cannot do and what the reader of *Go Down, Moses* is constantly asked to do. In addition, the multiple interpretations of Ben these metaphors suggest point to the ambiguity raised by an important question in the story: Isaac wishes to learn humility and patience from Ben (196), but does he? Does his later repudiation somehow carry forward what Ben stands for, or does it betray it?

Isaac must leave his gun, watch, compass, and stick in a clearing before he is granted the sight of Old Ben (206–9). First, he gives up his gun in order to approach "the bear's heretofore inviolable anonymity" (207). But leaving the gun is not enough: "He stood for a moment—a child, alien and lost in the green and soaring gloom of the markless wilderness. Then he relinquished completely to it. It was the watch and the compass. He was still tainted. He removed the linked chain of the one and the looped thong of the other from his overalls and hung them on a bush and leaned the stick beside them and entered it" (208). Then he "sees" Old Ben:

> Then he saw the bear. It did not emerge, appear: it was just there, immobile, fixed in the green and windless noon's hot dappling, not as big as he had dreamed it but as big as he had expected, bigger, dimensionless against the dappled obscurity, looking at him. Then it moved. It crossed the glade without haste, walking for an instant into the sun's full glare and out of it, and stopped again and looked back at him across one shoulder. Then it was gone. It didn't walk into the woods. It faded, sank back into the wilderness without motion as he had watched a fish, a huge old bass, sink back into the dark depths of its pool and vanish without even any movement of its fins. (209)

The "dappled obscurity" of the woods and "dark depths" of the pool are fitting images for the elusive kind of knowledge Ben represents. Isaac cannot approach such knowledge armed with the machines of civilization, but when he sees the bear he cannot follow it into the "dark depths" of the woods, either, even without these mechanical things. This scene is not so much a revelation of a mystery to Isaac, as most readings assert, but rather the statement of a mystery Isaac will never penetrate. The bear looks over his shoulder, backward, at Isaac, as he retreats to where Isaac cannot follow, to where Isaac cannot "see."

Part 2 begins with the repetition of "So he should have hated and feared Lion." Ben is to be hunted because he has killed a colt of the Major's, but he is innocent of the crime. The real culprit is the dog Lion, which Sam knows, and when Lion is caught shortly thereafter, he is groomed to be the slayer of Old Ben. Major de Spain says, " 'He has broken the rules . . . He has come into my house and destroyed my property, out of season too. He broke the rules. It was Old Ben, Sam.' Still Sam said nothing" (214). For when Sam sees Lion's footprint, he

> had known all the time what had made the tracks and what had torn the throat out of the doe in the spring and killed the fawn. It had been foreknowledge in Sam's face that morning. *And he was glad,* he told himself. He was old. *He had no children, no people, none of his blood anywhere above earth that he would ever meet again. And even if he were to, he could not have touched it, spoken to it, because for seventy years now he had had to be a negro. It was almost over now and he was glad.* (215)

The connection between the death of the wilderness through the "betrayal" of Old Ben and the whites' betrayal of the black man is obvious. To Sam, Lion's eyes are full of a "cold and almost impersonal malignance like some natural force" (218). Sam knows Old Ben's time has come, and so has his own. Sam knows things Isaac will never know, and he cannot speak them.

Part 3 of "The Bear" begins in cold December, with Boon and Isaac going into town to fetch supplies and, in Boon's case, to get drunk. Boon's behavior supplies an oddly humorous beginning for the section that will see the death of Old Ben, but the focus on Boon is not just for the sake of humor. Boon, wholly without "meanness or generosity or viciousness or gentleness or anything else" (227), kills the god, Ben, not out of design, like the others and their hunting ritual, but out of passionate fear for the death of his adored Lion. Boon acts out of emotion and with knowledge only of his immediate loyalties; his lack of ratiocination makes him a strong contrast to Isaac, who does not act when he should. These three, Lion, Ben, and Boon, are all part of a world of legend; the men on the train talk "about Lion and Old Ben as people later would talk about Sullivan and Kilrain and, later still, about Dempsey and Tunney" (230). When Ben is hunted down, an assembled community of neighbors, swamp dwellers, small farmers, and even townsfolk gathers to witness the mysterious event (236). In this scene Boon seemingly represents and acts for community.

Although Boon tells Isaac that he "dont never seem to think of nothing you want" while they are in town (232), Isaac does want the woods: "He felt the old life of the heart, as pristine as ever, as on the first day; he would never lose it, no matter how old in hunting and pursuit: the best, the best of all breathing, the humility and the pride" (233). As Boon is in the bar drinking and Isaac is wishing he were back on the train headed south for the woods, Isaac thinks of his grandfather, who, in Memphis as "a member of Colonel Sartoris' horse in Forrest's command, [rode] up Main street and (the tale told) into the lobby of the Gayoso Hotel where the Yankee officers sat in the leather chairs spitting into the tall bright cuspidors and then out again scot-free" (234). His daydream is interrupted by Boon, "wiping his mouth on the back of his hand" and ready to go home. Isaac's thinking of this family legend at this point in the story further extends the contrast between Isaac and Boon. Isaac's dreams of family glory are all dreams; he soon sheds his practical loyalty to his family. Boon, drunk and witless, is free of the restraints that plague Isaac. Boon may act out of blind devotion, but he acts—while Isaac watches.

Courage seems to require lack of judgment for Boon and Lion (as it did earlier for the fyce dog). Both act out of passion and without "judgment": "*Maybe that's what courage is,*" thinks Isaac (239). Isaac's paralyzing judgment causes him not to shoot the bear when he has the chance. It also seems that he does not have time to *decide* to shoot or not to shoot, for in the hunt section of Part 3 the narrator gives us only a frenetic series of grotesque images rather than relating a clear sequence of events, emphasizing action and reaction rather than thought. As Isaac rides, "The woods had opened, they were going fast, the clamor faint and fading on ahead; they passed the man who had fired—a swamper, a pointing arm, a gaunt face, the small black orifice of his yelling studded with rotten teeth" (238). The breathless, episodic narration of the chase does not give Isaac or the reader time to know exactly what is happening until Ben falls, stabbed by Boon after Lion's attack: "It fell just once. For an instant they almost resembled a piece of statuary: the clinging dog, the bear, the man stride its back, working and probing the buried blade. Then they went down. . . . It didn't collapse, crumple. It fell all of a piece, as a tree falls, so that all three of them, man dog and bear, seemed to bounce once" (241). Suddenly Isaac remembers that he saw Sam fall face down before Boon began to run at Ben.

The dying Sam, arduously transported through the rainy night in a wagon with the huge dead bear tied behind, cries out " 'Let me out, master. . . . Let me go home,' " echoing Isaac's earlier demand that Sam be let out of his "cage." Although the "boy was not there," he can see Sam suffer: "but Sam's eyes were probably open again on that profound look which saw further than them or the hut, further than the death of a bear and the dying of a dog" (245). Like Darl in *As I Lay Dying* and Quentin and Shreve in *Absalom, Absalom!* Isaac sees events occurring when he is not present, but he does not necessarily see their significance for himself. Sam dies childless, peopleless, alone, as Isaac will. But Sam's death a few days after his collapse is a mystery that neither Isaac nor the narrator ever reveals—Isaac demands to stay at the camp with Sam and Boon, and when Cass returns for him, Cass finds Sam dead and Boon apparently responsible. Cass demands the truth of Boon but is met with Isaac's cry, " 'Leave him alone! . . . Goddamn it! Leave him alone!' " (254). This section ends similarly to Parts 4 and 5 (as well as "Pantaloon in Black"), which also conclude with a denial of knowledge rather than an explanation, with isolation rather than community.

The narrator begins Part 4, "then he was twenty-one" and "he could say it. . . . Relinquish" (254), and Isaac spends the first few pages loudly justifying his giving up the plantation. He is more strident at twenty-one than he was at sixteen but not much improved as a partner in dialogue. There follows an argument with Cass about giving up the land (256–61), then the ledgers section (261–82), which also contains the marriage of Fonsiba and her inheritance from Isaac (274–81). The discussion with Cass continues (282–300), in which Isaac's historical and religious arguments are countered by Cass's pragmatism. The story moves on to Hubert's legacy (300–8), Isaac's loan from Cass (308–9), and Isaac's marriage (309–15), which together grimly comment on the concept of inheritance. The section ends with Isaac's wife's bitter laughter.

At the end of "Was" the betting resulted in Buck's not having to marry Sibby, and, similarly, at the end of Part 4 it only seems as though Isaac agrees not to give up his farm as part of a bargain with his wife. She goads him into sex with her and threatens to deny him if he will not say "yes" to keeping his farm. He refuses at first, then "he said Yes and he thought, *She is lost. She was born lost. We were all born lost.*" He seems to agree to keep the plantation, but of course he does not keep his land for long. Afterward, she turns from him and says, " 'And that's all. That's all from me. If this dont get you that son you talk about, it wont be mine:' lying on her side, her back to the empty rented room, laughing and laughing" (315). They both do the opposite of what they seem to agree to do, and the confusion, like so many other such confusions in *Go Down, Moses*, is never explained.

Part 4 seems more a part of the entire novel than of the story "The Bear," as it is the genealogical center of the book. Reed finds Part 4 to be about "the unfitness of the world for a perfect abstraction," and the "unfitness" of Part 4 of "The Bear," its disruptive effect in the story, suggests the "unfitness"—the failure—of Isaac's plan.[11] Narrative "unfitness" makes negativity a key to meaning: Part 4 only purports to contain the answers to the reader's questions about Isaac's motives. That the answers should be very difficult to get at, if they can be described at all, and that they are contradictory, "fits" beautifully with the novel's overall intentions concerning knowledge.

The causal relationship of the hunt of Part 3 to the renunciation of Part 4 lingers somewhere in the gap between the two parts. Isaac's received knowledge from Sam Fathers's wilderness and his discovery at age sixteen of the incest in his family reveal a complex knowledge he cannot reconcile. Yet his own role as author in the ledgers should indicate to him that he is more connected with his family than he thinks; fittingly, Part 4 stresses Isaac's connections more than any believable reasons for his repudiation. Even though Isaac says he can be free, it becomes increasingly clear that he does not escape the knowledge of evil his family's sins force upon him.

The arguments with Cass (256–61, 282–300) take up most of the section. Most of the argument is about ownership and authority, specifically about whether people can own land. But a lot of it is topical—" 'Not to mention 1865' " and " 'More men than Father and Uncle Buddy' " (261)—as they argue about the South and what it should be like now. Isaac and Cass try to understand their circumstances as part of a divine plan. The difference in them is in what each proposes to do about such judgment. Although it is voiced, the argument section is not a dialogue. Much of the time Isaac seems incoherent. His statements sound illogical and grandiose, and he fails to make important distinctions. Cass wearily reiterates that neither he nor Isaac will ever be free: " 'No, not now nor ever, we from them nor they from us. So I repudiate too. I would deny even if I knew it were true. I would have to. Even you can see that I could do no else. I am what I am; I will be always what I was born and have always been. And more than me' " (299–300). Cass is saying that everyone is in a position to "repudiate," but no one really can. All are already part of "His first plan which failed"; all are part of the sinful human race. There is no place for further renunciation.

Their arguments about the Civil War are separate and joint attempts to understand the darkness in their present lives. Isaac sees slavery, sin, ownership, fall, war, and renunciation as personal—his view of Providence accords him the role of finally refuting the problem of ownership. He believes that God gave men the land to use humbly, but they abused it by selling it and by selling human beings to work on it. Thus God has taken the land away in punishment for the white men's sins, bringing the war upon them to burn out the evil they have wrought. He has chosen Isaac to renounce ownership:

> "—when He used the blood which had brought in the evil to destroy the evil as doctors use fever to burn up fever, poison to slay poison. Maybe He chose Grandfather out of all of them He might have picked. Maybe He knew that Grandfather himself would not serve His purpose because Grandfather was born too soon too, but that Grandfather would have descendants, the right descendants; maybe He had foreseen already the descendants Grandfather would have, maybe he saw already in Grandfather the seed progenitive of the three generations He saw it would take to set at least some of His lowly people free—." (259)

Isaac's knowledge of what God has had in mind for him allows him to argue for the virtues of the blacks (295). He sincerely believes that somehow he is helping the black people by refusing to inherit his land, but exactly how they are to benefit is not clear: " 'It will be long. I have never said otherwise. But it will be all right because they will endure—' " (299).

In the midst of the argument, Isaac flashes back to the time he did not shoot the bear, and Cass quotes from "Ode on a Grecian Urn":

> *"She cannot fade, though thou hast not thy bliss," McCaslin said: "Forever wilt thou love, and she be fair." "He's talking about a girl," he said. "He had to talk about something," McCaslin said. Then he said, "He was talking about truth. Truth is one. It doesn't change. It covers all things which touch the heart—honor and pride and pity and justice and courage and love. Do you see now?"* (297)

Cass knows better than Isaac not only why Isaac did not shoot the bear but also why he wants to give up his plantation: like the youth in the poem, Isaac wants things to stay pure. To preserve something pure, Isaac feels he must relinquish his claims on his land, must give up the striving for community altogether. To let go, never to know, never to touch or to grasp, is Isaac's plan for living—the alternative, engagement in "real life," he feels, is doomed to sin and failure. But, of course, his dream is doomed to be only a dream. For Isaac it is all or nothing—either become a designer or withdraw completely. Unlike Maggie Verver, he can locate no other alternatives, no middle ground. Rather, like John Marcher in *The Beast in the Jungle,* he tries to live above the ordinary lives of error and pain of the rest of humanity.

In the argument section key words include the negatives: "relinquish" (256), "dispossessed" (258), and "escape" (283). As one might expect from Faulkner, the arguments, which are supposed to contain the reasons Isaac gives up his plantation and thus Isaac's most important motives, give the reader more the style of the argument than the substance. The arguments are built on contradiction and negation so that Isaac's arguments on his fulfilling Providence through renunciation, instead of being merely illogical on his part, seem designedly so on the author's part. Furthermore, one wonders why the narrator introduces each debater's comments with his name, "and McCaslin" and "and he" on the line above the actual speaker's comments, following the previous speaker's passage. This has the effect of separating the speaker from his speech, confusing the two speakers, highlighting each speaker's words all to themselves. There are many, many negative constructions:

> "That nevertheless and notwithstanding old Carothers did own it. Bought it, got it, no matter; kept it, held it, no matter; bequeathed it: else why do you stand here relinquishing and repudiating? Held it, kept it for fifty years until you could repudiate it, while He—this Arbiter, this Architect, this Umpire—condoned—or did He? looked down and saw—or did He? Or at least did nothing: saw, and could not, or did not see; saw, and would not, or perhaps He would not see—perverse, impotent, or blind: which?" (258)

Contradiction is a warning that no synthetic interpretation will suffice. Not the least of the negatives in the arguments is that though one recognizes that Isaac is wrong, one still cannot help sympathizing with him and even admiring him. In so many ways Isaac McCaslin is a negative hero.

Just when the reader is ready for the ledgers' long-delayed knowledge, they appear in all their dense, allusive mystery. Containing the poisonous knowledge Isaac hates to admit and the knowledge that keeps him from entering his community, the ledgers are a mystified epistemology, a dark center of the novel. One must remember just how mysterious the ledgers were in one's first reading of the book. Though as ledgers they purport to offer facts, they present knowledge as elusive, dangerous, hard won—and knowledge in *Go Down, Moses* is like that. The reader has to enter the text very actively indeed to puzzle out the ledger sequence, along with the horrified Isaac, to construct its meaning. It is very important, too, that not every entry has any direct bearing on the story of L. Q. C.'s incest. There is no single "solution" to this puzzle; indeed, the difficulty of penetration suggests a parallel with the mystery of Ben. The ledgers contain ultimately destructive knowledge for Isaac, the major forms of design in the novel: personal design, historical design, and genealogical design. In penetrating these secrets, Isaac turns away from his fellow humans, just as he was led to do by his knowledge of the wilderness.

Isaac recoils sharply from the sexual knowledge of the ledgers. He will not be a part of this kind of knowledge, and he will not eat his "bitter fruit." He will not admit that he has already eaten of it and that he cannot escape knowledge of sin by denying it. He is not able to accept, as he earlier urged Cass to do, "the heart's truth out of the heart's driving complexity." Neither communal nor sexual ties can hold his heart, for even after he reads the ledgers, Isaac believes he is free of the curse on the land because he has chosen to repudiate it—" 'I am free.' " But Cass again reminds him that no matter what is contained in his ledger account in heaven, here on earth no man is free of " 'the frail and iron thread strong as truth and impervious as evil and longer than life itself and reaching beyond record and patrimony both to join him with the lusts and passions, the hopes and dreams and griefs, of bones whose names while still fleshed and capable even old Carothers' grandfather had never heard' " (299). This passage recalls an earlier image of the "threads" of cotton that are "frail as truth and impalpable as equators yet cable-strong to bind for life them who made the cotton to the land their sweat fell on" (294). The connection between sexuality and the land is apparent in these passages—both as regards L. Q. C.'s "lusts and passions" and Isaac's wife, with her bargain of sex for land. But we, not Isaac, recognize this. He does not realize that no one is free of family or community, as far back as those stretch in time—Sam Fathers, Isaac's "liberator," made this clear. Cass answers Isaac's last argument: " 'You said how on that instant when Ikkemotubbe realised that he could sell the land to Grandfather, it ceased forever to have been his. All right; go on: Then it belonged to Sam Fathers, old Ikkemotubbe's son. And who inherited it from Sam Fathers, if not you? co-heir perhaps with Boon, if not of his life maybe, at least of his quitting it?' " But Isaac only responds again, " 'Yes. Sam Fathers set me free' " (300).

The deadlock is resolved by the narrator, who follows this exchange immediately:

> And Isaac McCaslin, not yet Uncle Isaac, a long time yet before he would be uncle to half a county and still father to no one, living in one small cramped fireless rented room in a Jefferson boarding-house where petit juries were domiciled during court terms and itinerant horse- and mule-traders stayed, with his kit of brand-new carpenter's tools and the shotgun McCaslin had given him with his name engraved in silver and old General Compson's compass (and, when the General died, his silver-mounted hunting horn too) and the iron cot and mattress and the blankets he would take each fall into the woods for more than sixty years and the bright tin coffeepot. (300)

This introduces the section on Hubert's legacy, the silver chalice and gold coins that are transformed into IOU's on scraps of paper in an old tin coffeepot, and it alludes to Isaac's failure just at the high point of his argument. The objects described in this passage as being in his rented room represent the major metaphors of the book, recalling the book's thematic patterns of hunting, gambling, and marriage—all powerful designs. Instead of the fire and the hearth, his room is fireless. The gun and compass remind us that those were the objects he had to give up to confront Old Ben. The hunting horn will reappear in "Delta Autumn," as will the iron cot, a symbol of Isaac's sterile and lonely life, and the bare rented room. All of this denies most emphatically that Isaac is "free."

Things do not work out as Isaac envisioned them; his repudiation does not make him happy—nor does it improve things for anyone else. The only time Isaac really helps the black people to whom he feels responsible is when he is distributing L. Q. C.'s legacies to them, not when he is alone in his little room remembering past glories. And, as noted earlier, things do not turn out as Isaac hoped in part because he has not reckoned on what his wife wants (314–15). Her rejection of him is one of the most painful and puzzling events in the book. Part 4 closes with impotence, sterility, and despair, a forecast of the line in "Delta Autumn" the black woman speaks to Isaac: " 'Old man, have you forgotten everything you ever knew about love?' " Isaac is less free than ever at the end of this section: "And that was all: 1874 the boy; 1888 the man, repudiated denied and free; 1895 and husband but no father, unwidowered but without a wife, and found long

since that no man is ever free and probably could not bear it if he were"
(281).

In a 1955 interview, Faulkner voiced a judgment against Isaac: Isaac
gave up, evaded his responsibility to his community. As Faulkner demonstrates in this and other works, when people like Isaac abdicate their
responsibilities, the designs of the L. Q. C. McCaslins succeed. In *Go Down,
Moses*, the Edmonds are clearly not fit to run the plantation, as Roth's
agonies show. Isaac's action was not a heroic renunciation but a cowardly
retreat:

> FAULKNER: And who are *your* favorite characters?
> Q (startled): Isaac McCaslin in "The Bear."
> FAULKNER (smiling a little, very quick and direct): Why?
> Q: Because he underwent the baptism in the forest, because he
> rejected his inheritance.
> FAULKNER: And do you think it's a good thing for a man to
> reject an inheritance?
> Q: Yes, in McCaslin's case. He wanted to reject a tainted
> inheritance. You don't think it's a good thing for him to have
> done so?
> FAULKNER: Well, I think a man ought to do more than just
> repudiate. He should have been more affirmative instead of
> shunning people.
> Q: Do you think that any of your characters succeed in being
> more affirmative?
> FAULKNER: Yes, I do. There was Gavin Stevens.[12]

Isaac's absence from his rightful place was a failure of knowledge. Isaac
could not hold together in his mind the knowledge of good and evil, and
not to be able to do that is not to be human. Isaac's letting go of the land
follows the novel's pattern of release, of stepping back from knowledge,
and yet he ends by enforcing a personal design, like L. Q. C. McCaslin. Real
relinquishment, the novel suggests, is acceptance of contradiction, not a
refusal to see it; real relinquishment is forgiveness. In relinquishing good to
fight evil, Isaac does no good and allows evil to continue, as Roth's
repetition of L. Q. C.'s sins shows. Had Isaac acted communally, Faulkner
suggests, he might have learned to forgive, endure, and prevail.

Part 5 takes place three years before Isaac's repudiation and two years
after the deaths of Old Ben and Sam. Isaac revisits the site of the hunt. The

land has now been sold to the lumber company, the railroad is running, and the wilderness is disappearing. Only Sam's and Lion's grave markers are untouched, "lifeless and shockingly alien in that place where dissolution itself was a seething turmoil of ejaculation tumescence conception and birth, and death did not even exist" (327). For Isaac, the fecund wilderness is still alive, even as it is threatened: "There was no death, not Lion and Sam: not held fast in earth but free in earth and not in earth but of earth, myriad yet undiffused of every myriad part" (328). Isaac's views are a strong contrast with Boon's imbecilic " 'Get out of here! Dont touch them! Dont touch a one of them! They're mine!' " as he hammers his dismembered gun in preparation for shooting a whole tree full of squirrels at the end of Part 5. Neither Isaac's entrapment in the past nor Boon's brutish activity is a satisfactory form of knowledge in the end.

The a-chronological Part 5 and "Pantaloon in Black" are the only stories in the novel out of temporal order, and they perform a special function: they cast doubt on the major themes of the book. This section tells us that the wilderness is dying and that presumably out of respect for it and for Sam Fathers's sacrifice (and out of revulsion at Boon's absurd "ownership" of the squirrels), Isaac will renounce the plantation. The real function of Part 5 would appear to be, then, to answer the question Part 4 tries to answer: Why does Isaac give up his land? Part 5 should add to our understanding of his reasons. It does elevate Isaac's renunciation of ownership by contrast to Boon and the squirrels, but it contains elements that deny all that. For example, when Isaac salutes the snake ("Oleh, Grandfather"), he seems to be recognizing the existence of evil and accepting it. A biblical symbol of evil, the snake also suggests L. Q. C.'s sexual sins, and it is also compared to other symbols of knowledge, including the train, as Ben was (318). The snake is "evocative of all knowledge and an old weariness and of pariah-hood and of death" (329). It would seem that in "accepting" the snake Isaac will be able to live with his knowledge of the evil of his grandfather and continue nevertheless to live in a community in which he has responsibilities to others. But of course this does not prove to be the case. In Part 5, as elsewhere, denial and negativity keep pushing the reader's search for knowledge about Isaac's reasons just out of reach; for everything asserted in *Go Down, Moses* there exists its opposite, and knowledge for the reader is never more difficult than Isaac's mysterious salute to the snake. The snake also recalls Rider's being "snake bit," and perhaps its presence here links that story's mode of denial and negativity to "The Bear." It would seem that Isaac can deal with evil in the woods but not in his own family. A literary descendant of Young Goodman Brown, he cannot live in a community with evil, and thus he lives in no community at all.

" 'It was a doe,' he said' ": "Delta Autumn"

In this story hero and reader find themselves in the delta:

> He had watched [the wilderness] not being conquered, destroyed, so much as retreating since its purpose was served now and its time an outmoded time, retreating southward through this inverted-apex, this ∇-shaped section of earth between hills and River until what was left of it seemed now to be gathered and for the time arrested in one tremendous density of brooding and inscrutable impenetrability at the ultimate funnelling tip. (343)

Isaac, like the wilderness, is unconquered but retreated, outmoded, and doomed. The time of year is autumn, not cold December as in Part 3 of "The Bear," which was followed by spring—but autumn, pointing toward despair. The opening, "Soon now they would enter the delta," recalls the previous four stories' "first" and "this time" openings, and indeed "Delta Autumn" begins its second paragraph with "At first." "Delta Autumn" is in many ways the logical conclusion to *Go Down, Moses*—logical, that is, but not inevitable. It represents the lowest point of the novel; it is what "Go Down, Moses" substitutes for as a conclusion. If the novel ended with the "funnelling tip" of "Delta Autumn" it would be a different book indeed. That the ∇ symbol Faulkner uses is an *inverted* delta seems fitting as we consider what an inversion of Isaac's love for the land this story gives us. The delta Δ as a symbol of community broadens to inclusiveness only in "Go Down, Moses."

"At first" Isaac experiences the "familiar sensation" of entering the wilderness, though the actual experience has changed. Wagons used to carry the young men and "the guns, the bedding, the dogs, the food, the whisky, the keen heart-lifting anticipation of hunting." But now, "the territory in which game still existed drawing yearly inward as his life was drawing inward, until now he was the last of those who had once made the journey in wagons" (335). In "Delta Autumn" Isaac is suddenly presented as an old man; most of his adult life has been left out of the novel. What is suggested is that he had a lonely life after the failure of his marriage and that the self-conscious humility of his trade as carpenter has not redeemed his wasted adulthood. Fighting time by riding several hundred miles with the others in an automobile to get to the receding wilderness is for Isaac a deep despair, but he lives for it all the same. That which he depended on and loved is dying, and the men who hunt it are as decayed morally as the wilderness is physically. The killing of does will be the symbol for the degeneration of the men, and Isaac repeatedly thinks, "better men hunted then." But did they? Was L. Q. C. "better" because he was even further back in time? Was L. Q. C. "better" than Cass? And did not L. Q. C. hunt "does"? Isaac's notions of the past and his nostalgia for the land are both moving and foolishly romantic.

As in "Was," marriage is once again juxtaposed with hunting. As Isaac lies on his iron cot in the tent the first night, he thinks of his wife as well as his never-conceived son: "The first and last time he ever saw her naked body, himself and his wife juxtaposed in their turn against that same land, that same wrong and shame from whose regret and grief he would at least save and free his son and, saving and freeing his son, lost him" (351). He also thinks he "lost her, because she loved him. But women hope for so much. They never live too long to still believe that anything within the scope of their passionate wanting is likewise within the range of their passionate hope" (352). We never learn much about Isaac's wife, but one does not have to remember much at all about her brief appearance in the book in Part 4 of "The Bear" to recognize how wrong Isaac has been. He did not lose her because she loved him, and it is he who could be described as someone with a "passionate hope" for "too much." They both love the same thing, land, though for different reasons. (His hunting partners, despite the moral lapse of which he accused them, seem "more his kin than any. Because this was his land" [352].] Marriage is emphasized not only in Isaac's bitter recall of his own marriage and in Roth's cruel abandonment of his mistress and child but even in the topography itself. Isaac looks out of the car window at "the small and irregular fields which a year ago were jungle and in which the skeleton stalks of this year's cotton stood almost as tall and rank as the old cane had stood, as if man had to marry his planting to the wilderness in order to conquer it" (342). This "marriage," like Isaac's and Roth's, is a tragic one, and it reveals the continuing failure of Isaac's design.

In "Delta Autumn," Isaac is again confronted with racial and sexual injustice. Roth is a grandson of Cass; his cast-off mistress is a granddaughter of James Beauchamp ("Tennie's Jim"), son of Turl and Tennie and brother of Lucas, and yet another descendant of L. Q. C. This makes the woman and Roth distant cousins and makes her a niece of Isaac's. The liaison between her and Roth closes up the two branches of the family, black and white. But once again the "other" is treated like an animal, like Turl or Rider. To the men, she is just a doe, " 'one that walks on two legs—when she's standing up, that is. Pretty light-colored, too,' " as Will Legate crudely puts it (337).

This repetition of L. Q. C.'s design shows not only the futility and failure of Isaac's plan but also his responsibility for many of the wrongs of the present. His absence has made a weak man a community leader, and abuses of women and blacks continue. Isaac is appalled by Roth's shabbiness, but he does the dirty work himself, paying off the black woman for Roth and sending her up North to her "own people." Isaac's telling her to leave the South and "marry a man in your own race, . . . forget all this, forget it ever happened, that he ever existed" (363) is a rejection of her as one of his own responsibilities and as a human being, for she is one of the many blacks he presumed to "save," and she is a member of his own family. She even calls him Uncle Isaac. Isaac must commit the sin he strove to avoid: denying the human, familial connection between members of his family, the same sin that damns Thomas Sutpen. He repeats his earlier rejection of community—his giving up his plantation—in sending her away with the money. Because Isaac reacts with amazement, outrage, and pity for the woman, but does what Roth asks anyway, the hunting horn he gives her is a fitting symbol of his emptiness and impotence. He is described throughout the scene as weak, pale, skinny, and old; he is shrill and petulant. In answer to his advice to forget and to leave, the woman drowns his puny discourse by delivering to him the most resounding question in the novel, " 'Old man,' she said, 'have you lived so long and forgotten so much that you dont remember anything you ever knew or felt or even heard about love?' " (363). Indeed, Isaac has forgotten love, the "other thing" besides humility and pride that he knew he needed but knew he did not have. Isaac has never had love: "Had not Sam Fathers already consecrated and absolved him from weakness and regret too?—not from love and pity for all which lived" (182).

In "The Bear" Isaac associates the death of Old Ben with the discovery of evil in his family. Here in "Delta Autumn" the destruction of the wilderness is yoked together with Roth's indifference to the woman and child and Isaac's own inability to help her. It seems that old L. Q. C. has won at last—he is the "old obsolescence" Faulkner associates with Old Ben in an interview.[13] But L. Q. C.'s design does not prevail in the novel. Perhaps he could be said to have won if the book ended with "Delta

Autumn." Isaac's design tried to prevent L. Q. C.'s design from winning, but Isaac's design fails to produce a desirable outcome itself.

Isaac is admirable, but he loses; he lives only long enough to watch his community with the hunters disintegrate like his beloved wilderness. The "ruined woods I used to know dont cry for retribution! he thought: The people who have destroyed it will accomplish its revenge" (364). Exploitation of land leads to exploitation of human beings. The story makes Isaac's defeat explicit, not only in the young woman's words but also in Roth's: " 'So you've lived almost eighty years,' Edmonds said. 'And that's what you finally learned about the other animals you lived among. I suppose the question to ask you is, where have you been all the time you were dead?' " (345).

Though he once calls the woods "his land" (352), Isaac still believes he did right—that one cannot own the land. His negative design shows up in his dreams of a land enduring beyond "the mathematical squares of rank cotton for the frantic old-world people to turn into shells to shoot at one another. . . . It belonged to all; they had only to use it well, humbly and with pride" (354). A terrible war is about to erupt, as the story reminds us, but though Isaac senses doom he pointedly avoids the other men's conversations about Hitler. This response to the war, as to "progress," including the destruction of the woods, is willfully blind. Isaac is a person who does not want to know what he does know—so he refuses to act on his knowledge. Isaac lost his power to act when he gave up his inheritance, for to act without personal design in this novel one must act as a member of a community, as Gavin and Mollie do. He was right to fear the exercise of personal design, but he was wrong not to realize that he could have been saved by joining his community. At the end of his life he has no community but a group of quarrelsome, petty amateur hunters who patronize and ignore him. Isaac is inviolate and alone—and he is a remarkably thorough failure. Sundquist aptly calls Isaac's repudiation "fratricidal," like that of Henry Sutpen, and "self-devouring," like that of Quentin Compson, because it "[asserts] that racial distinctions cannot be overcome, that the responsibility for them can only be renounced." [14] Quietly but dramatically underscoring the description of Isaac's land with the fratricide taking place on a grand scale in World War II Europe, "Delta Autumn" makes Isaac's passivity in the face of evil seem all the more a failure.

By "Delta Autumn," Isaac fails all his communities—his wife, his family, his neighbors, his land, even the moral beliefs for which he sacrificed. Most of all "Delta Autumn" shows that Isaac has failed his substitute son, Roth. The black woman tells Isaac that he spoiled Roth " 'when you gave to his grandfather that land which didn't belong to him, not even half of it by will or even law' " (360). In this story, Roth, a mixture of good and evil as he was in "The Fire and the Hearth," not only duplicates L. Q. C.'s sins but forces Isaac to duplicate them too through his participation. The unwanted knowledge that he is part of the sins of his fathers is brought home to Isaac here as it never has been thus far—he has known it all along but has refused to number himself among the sinners until now. Isaac's romantic view of man as lone hunter has ironically degenerated into Roth's "running does."

" 'It's our grief' ": "Go Down, Moses"

"Go Down, Moses," the title piece, offers a song of redemption and freedom. At last, here, voices in dialogue replace designers' consuming visions. The hermeneutic structure of the spiritual here echoes the events of the whole book, with its harmony, its choral repetitions, its group effort, and its improvisation. The spiritual addresses the future of the community of black and white people, of men and women, of old and young, which is also the subject of the story. The major themes of the novel reappear subtly changed. Hunting becomes the act of bringing Butch Beauchamp home; slavery is replaced by the joining of the whites and blacks into a community; marriage shows up through the value of family love, particularly with Mollie, and through the funeral as family ritual. The wilderness has become the town, and the most significant change is the stress on the common experience of blacks and whites. Myra Jehlen notes that throughout the novel blacks and whites lead equally problematic lives in the confused southern society and that the theme in "Go Down, Moses" is more than ever concerned with family—races are brought together by their very divisions.[15] Indeed, in the final story, blackness and whiteness are simultaneously addressed by the enduring and prevailing Mollie and the good-natured if awkward Lawyer Stevens.

This story, like all the others, is carefully connected to all the other stories. The opening image, "the face was black, smooth, impenetrable; the eyes had seen too much" (369), connects Mollie's face with other faces in previous stories, especially Lucas's and Sam Fathers's, and gives us an opening image we cannot "penetrate," only address. There are more black victims: a third cousin to the woman in "Delta Autumn," Butch

Beauchamp is also a grandson of James Beauchamp. He is comparable to Rider in his anonymity; he is identified only by a census taker, a representative of institutional community. But in spite of Butch's death, the recurring image of the fire and the hearth sets the tone for the story. The theme now is one of new hope for the future and for the community. The year is 1942, and Jefferson is growing. An outsider, Gavin Stevens, enters the story to help set things right and help bring the community together.

Gavin learns from Mollie the value of her wise innocence, and this quality of understanding on both their parts comes to dominate the conclusion, as Lucas's transformation dominates the conclusion of "The Fire and the Hearth." At the end of "Go Down, Moses," she wants the story of Butch's death and funeral in the paper: " 'You put it in de paper. All of hit' " (383). We might very well imagine that the novel itself is that "all of hit." Indeed, when *Go Down, Moses* was in progress and Faulkner was asked about its subject, he said it was about " 'a Negro funeral.' "[16] Mollie's wisdom and Gavin's understanding replace Lucas's game-playing and Isaac's complicated design: "*It doesn't matter to her now. Since it had to be and she couldn't stop it, and now that it's all over and done and finished, she doesn't care how he died. She just wanted him home, but she wanted him to come home right. She wanted that casket and those flowers and the hearse and she wanted to ride through town behind it in a car*" (383). Even if Mollie "had known what we know even" she would still have wanted it told. Why? Mollie wants the community to know what happened to Butch for a reason, and part of the reason involves the future of other young black men and women in the community. This communal, dialogic urge replaces Isaac's solitary knowledge. Oddly, instead of Isaac's own funeral ending the book, as one might expect since he is the character we know the most about, a stranger's funeral is presented, and another stranger becomes a new hero. The constant element is Mollie, who inspires Gavin to know and act within community.

Women are at their strongest in this story, especially Mollie and Miss Worsham, and their importance here reflexively strengthens their importance throughout the novel. The figure of Mollie takes on mythic proportions, and even Miss Worsham becomes larger than life: her "expression was neither shocked nor disapproving. It merely embodied some old, timeless, female affinity for blood and grief" (376). According to Brooks, women typically "embody and express" the claims of community in Faulkner's work.[17] Mollie and Miss Worsham bring powerful dialogue to this novel, and they accordingly bring a new version of community. As Lambert Strether learns from Maria Gostrey, Gavin learns from the two old women, one black and one white—and so does the reader. In their fireside chanting, the mourners of this story preserve difference and yet manage to act as a community. To Gavin and the reader, they teach the meaning of knowing "grief."

One of the greatest lessons the nascent community of "Go Down, Moses" offers is the value of knowing what to sacrifice, when, why, and for whom. Many characters in the story make sacrifices for community. The editor pays for copy he does not print, and he and Gavin are away from work all day. Mollie's long, hot trek parallels her journey to Roth in "The Fire and the Hearth" for a divorce, and this time she again toils for someone else. Miss Worsham gives what little money she has. All of this is for Butch, who is glimpsed only once at the beginning, but he too is a sacrifice, for Mollie mourns her Benjamin sold by Pharoah, Roth, into Egypt.

Some readers are troubled by what they call this story's "failure" as a conclusion to the novel. It may seem too sentimental, too comic and light, and it suddenly presents new characters and a new hero. Can "Go Down, Moses" ameliorate the sins of the past? Gavin's victory, like Maggie Verver's, is questionable in its limitations. Gavin appears in many of Faulkner's other books, including *Knight's Gambit*, *Light in August*, the Snopes trilogy, and *Intruder in the Dust*.[18] His manifestations differ: he seems clearly to be Faulkner's mouthpiece in *Knight's Gambit* and *Go Down, Moses*, but it would be a mistake to read him this way in *Light in August*, *The Town*, and some others. In the Snopes trilogy, despite his role as community defender, Gavin becomes an absurd, quixotic character who is heavily satirized. In *The Town*, for example, he is a courtly lover in love with "life-denying idealism," as Brooks notes, instead of real women. But Gavin is more successful in *Go Down, Moses*, for though his victory is a compromised one, it is in keeping with the manner in which other elements in this novel qualify each other.[19] This also helps explain the need for the comedy of the ending. The romantic bungler from *The Town* is in *Go Down, Moses* a competent member of his community, but he also demonstrates those "human" qualities, those "failures" he experiences in the other books.

Gavin in *Go Down, Moses* is Faulkner's finest Gavin. Gavin in *Intruder in the Dust*, which followed *Go Down, Moses*, has changed for the worse. As Sundquist has pointed out, in the later novel Gavin comes off as an apologist, gradualist, and paternalist.[20] But the theme of failure works in *Go Down, Moses* because the reader is brought into the process *through* the characters' failures, and this is not the case with the more traditionally structured *Intruder in the Dust*.[21] In *Go Down, Moses* Gavin is clearly on *our* plane, and his pragmatism and ability to compromise appear in stark contrast to Quentin's and Isaac's rarefied moral positions. Gavin is one of "the people."

In this concluding story Isaac is wrong, and something has to replace him. Isaac's plan has failed; Roth demonstrates this yet again in his driving Butch off the plantation. Mollie calls her "son" Roth "Pharaoh"; loveless though he is, Isaac, one feels, would never be called "Pharaoh." But Gavin has not forgotten love. He not only engineers the funeral, collects the money and gets most of it from himself and his friend the editor, organizes the transport of the body, and goes to call on the stricken relatives, but he also lies to Miss Worsham about how much money they need for the funeral so as not to embarrass her in the matter of her contribution. As carnivalized heroes, he and the editor blunder here and there, most significantly when they think Mollie would not want it in the paper, but they prevail as they continue through dialogue to reassert and uphold community. This story clearly demonstrates the tendency in Faulkner's late fiction for an optimistic ending in spite of the knowledge of evil in the past. The characters of "Go Down, Moses" endure, and in some small but hopeful ways, they do prevail. Never again would Faulkner achieve such a dialogic balance of failure and hope.

When Gavin comes to join the grievers around the fire and the hearth, he realizes he does not understand their chanting, and this makes him very uncomfortable. Mollie cannot hear or see Gavin when he visits them upstairs. He leaves, apologizing to Miss Worsham, " 'I'm sorry. . . . I ask you to forgive me. I should have known. I shouldn't have come.' 'It's all right,' Miss Worsham said. 'It's our grief' " (381). He was right to come, she suggests, because he shares in the communal grief. Such love surmounts Isaac's humility and pride and proves to be the only lasting form of expiation for the white community's sins. This love does not necessarily understand, and it can be a "dangerous" form of knowledge as well (as Rider's case demonstrates), but it alone in the end allows men and women to continue struggling in the face of despair.

As a representative of the public, Gavin replaces Isaac as the novel's conscience. At first he cares little about Butch: " 'I just hope, for her sake as well as that of the great public whom I represent, that [Butch's] present trouble is very bad and maybe final too——' " (374). But when he is confronted with Mollie, he thinks, " 'So it seems I didn't mean what I said I hoped.' " When she talks to him, he is immediately at her service, as he also is when he talks to Miss Worsham, who persuades him to bring the body home and not to tell Mollie what has become of Butch. Gavin is clearly not driven by high ideals as much as he is convinced to act morally by encountering a person in need. Unlike the true idealist, Isaac, Gavin has no design, but he gets things done. Mollie, Miss Worsham, and Gavin are communal doers. They are undeterred when they find out that Butch is a murderer, and they act before evil overcomes them. Isaac, in contrast, does no evil, yet he also does no good. The characters of the last story demonstrate once again that Isaac's withdrawal is an inadequate response to the evils of a closed, designed form of "doing."

In the last story communality replaces personal weakness as well as personal design. Although "Was" and "Go Down, Moses" have similar endings, the value of human life is powerfully contrasted in the first and last stories. In "Was," the comedy of the manhunt offers no hope for human improvement. "Go Down, Moses," another comic story about a manhunt, voices a different note. Here, one finds comedy in the redemptive sense instead of burlesque or grotesque—and it has taken the whole book to get this far. This story opens up Jefferson to the world: the whites have changed, and so have the blacks, as they seek help beyond Edmonds. They seek it from their family, the Worshams, and from Gavin, the representative of the public, the town lawyer. And Mollie wants "all of hit" in the paper. "Go Down, Moses," a reversal of "Delta Autumn," supplies a constructive tone to the whole novel. Community prevails.

The title story is thus necessary for the end of the novel because it gives hope for the future and offers against design an alternative to renunciation. Isaac's plan fails, but his beliefs hold out and give meaning to the actions of those who follow him and his generation; even if he cannot act on his beliefs, someone else can. And Isaac's spirit gives meaning and resonance to the events of the last story through negativity. That which Isaac does not have, love, is made to seem even more necessary to the future through its absence from Isaac's past. "Go Down, Moses" alone might not mean a great deal, but in its context in the novel, it is a moving testament of hope, embodying Faulkner's words: "Man must be completely free in spirit. But freedom, true freedom, extends only to where the next individual's freedom stops. That is, to be completely free is not to be completely ruthless, completely heedless. He must be free within a pattern of responsibility always."[22]

Isaac McCaslin fails because he tries to step outside the pattern of responsibility in which he lives. This idea is also a structural secret of the novel. The narrator has made it very difficult for the reader to discover the careful "freedom within a pattern" of the book. In contrast to the communal knowledge arrived at by author, narrator, and reader, Isaac constructs a transcendent view of the world and stays with it in lonely isolation. Isaac is not finally open to the new combinations, interpretations, and resonances of knowledge addressed by the reader of *Go Down, Moses*.

In a tense moment, Marlow in Conrad's *Heart of Darkness* lies to Kurtz's Intended and gives up his personal design of hating lies to save another human being; he thus sacrifices his personal code of honor for her salvation. Likewise, in James's and Faulkner's moral worlds, designs must fail in order to give meaning to what follows them, as Old Ben must die to live forever. The human community is presented by these authors as a metadesign that reasserts itself at the end of their novels as an escape from the designs of self-consciousness. Gavin's and Mollie's communal design in "Go Down, Moses" is the way of the future. Although it is a design—the brotherhood and sisterhood of humankind—it is transpersonal and variously composed of separate individuals, each retaining his or her own differences. As in all of James's and Faulkner's late novels, each individual voice contributes to the dialogue, in exactly the same way the readers, on another level, contribute to the whole of the fiction along with the author and narrator. One learns from James and Faulkner, more than anything else, that it is "the people," the community of the spiritual, "Go Down, Moses," who must be saved, not oneself alone.

Notes

CHAPTER 1: CONTEXTS FOR DIALOGUE

1. Richard Rorty, *Philosophy and the Mirror of Nature* (Princeton: Princeton University Press, 1979), 7–8. Vincent Leitch has characterized the American intellectual scene of the 1960s and 1970s as uniquely suited to a flowering of hermeneutics. Approaches arising from this era as part of a "renaissance" of diversification share most significantly their "antinomianism" in their attack on New Criticism. Leitch links developments in American literary theory to interpretations of Martin Heidegger's and Hans-Georg Gadamer's work, which replaced an older hermeneutic tradition rooted in the writings of F. D. E. Schleiermacher and Wilhelm Dilthey. Although E. D. Hirsch, among others, followed the older tradition, a "new hermeneutics" that completely denied objectivity evolved, "privileg[ing] the speaking voice over the dead letter," as Leitch puts it. *American Literary Criticism from the Thirties to the Eighties* (New York: Columbia University Press, 1988), 182–210. On the new hermeneutics, see also Richard E. Palmer, *Hermeneutics: Interpretation Theory in Schleiermacher, Dilthey, Heidegger, and Gadamer* (Evanston: Northwestern University Press, 1969); and Walter J. Ong, S.J., *The Presence of the Word: Some Prolegomena for Cultural and Religious History* (New Haven: Yale University Press, 1967). Palmer argues that "literary works are best regarded . . . not primarily as objects of analysis but as humanly created texts which speak" (7); Part III of his book deals specifically with questions of American literary interpretation. Other important resources for applying hermeneutic philosophy to literary studies include Tzvetan Todorov, *Symbolism and Interpretation*, trans. Catherine Porter (Ithaca: Cornell University Press, 1982); Paul Ricoeur, *The Conflict of Interpretations: Essays in Hermeneutics*, ed. Don Ihde (Evanston: Northwestern University Press, 1974); Roy J. Howard, *Three Faces of Hermeneutics* (Berkeley and Los Angeles: University of California Press, 1982); and Kurt Mueller-Vollmer, *The Hermeneutics Reader: Texts of the German Tradition from the Enlightenment to the Present* (New York: Continuum, 1985).

2. Rorty, *Philosophy*, 35–46, 162–63, 156, 316–17.

3. Ibid., 388–89, 378. One of Rorty's most important predecessors on these points is Josiah Royce. In *The Problem of Christianity* (Chicago: University of Chicago Press, 1918, 1968), Royce tells us that "whatever else men need, they need their communities of interpretation," on which "every ideal good" depends. Royce, a religious philosopher and contemporary of James, departs from William James, Charles Peirce, and John Dewey on the open-endedness of pluralism and prag-

matism when he attempts to maintain belief in absolutes—within the freedom of what he called "the Will to Interpret." Stressing loyalty to community as the foundation of the human enterprises of science, morality, religion, government, and business, Royce offers "Beloved Community" as an avenue toward redemption of humankind, for such a community breaks what he calls the tragic circle of individual design or "disloyalty." Despite the force of his belief in Spirit as a living unity, there is an unresolved tension in Royce's thought between completion and change, between the individual and the community, a typically American tension.

4. See Harold Bloom, *The Anxiety of Influence: A Theory of Poetry* (New York: Oxford University Press, 1973), for a suggestive treatment of this idea.

5. Larzar Ziff, *Puritanism in America: New Culture in a New World* (New York: Viking, 1973), 112, 5, 30.

6. Ibid., 66.

7. Ibid., 105–6.

8. See ibid., 122.

9. Warner Berthoff, *A Literature Without Qualities* (Berkeley and Los Angeles: University of California Press, 1979); Sacvan Bercovitch, *The Puritan Origins of the American Self* (New Haven: Yale University Press, 1975); and Emory Elliott, *Revolutionary Writers: Literature and Authority in the New Republic, 1725–1810* (New York: Oxford University Press, 1982), 12–13.

10. Elliott, *Revolutionary Writers*, 14–16.

11. Ibid., 16–17, 48–50.

12. Richard Poirier, *A World Elsewhere: The Place of Style in American Literature* (New York: Oxford University Press, 1966), 15–16, 21–24, 77–78.

13. Henry James, *The American Scene*, ed. Leon Edel (Bloomington: Indiana University Press, 1968).

14. Leon Edel, *Henry James*, 5 vols. (New York: Avon, 1972), 5:317.

15. Peter Buitenhuis, "Henry James on Hawthorne," *New England Quarterly* 32 (June 1959): 222–23.

16. Edel, *Henry James*, 1:14–15.

17. Ibid., 1:15–16.

18. Dayton Kohler, "William Faulkner and the Social Conscience," *College English* 2 (December 1949): 119–27.

19. Joseph Blotner, *Faulkner: A Biography* (New York: Random House, 1974), 1324–25.

20. William Faulkner, Nobel Prize Award Speech, in *The Faulkner Reader* (New York: Random House, 1954), 3–4.

21. Blotner, *Faulkner*, 1366–67.

22. Ibid., 869.

23. Leo Marx, *The Machine in the Garden* (New York: Oxford University Press, 1964), 15–17, 24–26, 42–43, 69, 72, 92, 97–100, 143–44.

24. Georg Lukacs, *History and Class Consciousness*, trans. Rodney Livingstone (Cambridge, Mass.: MIT Press, 1971); Carolyn Porter, *Seeing and Being: The Plight of the Participant Observer in Emerson, James, Adams, and Faulkner* (Middletown, Conn.: Wesleyan University Press, 1981), xii–xiv, 280.

25. Anne Norton, *Alternative Americas: A Reading of Antebellum Political Culture* (Chicago: University of Chicago Press, 1986), 1–6.

26. Ibid., 7.

27. Wendy Barker, *Lunacy of Light: Emily Dickinson and the Experience of Metaphor* (Carbondale: University of Southern Illinois Press, 1987).

28. Mikhail Bakhtin, *Problems of Dostoevsky's Poetics*, trans. Caryl Emerson, intro. Wayne C. Booth, Theory and History of Literature, Vol. 8 (Minneapolis: University of Minnesota Press, 1983); and Mikhail Bakhtin, *The Dialogic Imagination: Four Essays*, ed. and intro. Michael Holquist, trans. Caryl Emerson and Michael Holquist (Austin: University of Texas Press, 1981). Two recent books argue that Bakhtin can lead us to a new appreciation of heterogeneity in American literature. In *The Unusable Past* (New York: Methuen Books, 1986), Russell J. Reising is moved by Bakhtin toward a new appreciation of neglected " 'social' or mimetic writers," particularly those minority writers addressing social inequality and oppression. He uses Bakhtin as a strategy for reassessing works in their historical and economic settings. The "dialogization of inadequately examined divisions in the American canon" would yield, he says, "a new understanding of the interrelationships of now nearly mutually exclusive writers, themes, and world views" (2–6, 9–10, 235). Dale M. Bauer, in *Feminist Dialogics: A Theory of Failed Community* (Albany: State University of New York Press, 1988), stresses the necessity of tension between the central and the marginal in a dialogic community, specifically as she defines the "other" as the female voice. Bauer finds certain heroines—including Maggie Verver—engaging in a "battle among voices" where there are "no interpretive communities willing to listen to women's alien and threatening discourse." Bauer's effort is to generate a feminist dialogics that will get these heroines "back into the dialogue in order to reconstruct the process by which [they were] read out in the first place" (3–4). I think James and Faulkner have already done this, for their novels metafictively enact a dialogue with readers that furnishes the interpretive dialogics and are already subverted by the "other." Bauer prefers the "ideological directness" of the "conclusive" conclusions of Edith Wharton's *House of Mirth* and Kate Chopin's *Awakening* over the more ambiguous conclusions of Nathaniel Hawthorne's *Blithedale Romance* and James's *Golden Bowl*. She calls Hawthorne's and James's works too "mystifying" and at the same time too "Utopian," but it seems to me that a *metafictive* reading of James and Hawthorne using Bakhtin's "dialogism" better enables readers to appreciate such "mystery." Another interesting pairing of Bakhtin and James is Annette Larson Benert's "Dialogical Discourse in 'The Jolly Corner': The Entrepreneur as Language and Image," *Henry James Review* 8 (Winter 1987): 116–25.

29. Bakhtin, *The Dialogic Imagination*, 261–62, 291; Holquist, "Introduction," ibid., xxxi.

30. Ibid., 38–40.

31. Ibid., 338–39, 342.

32. Ibid., 17.

33. Ibid., 59, 6–7, 68.

34. Quoted in Caryl Emerson, "The Tolstoy Connection in Bakhtin," *PMLA* 100 (1985): 68–80.

35. Bakhtin, *Problems*, 7–8, 18–20, 29, 82–85.

36. Ibid., 28–30.

37. Edel, *Henry James*, 2:212.

38. For additional discussion of Bakhtin's theories in practical criticism see Gary Saul Morson, ed., Forum on Mikhail Bakhtin, *Critical Inquiry* 10 (December 1983): 225–320, particularly Caryl Emerson's "The Outer Word and Inner Speech: Bakhtin, Vygotsky, and the Internalization of Language" and Susan Stewart's "Shouts on the Street: Bakhtin's Anti-Linguistics." See also Morson, "The Heresiarch of *Meta*," *PTL: A Journal for Descriptive Poetics and Theory of Literature* 3 (1978): 407–27.

39. James's and Faulkner's reading of Russian literature was an important influence on their work. In an early review essay, James discussed many features of Ivan Turgenev's work (and the Russian novel in general) that correspond to features of his own—and to Faulkner's. In Faulkner's case, the strongest associations are with Fyodor Dostoevsky. Faulkner said several times in interviews that he reread Dostoevsky's *Brothers Karamazov* every year. In an interview with a reporter from the University of Virginia *College Topics*, Faulkner was asked about "the subject of the novel and its inevitable breakdown." He said that in the novel of the future, there will be no straight exposition, but only "soliloquies or speeches of the characters, those of each character printed in a different colored ink. Something of the play technique will thus eliminate much of the author from the story." In his view of the "new novel," it seems, Faulkner out-Bakhtins Bakhtin: even Bakhtin does not take dialogicity as far as Faulkner's colored inks. See Edel, *Henry James*, 2:204–7; Henry James, "Ivan Turgenev's Virgin Soil," *Nation*, 26 April 1877, reprinted in Henry James, *Literary Reviews and Essays on American, English and French Literature*, ed. Albert Mordell (New York: Grove Press, 1957), 190–97; and William Faulkner, in *Lion in the Garden: Interviews with William Faulkner, 1926–1962*, ed. James B. Meriwether and Michael Millgate (Lincoln: University of Nebraska Press, 1968), 284, 18. See also Tatiana Morozova, "Faulkner Reads Dostoevsky," *Soviet Literature* 12 (1981): 176–79; and Jean Weisgerber, *Faulkner and Dostoevsky: Influence and Confluence*, trans. Dean McWilliams (Athens: Ohio University Press, 1974). Morozova and Weisgerber trace connections between Faulkner's and Dostoevsky's humanism, their similar social settings, and their techniques of polyphony and ambiguity.

40. James's and Faulkner's novels may be read in one other context. New ideas about problems of knowledge in literary theory are paralleled by recent issues and theories of knowledge in pedagogy. The new emphasis on dialogics as a hermeneutics appropriate to language studies in general has been for several years among the most widespread developments in the teaching of writing in composition or literature classes. In the handling of epistemological problems of authority and interpretation, developments in teaching and composition theory are related to social and cultural approaches such as feminism and canon reform, as well as reader-response criticism, deconstruction, the newly reexamined "humanism" of scholars such as Wayne C. Booth, and the responses to literary communities of interpretation as defined by Stanley Fish. Steven Mailloux has called for a "rhetorical hermeneutics"

for all linguistic endeavors, and Don H. Bialostosky has proposed dialogics as a model for all academic discourse. In many cases growing directly out of literary theory, developments in teaching writing such as "collaborative learning" and "writing across the curriculum" ask all participants in language to acknowledge their communities of knowledge and treat thought and writing as social processes. The more one explores the theories supporting such techniques in the classroom, the more one finds "hermeneutics" to be a useful descriptive term for referring to many of our endeavors in American literature and language studies. The recent pedagogical emphasis on revision and the sense of an audience alone speaks strongly for this relationship. See Wayne C. Booth, *Critical Understanding: The Powers and Limits of Pluralism* (Chicago: University of Chicago Press, 1979); Booth, M. H. Abrams, and J. Hillis Miller, "The Limits of Pluralism," *Critical Inquiry* 3 (Spring 1977): 407–47; Booth, "LITCOMP: Some Rhetoric Addressed to Crypto-rhetoricians about a Rhetorical Solution to a Rhetorical Problem," in *Composition and Literature: Bridging the Gap*, ed. Winifred Byran Horner (Chicago: University of Chicago Press, 1983), 57–80; Booth, "A New Strategy for Establishing a Truly Democratic Criticism," *Daedalus* 112 (Summer 1983): 193–214; Stanley Fish, *Is There a Text in This Class?: The Authority of Interpretive Communities* (Cambridge, Mass.: Harvard University Press, 1980); Fish, "A Reply to Eugene Goodheart," *Daedalus* 112 (Summer 1983): 233–37; and Fish, "Transmuting the Lump: *Paradise Lost*, 1942–1982," in *Literature and History: Theoretical Problems and Russian Case Studies*, ed. Gary Saul Morson (Stanford: Stanford University Press, 1986), 33–56. For more recent ideas on hermeneutics in pedagogy, see Steven Mailloux, "Rhetorical Hermeneutics," *Critical Inquiry* 11 (June 1985): 620–42; and Don H. Bialostosky, "Dialogics as an Art of Discourse in Literary Criticism," *PMLA* 101 (October 1986): 788–97. For the most definitive work on collaborative learning, see Kenneth Bruffee, "Collaborative Learning: Some Practical Models," *College English* 34 (February 1973): 634–43; Bruffee, "Liberal Education and the Social Justification of Belief," *Liberal Education* 68 (Summer 1982): 95–114; Bruffee, "Writing and Reading as Collaborative or Social Acts: The Argument from Kuhn and Vygotsky," *Proceedings of the Skidmore Conference on Writing and Thinking* (Urbana: National Council of Teachers of English, 1983); and Bruffee, *A Short Course in Writing*, 2d ed. (Cambridge, Mass.: Winthrop Publishers, 1980). Elaine Maimon has been an important figure in the development of writing across the university programs. See her "Maps and Genres: Exploring Connections in the Arts and Sciences," in *Composition and Literature*, ed. Horner, 110–25; and Maimon, et al., *Writing in the Arts and Sciences* (Boston: Little, Brown, 1984). Another good source is Toby Fulwiler and Art Young, eds., *Language Connections: Writing and Reading Across the Curriculum* (Urbana: National Council of Teachers of English, 1982).

CHAPTER 2: KNOWLEDGE AS INTEREST AND DESIGN

1. Raymond Williams, *Keywords: A Vocabulary of Culture and Society* (New York: Oxford University Press, 1979), 143–44.

2. *The Compact Edition of the Oxford English Dictionary*, s.v. "interest."

3. Leon Edel, Introduction, *Henry James: Selected Fiction* (New York: E. P. Dutton, 1953), xvi.

4. Nathaniel Hawthorne, "Rappaccini's Daughter," in *The Complete Novels and Selected Tales of Nathaniel Hawthorne*, ed. Norman Holmes Pearson (New York: Modern Library, 1937, 1965), 332.

5. Henry James, "The Art of Fiction," in *The Portable Henry James*, rev. ed., ed. Morton Dauwen Zabel (New York: Viking/Penguin, 1979), 394.

6. William Faulkner, *Absalom, Absalom!* (New York: Random House, 1936), 263. Further references are cited in text.

7. David Bromwich traces the notion of "disinterest" in the literary criticism of William Hazlitt and Matthew Arnold to emphasize their legacy of "disinterest," cogently relating interest to design in art by sketching "part of a longer story about the invention of the literary object, and the sort of interest we are supposed to take in it." Bromwich's and Hazlitt's "disinterest" simultaneously invokes the double meanings of "interest" and "design." See "The Genealogy of Disinterestedness," *Raritan* 1 (Spring 1982): 62, 64–65, 83–84.

8. David Minter's use of "design" in this sense is suggestive for my own. He defines two kinds of intellectual heroes in American fiction, "designers" such as Hollingsworth and Sutpen and "interpreters" such as Coverdale and Quentin. He uses the term "interpreted design" to denote a literary work structured on the juxtaposition of these two heroes, one a person who dominates the action of his world, and one through whose interpreting mind we get the story of the designer. Thoreau, Hawthorne, and Adams, Minter finds, attempted to discover "more complex, more truly redemptive" modes of interpretation than did their eighteenth-century predecessors. In the fiction of James, Fitzgerald, and Faulkner, Minter notes even greater valuing of interpretation over mere successful design. Interpreting, not further designing, becomes "a means of taming unexpected and unacceptable failure." *The Interpreted Design as a Structural Principle in American Prose* (New Haven: Yale University Press, 1969), 3–6.

9. Edel, *Henry James*, 2:178; 1:36, 47, 115–16.

10. Quentin Anderson, *The American Henry James* (New Brunswick: Rutgers University Press, 1957), xiii, 3–6.

11. William James to Henry James, 4 May 1907, in *The Letters of William James*, 2 vols., ed. Henry James (Boston: Atlantic Monthly Press, 1920), 2:278.

12. William James to Henry James, 22 October 1905, quoted in Ralph Barton Perry, *The Thought and Character of William James*, 2 vols. (Boston: Little, Brown, 1935), 1:424.

13. Henry James to William James, 23 November 1905, in *The Letters of Henry James*, 2 vols., ed. Percy Lubbock (New York: Scribner's, 1920), 2:43.

14. Victor Strandberg, "Faulkner's God: A Jamesian Perspective," in his *A Faulkner Overview: Six Perspectives* (Port Washington, N.Y.: Kennikat Press, 1981), 89–90, 104–6, 112–13.

15. Henry James, *Hawthorne*, English Men of Letters Series (London: Macmillan, 1879; Ithaca: Cornell University Press, 1956), 113–14, 136–40.

16. Richard H. Brodhead argues that writers in America in the decades after 1860 "moved into a field rather massively dominated by the figure of Hawthorne." James was "more than familiar with Hawthorne's writing"—he was "possessed of it." But Hawthorne's influence is ambiguous: his followers easily "engage him at the level of his subject matter" (including the regional types and social situations that occur in local color fiction), but "his effect on the followers who to any extent reactivate the imaginative procedures of his fiction tends to be highly disruptive" in that the realist authors "who re-create the deep logic of his fiction find that they have revived, within their work, a voice that calls the validity of their own procedures strenuously into question." "Hawthorne among the Realists: The Case of Howells," in *American Realism: New Essays*, ed. Eric J. Sundquist (Baltimore: Johns Hopkins University Press, 1982), 25–27.

17. F. O. Matthiessen argues that James's dissatisfaction with Hawthorne's use of allegory and romance led him to develop his own peculiar "dense symbols," his ambiguity. *American Renaissance* (New York: Oxford University Press, 1941), 292–305, 351–68.

18. Philip Rahv, "The Dark Lady of Salem," *Partisan Review* 8 (September-October 1941): 362–81.

19. Alexander Cowie explains that James and Hawthorne primarily reacted to "the spiritual domination of one character by another": Zenobia and Priscilla, Kate and Milly, Olive and Verena. Randall Stewart correspondingly notes that like Hawthorne and Melville, James is a "counter-romantic," who, recognizing original sin, does not "apotheosize the self . . . but warn[s] against its perversities." Dissatisfied with the inflation of the individual in nineteenth-century romanticism, these writers dramatize the dangers of "self-trust" and "the miseries of the overcultivated Ego." J. A. Ward calls the harmful domination of one person over another *the* subject of Hawthorne's and James's work; what James called "omnivorous egoism" is his version of Hawthorne's "Unpardonable Sin." See Cowie, *The Rise of the American Novel* (New York: American Books, 1948), chap. 16; Stewart, *American Literature and Christian Doctrine* (Baton Rouge: Louisiana State University Press, 1958), 106; and Ward, "Henry James and the Nature of Evil," *Twentieth Century Literature* 6 (July 1960): 69. See also Watson Branch, "The Deeper Psychology: James's Legacy from Hawthorne," *Arizona Quarterly* 40 (Spring 1984): 67–74.

20. Nathaniel Hawthorne, Preface to *The Blithedale Romance*, ed. Seymour Gross and Rosalie Murphy (New York: Norton, 1978), 1–3. Rita Gollin has shown that much of Hawthorne's later concern about problems of authorial knowledge shows up in his *Notebooks*, particularly in his anxieties about formulating aesthetic responses to works of art; he complains frequently of his limited "receptive faculty" and compares the difficult process of apprehending art to that of constructing a work of fiction. "Hawthorne and the Anxiety of Aesthetic Response," *Centennial Review* 28–29 (Fall–Winter 1984): 94–103.

21. Hawthorne's and James's shared concerns about artistic design have been addressed by critics in very similar terms. See Maurice Beebe, *Ivory Towers and Sacred Founts: The Artist as Hero in Fiction from Goethe to Joyce* (New York: New York University Press, 1964), 18; Annette K. Baxter, "Independence vs. Isolation:

Hawthorne and James on the Problem of the Artist," *Nineteenth Century Fiction* 10 (1955): 226, 230; Edwin Fussell, "Hawthorne, James, and the 'Common Doom,'" *American Quarterly* 10 (1958): 441–49; and R. W. B. Lewis, *The American Adam* (Chicago: University of Chicago Press, 1955), 191–93.

22. Malcolm Cowley, "William Faulkner Revisited," *Saturday Review*, 14 April 1945, 13–16; and Terence Martin, *Nathaniel Hawthorne* (New York: Twayne, 1965), 177–80.

23. James, *Hawthorne*, 103–4.

24. See James B. Mellow, "Hawthorne's Divided Genius," *Wilson Quarterly* 6 (Spring 1982): 172–73, 162, 168. Mellow argues that like Faulkner, Hawthorne "made ambivalence a method," and "it was not simply a question of indecision or indifference or a means of escape from the hard social issues of the period—as some of his severest critics claimed."

25. Faulkner's works are often read through the medium of Hawthorne's. For example, Paul S. Stein finds that in *Go Down, Moses*, there are the "essentially good and pure land which exists as a contrary to a corrupt civilization" and the "other wilderness in the American tradition, embodied in the forest which Young Goodman Brown enters." The latter, the "Hawthornian wilderness" that "serves to reveal and reflect the darker side of man's own soul," is also Faulkner's mythic land, "a wilderness over which Ben's presence looms precisely as does Old Carothers' over the tamed land." Ike's initiation thus "fits well within an American tradition of such initiations: rites from which novices emerge profoundly *un*fit for life within their communities." These Hawthornian anti-initiations are "deeply traumatizing." "Ike McCaslin: Traumatized in a Hawthornian Wilderness," *Southern Literary Journal* 12 (1980): 69–70.

26. In the same essay as the "Say NO in thunder" passage, Melville wrote on Hawthorne as a "failure" and praised those authors who are not afraid to "fail" in a similar sense. Melville argues that without such a willingness to fail, an author cannot be great. Herman Melville, "Hawthorne and His Mosses," *New York Literary World*, 17 and 24 August 1850, reprinted in *The Writings of Herman Melville*, 10 vols., ed. Harrison Hayford et al. (Evanston and Chicago: Northwestern University Press and The Newberry Library, 1987), 9:239–53. One may question my neglect of Melville in favor of Hawthorne in this chapter, especially as one could argue that Melville's *Moby-Dick* is the greatest single hermeneutic novel ever written. But because this novel and other experimental hermeneutic works, such as *Pierre*, were not for the most part as available as Hawthorne's work in James's and Faulkner's early careers, the nineteenth-century influence comes much more clearly from Hawthorne. In addition, Hawthorne works with hermeneutic narratives more consistently from novel to novel than did Melville.

27. Bruce Michelson argues that *The House of the Seven Gables* is a multileveled work that may be seen simultaneously "as a ghost story, as a moral document, and as a kind of metafiction." "Hawthorne's House of Three Stories," *New England Quarterly* 57 (June 1984): 163–83. See also Kristin Brady, "Hawthorne's Editor/ Narrator: The Voice of Indeterminacy," *CEA Critic* 47 (Summer 1985): 27–38.

28. There are two other extended evaluations of Hawthorne by Henry James that demonstrate James's growing appreciation of Hawthorne: "Hawthorne's

French and Italian Journals," *Nation* 14 March 1872, pp. 172–73; and "Hawthorne," *Library of the World's Best Literature*, 30 vols., ed. Charles Dudley Warner (New York: R. S. Peale and J. A. Hill, 1896–97), 12:7053–61.

29. Tony Tanner, Introduction, *Hawthorne* by Henry James (London: Macmillan, 1967), 1–21.

30. James, *Hawthorne*, 3–4.

31. Marius Bewley, *The Complex Fate: Hawthorne, Henry James, and Some Other American Writers* (London: Chatto and Windus, 1952; New York: Gordian Press, 1967), 55–78; and Bewley, *The Eccentric Design: Form in the Classic American Novel* (New York: Columbia University Press, 1959), 9ff.

32. James, *Hawthorne*, 22–23.

33. Ibid., 24–25.

34. The faults in Hawthorne's writing are the sort James would painstakingly try to avoid in his own future work, but James criticizes Hawthorne for many of the same things for which he himself was to be criticized, particularly in his remarks on *The Scarlet Letter*. Ibid., 90–92.

35. Ibid., 120–23.

36. Blotner, *Faulkner*, 393, 379.

37. William Faulkner, *Vision in Spring*, ed. Judith Sensibar (Austin: University of Texas Press, 1984). Sensibar argues in *The Origins of Faulkner's Art* (Austin: University of Texas Press, 1984) that all of Faulkner's later work is rooted in his early poetry.

38. Carvel Collins, "Faulkner at the University of Mississippi," in *William Faulkner: Early Prose and Poetry*, comp. and ed. Collins (Boston: Atlantic Monthly Press, 1962), 3–38.

39. Blotner, *Faulkner*, 267.

40. Ibid., 240–45, 319–20.

41. Ibid., 393.

42. George P. Garrett, Jr., "An Examination of the Poetry of William Faulkner," *Princeton University Library Chronicle* 18 (Spring 1957): 124–35; reprinted in *William Faulkner: Four Decades of Criticism*, ed. Linda Welsheimer Wagner (East Lansing: Michigan State University Press, 1973), 45. An article by another critic demonstrates why critics have stayed away from Faulkner's poetry: it dismisses the poems as strictly derivative examples of "immature romanticism." See Harry Runyan, "Faulkner's Poetry," *Faulkner Studies* 3 (Summer–Autumn 1954): 23–29. See also Cleanth Brooks's discussion of Faulkner's pastoral poems in *William Faulkner: Toward Yoknapatawpha and Beyond* (New Haven: Yale University Press, 1978), 4–6, 17–18.

43. Garrett, "An Examination," 46, 53.

44. William Faulkner, *The Marble Faun* (Boston: Four Seas Co., 1924); reprinted as *The Marble Faun and A Green Bough* (New York: Random House, 1965), 12.

45. See Garrett, "An Examination," 46.

46. Faulkner, *Marble Faun*, 25.

47. Faulkner, "The Hill," in *William Faulkner*, ed. Collins, 90–92.

48. Faulkner, *Marble Faun*, 50.

49. Henry James, "The Papers," in James, *The Better Sort* (New York: Scribner's, 1903), 322. Edel calls "The Papers" a "brilliant if long-drawn-out prophecy of modern 'public relations.'" *Henry James*, 5:143.

50. Peter Conn, *The Divided Mind: Ideology and Imagination in America, 1898–1917* (Cambridge: Cambridge University Press, 1983), 21.

51. Edel, *Henry James*, 2:426–28.

52. Ibid., 3:333–34.

53. Walter Isle, *Experiments in Form: Henry James's Novels, 1896–1901* (Cambridge, Mass.: Harvard University Press, 1968), vii–viii, 16–17, 34.

54. Ibid., 17, 24–25.

55. Faulkner, *Lion in the Garden*, 255.

56. Faulkner, *Faulkner in the University*, ed. Frederick L. Gwynn and Joseph Blotner (Charlottesville: University Press of Virginia 1959), 23.

57. Ibid., 54–55.

58. Olga Vickery points out that, like Dostoevsky, "Faulkner distrusts reason and loves paradox, distrusts total understanding and seeks to preserve some element of mystery, plunges into the labyrinth of the unnatural and the morass of the soul, and hovers on the edge of the hallucinatory, of the spectral, always vulnerable to daemonic intrusions into what might prove, in the end, to have been merely a tissue of dreams." But like Tolstoy, Faulkner is "the poet of the land and of the rural setting, the man thirsting for the truth and engaging in excessive pursuit of it, the writer evoking the realness, the tangibility, the sensible entirety of concrete experience." Vickery asserts that Faulkner achieves the sort of artistic design James calls "The Figure in the Carpet" not merely through chronological rendering of events or the "essentially topographical arrangement" of stories, or exclusively through the focus on morality, social criticism, or philosophy. The all-important "texture," or pattern, is character. "William Faulkner and the Figure in the Carpet," *South Atlantic Quarterly* 63 (Summer 1964); reprinted ibid. 76 (Autumn 1977): 479–80, 492–96.

59. Blotner, *Faulkner*, 716, 1659.

60. Series of letters in May and June 1946 between Faulkner and Robert Linscott, quoted ibid., 1216.

61. Faulkner to Malcolm Cowley, 18 February 1946, in *The Faulkner-Cowley File: Letters and Memories, 1944–1962*, ed. Malcolm Cowley (New York: Viking, 1966), 89–90.

62. Faulkner to Malcolm Cowley, 10 February 1959, quoted in Blotner, *Faulkner*, 1721.

63. Cowley, Introduction, *The Portable Faulkner* (New York: Viking, 1946), 18.

64. Blotner, *Faulkner*, 1518–19.

65. Robert Coughlan's "The Private World of William Faulkner" (*Life* 35 [28 September 1953]: 118–36), based on an interview with Faulkner, contained much embarrassing personal information gleaned from Faulkner's acquaintances, especially a disaffected Phil Stone.

66. See Blotner, *Faulkner*, 1518–19.

67. Faulkner, Letter to the Editor, *New York Times*, 10 January 1955, quoted ibid., 1520.

68. Henry James, Preface to *The Golden Bowl*, in James, *The Art of the Novel*, ed. and intro. R. P. Blackmur (New York: Scribner's, 1934, 1962), 327–28.

69. Blackmur, Introduction to James, *The Art of the Novel*, xiii, xxix.

70. James, Preface to "The Lesson of the Master," in James, *The Art of the Novel*, 222.

71. Blackmur, Introduction to James, *The Art of the Novel*, xxv–xxvi.

72. James, Preface to *Portrait of a Lady*, in James, *The Art of the Novel*, 46–47.

73. Ibid., 56.

74. James, Preface to *The Princess Casamassima*, ibid., 64–65.

75. James, Preface to *Daisy Miller*, ibid., 268–70.

76. James, Preface to *The Wings of the Dove*, ibid., 292, 306.

77. James, Preface to *The Ambassadors*, ibid., 313–14.

78. Faulkner, *Lion in the Garden*, 61.

79. Ibid., 108.

80. Meriwether and Millgate, Introduction, ibid., xi.

81. Faulkner, in *Essays, Speeches, and Public Letters*, ed. James B. Meriwether (New York: Random House, 1965), 129, 133, 131.

82. Faulkner, *Lion in the Garden*, 206.

83. Ibid., 216.

84. Ibid., 200, 102–3, 70–73.

85. Ibid., 159–60.

86. Ibid., 58, 81. In *Quest for Failure: A Study of William Faulkner* (Ithaca: Cornell University Press, 1960; Westport, Conn.: Greenwood Press, 1972), Walter J. Slatoff offers a discussion of "failure" in Faulkner's fiction that spans his entire career. Slatoff's book is strong in demonstrating how Faulkner's imagery and syntax cause the reader to deal with contradictions embodied in Faulkner's oxymorons and antitheses, but it does not apply the idea of failure critically enough to Faulkner's themes and ideas. Stephen Oates, in his new biography of Faulkner, calls failure an important theme in Faulkner's life and career, particularly the sense in his fiction of white society in the South as a failure. *William Faulkner: The Man and the Artist, a Biography* (New York: Harper & Row, 1987), 180 and passim.

87. Faulkner, *Lion in the Garden*, 220–21.

Chapter 3: Failure to "Live": *The Ambassadors*

1. F. O. Matthiessen, *Henry James: The Major Phase* (New York: Oxford University Press, 1944).

2. See Edgar J. Burde, "*The Ambassadors* and the Double Vision of Henry James," *Essays in Literature* 4 (Spring 1977): 59–77.

3. Edel, *Henry James*, 5:69–70, 78–79.

4. James, Preface to *The Ambassadors*, in James, *The Art of the Novel*, 310.

5. Ibid., 315–18.

6. Ibid., 321. Richard Poirier offers a similar view of James's freedom of character. In *The Comic Sense of Henry James* (New York: Oxford University Press, 1967), Poirier distinguishes between James's "fixed" and "free" characters: fixed characters

exhibit a smooth perfection that masks internal emotional paralysis (Madame Merle, Gilbert Osmond), whereas free characters pursue idealistic values but fail to understand or achieve their goals (Isabel Archer, Lambert Strether). Free characters are left unexplained in the end and are associated with comedy, which Poirier defines as James's "best weapon in defense of . . . freedom" (249, 254–55, 94–95).

7. James, Preface to *The Ambassadors*, in James, *The Art of the Novel*, 322–23, 326.

8. Henry James, *The Ambassadors* (New York: Harper's, 1902, 1948), 64. Further references are cited in the text.

9. Charles Thomas Samuels, *The Ambiguity of Henry James* (Urbana: University of Illinois Press, 1971), 197.

10. Elsa Nettels, "*The Ambassadors* and the Sense of the Past," *Modern Language Quarterly* 31 (June 1970): 220–35.

11. See Frederick C. Crews, *The Tragedy of Manners: Moral Drama in the Later Novels of Henry James* (New Haven: Yale University Press, 1957), 49–50.

12. Ibid., 41–42.

13. Percy Lubbock's description of James's narrator as located somewhere behind the left shoulder of his main character reinforces this questioning of the single view. *The Craft of Fiction* (New York: Viking, 1957), 258.

14. Ruth Bernard Yeazell, *Language and Knowledge in the Late Novels of Henry James* (Chicago: University of Chicago Press, 1976), 22–25, 28–30.

15. Samuels, *Ambiguity*, 194.

16. The metafictive devices in *The Ambassadors* are quite extensive. The theater scenes occur in the context of a pattern of dramatic metaphors, which, like these scenes, comment on the fictionality of the novel (352, 379). There are also complicated patterns of book metaphors (55, 59–61, 65–66, 122–23, 206, 300, 375, 386, 393, 409, 413); of Strether as a writer—a letter writer (80, 179, 232); and of Strether as an artist (135, 142–43, 151, 157, 349–50, 380, 388). In addition, tone of voice is often described with a metafictive purpose (57, 66, 75, 153, 336, 377–78, 385).

17. Crews, *Tragedy*, 52.

18. See especially Matthiessen, *Henry James*, 39–42; Oscar Cargill, "*The Ambassadors*: A New View," *PMLA* 75 (1960): 439–52; U. C. Knoepflmacher, " 'O Rare for Strether!' *Antony and Cleopatra* and *The Ambassadors*," *Nineteenth Century Fiction* 19 (1964–65): 333–44; Crews, *Tragedy*, 42; and Edel, *Henry James*, 5:71ff.

19. James, Preface to *The Ambassadors*, in James, *The Art of the Novel*, 307–8.

20. Rachel Salmon, "Naming and Knowing in Henry James's 'The Beast in the Jungle': The Hermeneutics of a Sacred Text," *Orbis Litterarum* 36 (1981): 302–22.

21. James, Preface to *The Ambassadors*, in James, *The Art of the Novel*, 322.

22. Ibid., 322, 324.

23. Yeazell, *Language and Knowledge*, 69.

24. Crews calls Jeanne's "being sold for the sake of a title . . . appalling to [Strether's] romantic American soul," for Jeanne's slavery has " 'something ancient and cold in it.' " *Tragedy*, 50.

25. Yeazell, *Language and Knowledge*, 70–73.

26. Ibid., 69–71.

27. Crews, *Tragedy*, 39.

28. John Warner, " 'In View of Other Matters': The Religious Dimension of *The Ambassadors*," *Essays in Literature* 4 (Spring 1977): 93–94.

CHAPTER 4: COMMUNITY VERSUS DESIGN IN *ABSALOM, ABSALOM!*

1. Bakhtin, *Problems*, 58.

2. Hyatt Waggoner, *William Faulkner: From Jefferson to the World* (Lexington: University of Kentucky Press, 1959), 214. A more epistemologically reductive reading of Faulkner's narrative structure is that of Alma A. Ilacqua in "Faulkner's *Absalom, Absalom!*: An Aesthetic Projection of the Religious Sense of Beauty," *Ball State University Forum* 21, no. 2 (1980): 34–41. Ilacqua sees Shreve as one of the "elect," a person "selected" to view the "whole order" of this novel. He has "total vision" of the elect rather than the fragmentary vision of everyone else. Shreve illustrates, she claims, Faulkner's attempt to uphold an "Edwardsian" order in the universe. I would argue that Faulkner is doing just the opposite.

3. The exception is Faulkner's own direct presence in *Absalom, Absalom!* through the map of Yoknapatawpha County appended to the novel. But this presence only adds another transformative narrative feature, another narrator—Faulkner himself.

4. Joseph Reed, *Faulkner's Narrative* (New Haven: Yale University Press, 1973), 161–62. With the exception of a few passages such as this one, Reed strongly asserts a hermeneutic reading of Faulkner.

5. Bakhtin, *Dialogic Imagination*, 402–5.

6. Porter links Quentin's withdrawal to Sutpen's attempt to "encompass and transcend time," pointing to Sutpen's visual metaphors as support. As a contrast to Quentin's withdrawal from community, Porter offers a discussion of Judith Sutpen. *Seeing and Being*, 259–67, 270–71. John Irwin's Freudian analysis argues that Quentin's withdrawal in *Absalom, Absalom!* is primarily conditioned by his incestuous obsession with his sister Caddy in *The Sound and the Fury*; Quentin thus acts compulsively and without free will. Irwin's description of doubling and incest as images of self-enclosure within the individual and the family presents a closed system without possibility for exception, in this case a recapitulation of Freudian designs. The presence of the other in Faulkner does not always damn a character into dependence or obsession, but rather always asks to be addressed. The focus on Quentin as hero is here too exclusive for an overall reading of the novel. *Doubling and Incest/Repetition and Revenge: A Speculative Reading of Faulkner* (Baltimore: Johns Hopkins University Press, 1975), 1–5, 25–29, 59.

7. Judith acknowledges her "complex fate," Minter notes, and she clearly exemplifies the novel's larger pattern "of affront leading to design, design leading to action, action leading to failure (as well as to new affronts and new designs), failure leading to inquiry, and failed inquiry leading to imaginative interpretation." *Interpreted Design*, 191, 202–11, 216–17.

8. *Absalom, Absalom!*'s narrators reveal the "creation of truth inherent in the attempt to find it," a "public truth," comments Olga Vickery in "*Absalom, Absalom!*," in *The Novels of William Faulkner*, rev. ed. (Baton Rouge: Louisiana State University Press, 1964), 124–34.

9. The main narrator I call "narrator" and the storytelling characters "tellers."

10. Reed, *Faulkner's Narrative*, 67.

11. Cleanth Brooks, *William Faulkner: The Yoknapatawpha Country* (New Haven: Yale University Press, 1963), 296–97.

12. Names such as "the Kernel" are important throughout *Absalom, Absalom!* for names in general are designs in this novel. The lost war is called a "mounting tide of names of lost battles from either side—Chickamauga and Franklin, Vicksburg and Corinth and Atlanta" (345). Shreve habitually calls Miss Rosa "Aunt Rosa" or "the old dame." Quentin irritably corrects Shreve, " 'Miss Rosa, I tell you' " (176), but Shreve deliberately sticks to his own names for the characters. Rosa's name seems to be a point of contention among several other characters, too, including Wash, who calls her, disrespectfully, "Rosie." There is the mix-up between the names Cassandra and Clytemnestra. General Compson does not know what to call Judith when he is speaking to Charles Etienne St. Valery Bon—" 'he could not say "Miss Judith," since that would postulate the blood more than ever' " (204). And Judith herself asks Charles Etienne St. Valery Bon, who calls her "Miss Sutpen," to call her "Aunt Judith" (208), which he will not do. Similarly, Quentin imagines that Sutpen is concerned about his abandoned offspring, his vanished Henry, whose " *'name would be different and those to call him by it strangers' "* (182). Sutpen chose all their names as part of his design, even Charles Bon: " 'Charles Good. . . . That would have been part of the cleaning up, just as he would have done his share toward cleaning up the exploded caps and musket cartridges after the siege if he hadn't been sick (or maybe engaged).' " Sutpen could not " 'permit the child, since it was a boy, to bear either his name or that of his maternal grandfather.' " Jim Bond's name is the final irony in the Sutpen design; as Luster explains, "bond" is a " 'lawyer word. Whut dey puts you under when the Law ketches you' " (215). Bond's howling is the product of the inexorable working of the "Law" of the designs Sutpen starts for himself and those he finds he lives under like everyone else: "There was only the sound of the idiot negro left" (376). As Shreve senses, it is this sound that so torments Quentin in the end (377–78).

13. John Hagopian, "The Biblical Background of Faulkner's *Absalom, Absalom!*," *CEA Critic* 36, no. 2 (1974): 22–24. Another example of how readers are provoked to fill in negativity is supplied by Cleanth Brooks in "The Narrative Structure of *Absalom, Absalom!*," *Georgia Review* 29 (1975): 366–94. Faulkner, he says, intends the reader to know that Quentin learned of Bon's parentage from Henry—there were more words spoken between the two of them than appear in the text. See *Absalom, Absalom!*, 373.

CHAPTER 5: THE NEGATIVE DESIGN OF *THE GOLDEN BOWL*

1. Henry James, *The Golden Bowl* (New York: Scribner's, 1904; New York: Penguin Books, 1972), 395. Further references are cited in text.

2. James, Preface to *The Golden Bowl*, in James, *The Art of the Novel*, 327–29.

3. James, *The American Scene*, 12.

4. Mark Seltzer calls James's work a "double discourse" that actually reinforces existing power structures even as it seems to repudiate them. He has argued that in contrast to the repudiation of power so often associated with James's heroines, Maggie's representation of love as a value that normalizes power imbalances in her community actually furthers the designs of power she and her father have enacted all

along. See *Henry James and the Art of Power* (Ithaca: Cornell University Press, 1984), 14–16, 94–95. Yet Seltzer's analysis does not account for hints of Maggie's failure or her pain at the end; it does not adequately address James's and Maggie's extreme self-consciousness about the costs of design in the entanglement of love and power. Although Maggie certainly exercises a winning power, her design is an "antidesign" qualitatively different from Adam's. Seltzer tells us that in James's late novels "love and power are ways of saying the same thing." To the contrary, James's late novels are about why this is not so. Similarly, Porter says that *The Golden Bowl* depicts "a wholly reified world" in which individuals have become commodities and in which love is in danger of functioning only as an illusion to maintain the status quo. As Maggie works to save herself and her marriage, she becomes a doer like Adam. But Maggie's "negative" actions have entirely different goals and results from Adam's "working" for himself. *Seeing and Being*, 122–23, 130–36. Minter differentiates between Adam as the supreme designer of the novel and Maggie as its supreme "interpreter." Minter notes that as Maggie undoes and rearranges Adam's design, she is "able simultaneously to acknowledge [its] radical flaw and to retain devotion to perfection." *Interpreted Design*, 168–71. For me Maggie is the heroine and Maggie is "saved" because she is as scrupulous and self-conscious about having a design as James is, for this leads both of them to create metadesigns that are open in a way that mere personal designs are not.

5. Crews, *Tragedy*, 104.

6. Samuels, *Ambiguity*, 211.

7. Yeazell, *Language and Knowledge*, 107–8, 110–14.

8. Dorothea Krook, *The Ordeal of Consciousness in Henry James* (Cambridge: Cambridge University Press, 1967), 324.

9. Samuels, *Ambiguity*, 212.

10. Tzvetan Todorov, *Poétique de la prose* (Paris: Seuil, 1971), 153; Shlomith Rimmon, *The Concept of Ambiguity—The Example of James* (Chicago: University of Chicago Press, 1977), 231, 227–28; and Henry James, Preface to *The Aspern Papers*, in James, *The Art of the Novel*, 177. See also Joseph Wiesenfarth, *Henry James and the Dramatic Analogy* (New York: Fordham University Press, 1963), and Ralf Norrman, *The Insecure World of Henry James's Fiction: Intensity and Ambiguity* (London: Macmillan, 1982).

11. See Samuels, *Ambiguity*, 220–22.

12. Yeazell, *Language and Knowledge*, 118–20.

13. Samuels, *Ambiguity*, 210–11. Sallie Sears agrees: because "James could not assert positive values with any degree of . . . conviction," his "negative" vision indicates that "whatever James saw that seemed potentially beautiful had a kind of built-in abortive principle to it, contained the seeds of its own doom." *The Negative Imagination: Form and Perspective in the Novels of Henry James* (Ithaca: Cornell University Press, 1968), xii.

14. Daniel J. Schneider, *The Crystal Cage: Adventures of the Imagination in the Fiction of Henry James* (Lawrence: Regents Press of Kansas, 1978), 140, 146–47, 150–52.

15. Philip Sicker examines James's treatment of love relationships in his *Love and the Quest for Identity in the Fiction of Henry James* (Princeton: Princeton University

Press, 1980), arguing that James's morality as expressed through love relationships owes less to romantic models than to the acceptance of flux and of the female sensibility. James's women characters are nontraditional, distinguished more by their wit than their beauty or simplicity. Yet he believes Maggie Verver could succeed only in a very different society from the one James portrays. See Sicker, 1–20. Marcia Ian also differs with my characterization of Maggie's love. In "Consecrated Diplomacy and the Concretion of Self," *Henry James Review* 7 (Fall 1985): 27–33, and "The Elaboration of Privacy in *The Wings of the Dove*," *ELH* 51 (Spring 1984): 107–36, she identifies Maggie's development as that of a progressively "detached" self. Maggie's winning is Ian's focus. Yet *The Golden Bowl* refuses any such "winning" *or* "detachment," just as it discourages fusion of selves. It asks instead for dialogue, for which Maggie is ready at the end—the tragedy being that the Prince most likely is not. Like Strether, Maggie is a model for the reader, but *only* a model for further action. If the reader's participation is unaccounted for, there is a confusion between what James depicts and what he is saying by doing so.

16. Besides the economic, ocular, and drama metaphors of *The Golden Bowl*, other important image clusters include those derived from architecture and art, transportation, water, and cages. As in *The Ambassadors*, in *The Golden Bowl* the same metaphors are often used to describe the state of mind of several characters. According to Ora Segal, the narrator of *The Golden Bowl* emphasizes the "ironic parallelism of the reversed situations" of the characters by using, for example, the images of the bath, the cage, and the cup to describe Maggie's, the Prince's, and Charlotte's various situations. *The Lucid Reflector: The Observer in Henry James's Fiction* (New Haven: Yale University Press, 1969), 183.

17. Salmon, "Naming and Knowing," 302.

18. Ibid.

19. Ibid., 303–5.

20. Yeazell, *Language and Knowledge*, 92, 97–98.

21. Ibid., 98–99.

CHAPTER 6: *GO DOWN, MOSES*: DISSOLUTION OF DESIGN

1. Minter reminds us that *Go Down, Moses* could be said to define every text "as an ur-text and pre-text," which requires us "to begin making connections and patterns that we must then revise or even repudiate," including moral solutions to the moral problems it raises. *Interpreted Design*, 189–90.

2. William Van O'Connor finds that in *Go Down, Moses*, "in place of doom, of tragic inevitabilities, of Old Testament harshness, one finds a sense of hopefulness, a promise of salvation." Similarly, Stanley Tick believes that *Go Down, Moses* is a novel that "ultimately reveals a profound moral commitment on the part of its author." O'Connor, "The Wilderness Theme in Faulkner's 'The Bear,'" *Accent* 13 (1953): 12–20, reprinted in *William Faulkner: Three Decades of Criticism*, ed. Frederick J. Hoffman and Olga W. Vickery (East Lansing: Michigan State University Press, 1960), 323; and Tick, "The Unity of *Go Down, Moses*," *Twentieth Century Literature* 8

(1962): 67–73, reprinted in *William Faulkner: Four Decades of Criticism*, ed. Linda Welsheimer Wagner (East Lansing: Michigan State University Press, 1973), 328.

3. Eric J. Sundquist, *Faulkner: The House Divided* (Baltimore: Johns Hopkins University Press, 1983), ix–x, 140, 150–58.

4. In contrast to Sundquist, Reed praises *Go Down, Moses'* departure from the structure of *Absalom, Absalom!* Although it covers the same time period, he notes, its movement through time is different. In *Absalom, Absalom!* one is conscious of being in the present looking at the past throu_ 'ı Quentin's and Shreve's distance; the past is synthesized in their "present" narratives. The intricately related but separate stories of *Go Down, Moses* replace this structure with the "flux of events and the inflexibility of plan." This novel's structure thus allows the "baroquely" complex echoing, retracing, and recapitulation of *Absalom, Absalom!* without its obscurities of style. *Faulkner's Narrative*, 136.

5. This chart is now located in the Alderman Library at the University of Virginia. Also of "genealogical" interest, there is some evidence that James modeled Basil Ransom of *The Bostonians* directly after the man on whom Faulkner modeled L. Q. C. McCaslin. According to Edel, James was told that Lucius Q. C. Lamar, the senator from Mississippi, seemed to recognize something of himself in Ransom. James confessed that he had met him once or twice in Washington, and he was one of the few Mississippians with whom James had the pleasure of conversing. Edel, *Henry James*, 3:140.

6. William Faulkner, *Go Down, Moses* (New York: Random House, 1942), 33. Further references are cited in the text.

7. Bakhtin notes that symbols of gambling "were always part of the image system" of carnival symbols: "People from various (hierarchical) positions in life, once crowded around the roulette table, are made equal by the rules of the game and in the face of fortune, chance." Their behavior at the table does not correspond to their behavior in ordinary life, for the atmosphere is there one of sudden changes and reversals, crownings/decrownings: "The stake is similar to a *crisis*: a person feels himself *on the threshold*" of knowledge. *Problems*, 230–31.

8. Brooks, *William Faulkner: The Yoknapatawpha Country*, 275.

9. Reed, *Faulkner's Narrative*, 196.

10. Wesley Morris, *Friday's Footprint: Structuralism and the Articulated Text* (Columbus: Ohio State University Press, 1979), 71–73, 17, 21.

11. Reed, *Faulkner's Narrative*, 190–91.

12. Faulkner, *Lion in the Garden*, 225.

13. Ibid., 140.

14. Sundquist, *Faulkner*, 148. On Isaac's failed "freedom," see also Margaret M. Dunn, "The Illusion of Freedom in *The Hamlet* and *Go Down, Moses*," *American Literature* 57 (1984): 407–23; and Michael Millgate, *The Achievement of William Faulkner* (New York: Random House, 1966), 201–14.

15. Myra Jehlen, *Class and Character in Faulkner's South* (New York: Columbia University Press, 1976), 97–132.

16. Faulkner, *Lion in the Garden*, 48.

17. Brooks, *William Faulkner: The Yoknapatawpha Country*, 278. See also David

Williams, *Faulkner's Women: The Myth and the Muse* (Montreal: McGill-Queen's University Press, 1977), for discussion of the strengths of Faulkner's women.

18. Although Gavin does not appear in *Absalom, Absalom!*, Samuel Worsham Beauchamp in *Go Down, Moses* was originally named Henry Coldfield Sutpen, a grandson of a slave named Rosa Sutpen. Furthermore, the character of Isaac seemingly evolved from Quentin Compson, who was Faulkner's original protagonist in "Lion," "The Old People," "A Bear Hunt," and "A Justice." Sundquist, *Faulkner*, 131; and Blotner, *Faulkner*, 1040.

19. Brooks, *William Faulkner: The Yoknapatawpha Country*, 194, 197–98.

20. Sundquist, *Faulkner*, 131–32, 149.

21. As Morris observes, in *Go Down, Moses* "the complex structure of failed and successful interpretations" allows us to learn from the characters' limitations in each story; we may thus "achieve a sense of belonging" through participation in language. *Friday's Footprint*, 10–11.

22. Faulkner, *Lion in the Garden*, 206.

Bibliography

Anderson, Quentin. *The American Henry James*. New Brunswick: Rutgers University Press, 1957.

Bakhtin, Mikhail. *The Dialogic Imagination: Four Essays*. Edited and with an Introduction by Michael Holquist. Translated by Caryl Emerson and Michael Holquist. Austin: University of Texas Press, 1981.

————. *Problems of Dostoevsky's Poetics*. Translated by Caryl Emerson. Introduction by Wayne C. Booth. Theory and History of Literature, vol. 8. Minneapolis: University of Minnesota Press, 1983.

Barker, Wendy. *Lunacy of Light: Emily Dickinson and the Experience of Metaphor*. Carbondale: University of Southern Illinois Press, 1981.

Bauer, Dale M. *Feminist Dialogics: A Theory of Failed Community*. Albany: State University of New York Press, 1987.

Baxter, Annette K. "Independence vs. Isolation: Hawthorne and James on the Problem of the Artist." *Nineteenth Century Fiction* 10 (1955): 225–31.

Beebe, Maurice. *Ivory Towers and Sacred Founts: The Artist as Hero in Fiction from Goethe to Joyce*. New York: New York University Press, 1964.

Benert, Annette Larson. "Dialogical Discourse in 'The Jolly Corner': The Entrepreneur as Language and Image." *Henry James Review* 8 (Winter 1987): 116–25.

Bercovitch, Sacvan. *The Puritan Origins of the American Self*. New Haven: Yale University Press, 1975.

Berthoff, Warner. *A Literature Without Qualities*. Berkeley and Los Angeles: University of California Press, 1979.

Bewley, Marius. *The Complex Fate: Hawthorne, Henry James, and Some Other American Writers*. London: Chatto and Windus, 1952. New York: Gordian Press, 1967.

————. *The Eccentric Design: Form in the Classic American Novel*. New York: Columbia University Press, 1959.

Bialostosky, Don H. "Dialogics as an Art of Discourse in Literary Criticism." *PMLA* 101 (October 1986): 788–97.

Bloom, Harold. *The Anxiety of Influence: A Theory of Poetry*. New York: Oxford University Press, 1973.

Blotner, Joseph. *Faulkner: A Biography*. 2 vols. New York: Random House, 1974.

Booth, Wayne C. *Critical Understanding: The Powers and Limits of Pluralism*. Chicago: University of Chicago Press, 1979.

————. "LITCOMP: Some Rhetoric Addressed to Crypto-Rhetoricians about a Rhetorical Solution to a Rhetorical Problem." In *Composition and Literature:*

Bridging the Gap, edited by Winifred Bryan Horner, 57–80. Chicago: University of Chicago Press, 1983.

———. "A New Strategy for Establishing a Truly Democratic Criticism." *Daedalus* 112 (Summer 1983): 193–214.

Booth, Wayne C., M. H. Abrams, and J. Hillis Miller. "The Limits of Pluralism." *Critical Inquiry* 3 (Spring 1977): 407–47.

Brady, Kristin. "Hawthorne's Editor/Narrator: The Voice of Interdeterminacy." *CEA Critic* 47 (Summer 1985): 27–38.

Branch, Watson. "The Deeper Psychology: James's Legacy from Hawthorne." *Arizona Quarterly* 40 (Spring 1984): 67–74.

Brodhead, Richard H. "Hawthorne among the Realists: The Case of Howells." In *American Realism: New Essays,* edited by Eric J. Sundquist, 25–41. Baltimore: Johns Hopkins University Press, 1982.

Bromwich, David. "The Genealogy of Disinterestedness." *Raritan* 1 (Spring 1982): 62–92.

Brooks, Cleanth. "The Narrative Structure of *Absalom, Absalom!*" *Georgia Review* 29 (1975): 366–94.

———. *William Faulkner: The Yoknapatawpha Country.* New Haven: Yale University Press, 1963.

———. *William Faulkner: Toward Yoknapatawpha and Beyond.* New Haven: Yale University Press, 1978.

Bruffee, Kenneth. "Collaborative Learning: Some Practical Models." *College English* 34 (February 1973): 634–43.

———. "Liberal Education and the Social Justification of Belief." *Liberal Education* 68 (Summer 1982): 95–114.

———. *A Short Course in Writing.* 2d ed. Cambridge, Mass.: Winthrop Publishers, 1980.

———. "Writing and Reading as Collaborative or Social Acts: The Argument from Kuhn and Vygotsky." *Proceedings of the Skidmore Conference on Writing and Thinking.* Urbana: National Council of Teachers of English, 1983.

Buitenhuis, Peter. "Henry James on Hawthorne." *New England Quarterly* 32 (June 1959): 207–25.

Burde, Edgar J. "*The Ambassadors* and the Double Vision of Henry James." *Essays in Literature* 4 (Spring 1977): 59–77.

Cargill, Oscar. "*The Ambassadors*: A New View." *PMLA* 75 (1960): 439–52.

Collins, Carvel. "Faulkner at the University of Mississippi." In *William Faulkner: Early Prose and Poetry,* compiled and edited by Carvel Collins, 3–38. Boston: Atlantic Monthly Press, 1962.

Conn, Peter. *The Divided Mind: Ideology and Imagination in America, 1898–1917.* Cambridge: Cambridge University Press, 1983.

Coughlan, Robert. "The Private World of William Faulkner." *Life* 35 (28 September 1953): 118–36.

Cowie, Alexander. *The Rise of the American Novel.* New York: American Books, 1948.

Cowley, Malcolm, ed. *The Faulkner-Cowley File: Letters and Memories, 1944–1962.* New York: Viking, 1966.

———. Introduction to *The Portable Faulkner.* New York: Viking, 1946.

————. "William Faulkner Revisited." *Saturday Review,* 14 April 1945: 13–16.

Crews, Frederick C. *The Tragedy of Manners: Moral Drama in the Later Novels of Henry James.* New Haven: Yale University Press, 1957.

Dunn, Margaret M. "The Illusion of Freedom in *The Hamlet* and *Go Down Moses.*" *American Literature* 57 (1984): 407–23.

Edel, Leon. *Henry James.* 5 vols. New York: Avon, 1972.

————. Introduction to *Henry James: Selected Fiction.* New York: E. P. Dutton, 1953.

Elliott, Emory. *Revolutionary Writers: Literature and Authority in the New Republic, 1725–1810.* New York: Oxford University Press, 1982.

Emerson, Caryl. "The Outer Word and Inner Speech: Bakhtin, Vygotsky, and the Internalization of Language," *Critical Inquiry* 10 (December 1983): 245–64.

————. "The Tolstoy Connection in Bakhtin." *PMLA* 100 (1985): 68–80.

Faulkner, William. *Absalom, Absalom!* New York: Random House, 1936.

————. *Essays, Speeches, and Public Letters.* Edited by James B. Meriwether. New York: Random House, 1965.

————. *Faulkner in the University.* Edited by Frederick L. Gwynn and Joseph Blotner. Charlottesville: University Press of Virginia, 1959.

————. *Go Down, Moses.* New York: Random House, 1942.

————. *The Lion in the Garden: Interviews with William Faulkner, 1926–1962.* Edited by James B. Meriwether and Michael Millgate. Lincoln: University of Nebraska Press, 1968.

————. *The Marble Faun.* Boston: Four Seas Co., 1924. Reprint as *The Marble Faun and A Green Bough.* New York: Random House, 1965.

————. Nobel Prize Award Speech. In *The Faulkner Reader.* New York: Random House, 1954.

————. *Vision in Spring.* Edited by Judith Sensibar. Austin: University of Texas Press, 1984.

Fish, Stanley. *Is There a Text in This Class?: The Authority of Interpretive Communities.* Cambridge, Mass.: Harvard University Press, 1980.

————. "A Reply to Eugene Goodheart." *Daedalus* 112 (Summer 1983): 233–37.

————. "Transmuting the Lump: *Paradise Lost,* 1942–1982." In *Literature and History: Theoretical Problems and Russian Case Studies,* edited by Gary Saul Morson, 33–56. Stanford: Stanford University Press, 1986.

Fulwiler, Toby, and Art Young, eds. *Language Connections: Writing and Reading across the Curriculum.* Urbana: National Council of Teachers of English, 1982.

Fussell, Edwin. "Hawthorne, James, and the 'Common Doom.'" *American Quarterly* 10 (1958): 441–49.

Garrett, George P., Jr. "An Examination of the Poetry of William Faulkner." *Princeton University Library Chronicle* 18 (Spring 1957): 124–35. Reprint in *William Faulkner: Four Decades of Criticism,* edited by Linda Welsheimer Wagner, 44–54. Ypsilanti: Michigan State University Press, 1973.

Gollin, Rita. "Hawthorne and the Anxiety of Aesthetic Response." *Centennial Review* 28–29 (Fall–Winter 1984): 94–104.

Hagopian, John. "The Biblical Background of Faulkner's *Absalom, Absalom!*" *CEA Critic* 36, no. 2 (1974): 22–24.

Hawthorne, Nathaniel. Preface to *The Blithedale Romance,* by Nathaniel Hawthorne. Edited by Seymour Gross and Rosalie Murphy. New York: Norton,
1978.

————. "Rappaccini's Daughter." In *The Complete Novels and Selected Tales of
Nathaniel Hawthorne,* edited by Norman Holmes Pearson. 1937. Reprint. New
York: Modern Library, 1965.

Howard, Roy J. *Three Faces of Hermeneutics.* Berkeley and Los Angeles: University
of California Press, 1982.

Ian, Marcia. "Consecrated Diplomacy and the Concretion of Self." *Henry James
Review* 7 (Fall 1985): 27–33.

————. "The Elaboration of Privacy in *The Wings of the Dove.*" *ELH* 51 (Spring
1984): 107–36.

Ilacqua, Alma A. "Faulkner's *Absalom, Absalom!*: An Aesthetic Projection of the
Religious Sense of Beauty." *Ball State University Forum* 21, no. 2 (1980): 34–41.

Irwin, John. *Doubling and Incest/Repetition and Revenge: A Speculative Reading of
Faulkner.* Baltimore: Johns Hopkins University Press, 1975.

Isle, Walter. *Experiments in Form: Henry James's Novels, 1896–1901.* Cambridge,
Mass.: Harvard University Press, 1968.

James, Henry. *The Ambassadors.* New York: Harper's, 1902, 1948.

————. *The American Scene.* London: Chapman and Hall, 1907. Reprint. Edited by
Leon Edel. Bloomington: Indiana University Press, 1968.

————. "The Art of Fiction." In *The Portable Henry James,* rev. edition, edited by
Morton Dauwen Zabel. New York: Viking/Penguin, 1979.

————. *The Art of the Novel.* Edited and with an Introduction by R. P. Blackmur.
New York: Scribner's, 1934, 1962.

————. *The Golden Bowl.* New York: Scribner's, 1904; New York: Penguin, 1972.

————. *Hawthorne.* English Men of Letters Series. London: Macmillan, 1879;
Ithaca: Cornell University Press, 1956.

————. "Hawthorne." *Library of the World's Best Literature.* 30 vols. Edited by
Charles Dudley Wagner. Vol. 12: 7053–61. New York: R. S. Peale and J. A.
Hill, 1896–97.

————. "Hawthorne's French and Italian Journals." *Nation,* 14 March 1872: 172–73.

————. "Ivan Turgenev's Virgin Soil." *Nation,* 26 April 1877. Reprint in James,
Literary Reviews and Essays on American, English and French Literature, edited
by Albert Mordell, 190–97. New York: Grove Press, 1957.

————. *The Letters of Henry James.* 2 vols. Edited by Percy Lubbock. New York:
Scribner's, 1920.

————. "The Papers." In James, *The Better Sort.* New York: Scribner's, 1903.

James, William. *The Letters of William James.* 2 vols. Edited by Henry James.
Boston: Atlantic Monthly Press, 1920.

Jehlen, Myra. *Class and Character in Faulkner's South.* New York: Columbia University Press, 1976.

Knoepflmacher, U. C. " 'O Rare for Strether!': *Antony and Cleopatra* and *The
Ambassadors.*" *Nineteenth Century Fiction* 19 (1964–65): 333–44.

Kohler, Dayton. "William Faulkner and the Social Conscience." *College English* 2
(December 1949): 119–27.

Krook, Dorothea. *The Ordeal of Consciousness in Henry James*. Cambridge: Cambridge University Press, 1967.

Leitch, Vincent. *American Literary Criticism from the Thirties to the Eighties*. New York: Columbia University Press, 1988.

Lewis, R. W. B. *The American Adam*. Chicago: University of Chicago Press, 1955.

Lubbock, Percy. *The Craft of Fiction*. New York: Viking, 1957.

Lukacs, Georg. *History and Class Consciousness*. Translated by Rodney Livingstone. Cambridge, Mass.: MIT Press, 1971.

Mailloux, Steven. "Rhetorical Hermeneutics." *Critical Inquiry* 11 (June 1985): 620–42.

Maimon, Elaine. "Maps and Genres: Exploring Connections in the Arts and Sciences." In *Composition and Literature: Bridging the Gap,* edited by Winifred Bryan Horner, 110–25. Chicago: University of Chicago Press, 1983.

Maimon, Elaine, et al. *Writing in the Arts and Sciences*. Boston: Little, Brown, 1984.

Martin, Terence. *Nathaniel Hawthorne*. Twayne United States Authors Series, no. 75. New York: Twayne, 1965.

Marx, Leo. *The Machine in the Garden*. New York: Oxford University Press, 1964.

Matthiessen, F. O. *American Renaissance*. New York: Oxford University Press, 1941.

———. *Henry James: The Major Phase*. New York: Oxford University Press, 1944.

Mellow, James B. "Hawthorne's Divided Genius." *Wilson Quarterly* 6 (Spring 1982): 162–74.

Melville, Herman. "Hawthorne and His Mosses." *New York Literary World*, 17 and 24 August 1850. Reprint in *The Piazza Tales and Other Prose Pieces,* Vol. 9 of *The Writings of Herman Melville,* edited by Harrison Hayford et al., 239–53. 10 vols. Evanston and Chicago: Northwestern University Press and The Newberry Library, 1987.

Michelson, Bruce. "Hawthorne's House of Three Stories." *New England Quarterly* 57 (June 1984): 163–83.

Millgate, Michael. *The Achievement of William Faulkner*. New York: Random House, 1966.

Minter, David. *The Interpreted Design as a Structural Principle in American Prose*. New Haven: Yale University Press, 1969.

Morozova, Tatiana. "Faulkner Reads Dostoevsky." *Soviet Literature* 12 (1981): 176–79.

Morris, Wesley. *Friday's Footprint: Structuralism and the Articulated Text*. Columbus: Ohio State University Press, 1979.

Morson, Gary Saul. "The Heresiarch of *Meta*." *PTL: A Journal for Descriptive Poetics and Theory of Literature* 3 (1978): 407–27.

Mueller-Vollmer, Kurt. *The Hermeneutics Reader: Texts of the German Tradition from the Enlightenment to the Present*. New York: Continuum, 1985.

Nettels, Elsa. "*The Ambassadors* and the Sense of the Past." *Modern Language Quarterly* 31 (June 1970): 220–35.

Norrman, Ralf. *The Insecure World of Henry James's Fiction: Intensity and Ambiguity*. London: Macmillan, 1982.

Norton, Anne. *Alternative Americas: A Reading of Antebellum Political Culture*. Chicago: University of Chicago Press, 1986.

Oates, Stephen. *William Faulkner: The Man and the Artist, a Biography*. New York: Harper & Row, 1987.

O'Connor, William Van. "The Wilderness Theme in Faulkner's 'The Bear.'" *Accent* 13 (1953): 12–20. Reprint in *William Faulkner: Three Decades of Criticism*, edited by Frederick J. Hoffman and Olga Vickery, 322–30. East Lansing: Michigan State University Press, 1960.

Ong, Walter J., S. J. *The Presence of the Word: Some Prolegomena for Cultural and Religious History*. New Haven: Yale University Press, 1967.

Palmer, Richard E. *Hermeneutics: Interpretation Theory in Schleiermacher, Dilthey, Heidegger, and Gadamer*. Evanston: Northwestern University Press, 1969.

Perry, Ralph Barton. *The Thought and Character of Henry James*. 2 vols. Boston: Little, Brown, 1935.

Poirier, Richard. *The Comic Sense of Henry James*. New York: Oxford University Press, 1967.

———. *A World Elsewhere: The Place of Style in American Literature*. New York: Oxford University Press, 1966.

Porter, Carolyn. *Seeing and Being: The Plight of the Participant Observer in Emerson, James, Adams, and Faulkner*. Middletown, Conn.: Wesleyan University Press, 1981.

Rahv, Philip. "The Dark Lady of Salem." *Partisan Review* 8 (September–October 1941): 362–81.

Reed, Joseph. *Faulkner's Narrative*. New Haven: Yale University Press, 1973.

Reising, Russell J. *The Unusable Past*. New York: Methuen Books, 1986.

Ricoeur, Paul. *The Conflict of Interpretations: Essays in Hermeneutics*. Edited by Don Ihde. Evanston: Northwestern University Press, 1974.

Rimmon, Shlomith. *The Concept of Ambiguity—The Example of James*. Chicago: University of Chicago Press, 1977.

Rorty, Richard. *Philosophy and the Mirror of Nature*. Princeton: Princeton University Press, 1979.

Royce, Josiah. *The Problem of Christianity*. 1918. Reprint. Chicago: University of Chicago Press, 1968.

Runyon, Harry. "Faulkner's Poetry." *Faulkner Studies* 3 (Summer–Autumn 1954): 23–29.

Salmon, Rachel. "Naming and Knowing in Henry James's 'The Beast in the Jungle': The Hermeneutics of a Sacred Text." *Orbis Litterarum* 36 (1981): 302–22.

Samuels, Charles Thomas. *The Ambiguity of Henry James*. Urbana: University of Illinois Press, 1971.

Schneider, Daniel J. *The Crystal Cage: Adventures of the Imagination in the Fiction of Henry James*. Lawrence: Regents Press of Kansas, 1978.

Sears, Sallie. *The Negative Imagination: Form and Perspective in the Novels of Henry James*. Ithaca: Cornell University Press, 1968.

Segal, Ora. *The Lucid Reflector: The Observer in Henry James's Fiction*. New Haven: Yale University Press, 1969.

Seltzer, Mark. *Henry James and the Art of Power*. Ithaca: Cornell University Press, 1984.

Sensibar, Judith. *The Origins of Faulkner's Art*. Austin: University of Texas Press, 1984.

Sicker, Philip. *Love and the Quest for Identity in the Fiction of Henry James*. Princeton: Princeton University Press, 1980.

Slatoff, Walter J. *Quest for Failure: A Study of William Faulkner*. Ithaca: Cornell University Press, 1960; Westport, Conn.: Greenwood Press, 1972.

Stein, Paul S. "Ike McCaslin: Traumatized in a Hawthornian Wilderness." *Southern Literary Journal* 12 (1980): 69–70.

Stewart, Randall. *American Literature and Christian Doctrine*. Baton Rouge: Louisiana State University Press, 1958.

Stewart, Susan. "Shouts on the Street: Bakhtin's Anti-Linguistics." *Critical Inquiry* 10 (December 1983): 265–82.

Strandberg, Victor. "Faulkner's God: A Jamesian Perspective." In Strandberg's *A Faulkner Overview: Six Perspectives*, 89–116. Port Washington, N.Y.: Kennikat Press, 1981.

Sundquist, Eric J. *Faulkner: The House Divided*. Baltimore: Johns Hopkins University Press, 1983.

Tanner, Tony. Introduction to *Hawthorne*, by Henry James. London: Macmillan, 1967.

Tick, Stanley. "The Unity of *Go Down, Moses*." *Twentieth Century Literature* 8 (1962): 67–73. Reprint in *William Faulkner: Four Decades of Criticism*, edited by Linda Welsheimer Wagner, 327–34. East Lansing: Michigan State University Press, 1973.

Todorov, Tzvetan. *Poetique de la prose*. Paris: Seuil, 1971.

———. *Symbolism and Interpretation*. Translated by Catherine Porter. Ithaca: Cornell University Press, 1982.

Vickery, Olga. *The Novels of William Faulkner*. Rev. edition. Baton Rouge: Louisiana State University Press, 1964.

———. "William Faulkner and the Figure in the Carpet." *South Atlantic Quarterly* 76 (Autumn 1977): 479–96. (First published in *South Atlantic Quarterly* 63 [Summer 1964]: 318–35.)

Waggoner, Hyatt. *William Faulkner: From Jefferson to the World*. Lexington: University of Kentucky Press, 1959.

Ward, J. A. "Henry James and the Nature of Evil." *Twentieth Century Literature* 6 (July 1960): 65–69.

Warner, John. " 'In View of Other Matters': The Religious Dimension of *The Ambassadors*." *Essays in Literature* 4 (Spring 1977): 78–94.

Weisenfarth, Joseph. *Henry James and the Dramatic Analogy*. New York: Fordham University Press, 1963.

Weisgerber, Jean. *Faulkner and Dostoevsky: Influence and Confluence*. Translated by Dean McWilliams. Athens: Ohio University Press, 1974.

Williams, David. *Faulkner's Women: The Myth and the Muse*. Montreal: McGill-Queen's University Press, 1977.

Williams, Raymond. *Keywords: A Vocabulary of Culture and Society*. New York: Oxford University Press, 1979.

Yeazell, Ruth Bernard. *Language and Knowledge in the Late Novels of Henry James*. Chicago: University of Chicago Press, 1976.

Ziff, Larzar. *Puritanism in America: New Culture in a New World*. New York: Viking, 1973.

Index

Abrams, M. H., 197 n.40
Adams, Henry, 198 n.8; *The Education of Henry Adams,* 12
Ambiguity, xi, 41, 61, 65, 136–39, 142, 145, 147, 171–72, 198 n.17; mimetic and nonmimetic, 137
Amerigo. *See* James, Henry: *The Golden Bowl,* Prince Amerigo
Anderson, Quentin, 26
Antinomian Controversy, the, 4
Archer, Isabel, *See* James, Henry: *The Portrait of a Lady*
Arnold, Matthew, 198 n.7
Avoidance, 61, 64–65, 110
Aylmer. *See* Hawthorne, Nathaniel: *The Birthmark*

Bakhtin, Mikhail, 16–21, 23, 44, 55, 64, 74, 78, 84, 86–88, 100, 148, 157, 209 n.7; and the canon, 195 n.28; and feminist readings, 195 n.28; and practical criticism, 196 n.38; theory of language of, 18; theory of novel genre of, 17–18
—, works:
 "Author and Hero in Aesthetic Activity," 19
 The Dialogic Imagination, 17
 "Epic and Novel," 17
 Problems of Dostoevsky's Poetics, 17
Barker, Wendy, 13, 16
Barlow, Joel, 6
Barrace, Miss. *See* James, Henry: *The Ambassadors*
Bartram, May. *See* James, Henry: *The Beast in the Jungle*
Bauer, Dale M., 195 n.28
Baxter, Annette K., 199 n.21
Beauchamp, Butch (Samuel Worsham). *See* Faulkner, William: *Go Down, Moses*

Beauchamp, Fonsiba. *See* Faulkner, William: *Go Down, Moses*
Beauchamp, Henry. *See* Faulkner, William: *Go Down, Moses*
Beauchamp, Hubert Fitzhubert. *See* Faulkner, William: *Go Down, Moses*
Beauchamp, James (Tennie's Jim). *See* Faulkner, William: *Go Down, Moses*
Beauchamp, Lucas. *See* Faulkner, William: *Go Down, Moses*
Beauchamp, Mollie. *See* Faulkner, William: *Go Down, Moses*
Beauchamp, Sophonsiba. *See* Faulkner, William: *Go Down, Moses*
Beebe, Maurice, 199 n.21
Benert, Annette Larson, 195 n.28
Bercovitch, Sacvan, 6
Berthoff, Warner, 5
Bialostosky, Don H., 197 n.40
Bible, the, 1, 4, 111
Bilham, Mr. *See* James, Henry: *The Ambassadors*
Blackmur, R. P., 44–45
Blake, William, 129
Blotner, Joseph, 10–11, 34–35
Bon, Charles. *See* Faulkner, William: *Absalom, Absalom!*
Bon, Charles Etienne St. Valery. *See* Faulkner, William: *Absalom, Absalom!*
Bond, Jim. *See* Faulkner, William: *Absalom, Absalom!*
Booth, Wayne C., 196–97 n.40
Brackenridge, Hugh Henry, 6
Branch, Watson, 199 n.19
Breit, Harvey, 51
Brodhead, Richard H., 199 n.16
Bromwich, David, 25, 198 n.7
Brooks, Cleanth, 104, 154, 188, 206 n.13
Brown, Charles Brockden, 6

Bruffee, Kenneth, 197 n.40
Buitenhuis, Peter, 9
Bundren, Cash. *See* Faulkner, William: *As I Lay Dying*
Bundren, Darl. *See* Faulkner, William: *As I Lay Dying*
Bundren, Jewel. *See* Faulkner, William: *As I Lay Dying*

Canon, literary, x, 3; and novel as anticanonical, 17; reform, 3, 12, 196–97 n.40
Carnivalization, 17, 87, 157, 190
Castledean, Lady. *See* James, Henry: *The Golden Bowl*
Celebrityhood, 33, 39–44
Characters: as doubles, 19–20, 91, 98, 110; as *ficelles*, xii, xvi, 21, 55–58, 61, 65–66, 70, 73–83; free speech of, 19–20; as hearers and tellers, 84–85, 87–92, 101; as hermeneutic models, 21, 158; interests and designs of, 23–25; minority, 21, 82, 98, 73–83, 104–5, 159–62, 164–65; as privileged over plot, 42
Chase, Richard, 14
Chopin, Kate: *The Awakening*, 195 n.28
Civil War, the, 28, 91, 98–99, 106, 177
Clytie. *See* Faulkner, William: *Absalom, Absalom!*
Coldfield, Ellen. *See* Faulkner, William: *Absalom, Absalom!*
Coldfield, Rosa. *See* Faulkner, William: *Absalom, Absalom!*
Collaborative learning, 197 n.40
Community, 7, 14, 49–52, 63, 71, 77, 82, 91–93, 98, 100, 106, 113, 120–21, 123, 134–37, 147–48, 158–61, 169, 186–92; American diversity of, 15, 86–87; artist's role in, 21, 28–34, 37–39, 139; of authors, narrators, characters, and readers, xviii, 26, 44, 102–3; created through imagination, 72; created through negativity, 63; defined differently for James and Faulkner, xi–xii, defined in the American novel, 21; and disinterest, 25, 55; as failed in the South, 98; false design of, 104; of family, xv, 109, 160; Faulkner's definition of freedom within, 191–92;

of hearers and tellers, 97; individual and, 14, 20, 49–52, 91; James's and Faulkner's new models of, xii, 14; philosophical, ix; racism and, 150, 156, 163; reification of, 14; of tales, 149; through metaphor, 88; of voice, 16, 100–103, 113, women and, 104–5, 188–89
Compson, Benjy. *See* Faulkner, William: *The Sound and the Fury*
Compson, Caddy. *See* Faulkner, William: *Absalom, Absalom!*
Compson, General. *See* Faulkner, William: *Absalom, Absalom!*
Compson, Quentin. *See* Faulkner, William: *Absalom, Absalom*
Conn, Peter, 39
Conrad, Joseph, 105; *Heart of Darkness*, 192
Conversational metaphor: defined, 127. *See also* Dialogics
Cotton, John, 4–5
Coughlan, Robert, 202 n.65
Cowie, Alexander, 199 n.19
Cowley, Malcolm, 29, 43
Craft: James's and Faulkner's notions of, x–xi, 44–50
Crane, Hart, 27
Crews, Frederick, 62, 67, 81, 121, 204 n.24
Croy, Kate. *See* James, Henry: *The Wings of the Dove*

Deconstruction, 1, 196 n.40
Densher, Merton. *See* James, Henry: *The Wings of the Dove*
"Design," 57, 65–68, 70, 73, 77, 79–80, 85–86, 89, 108–12, 119–34, 136, 138, 144–45, 149–53, 155–57, 173, 179–81, 184–86, 188, 191–92, 198 n.8, 202 n.58; authorial design-as-antidesign, 18–21, 37, 46–48, 103, 114; of celebrityhood, 39; characters as antidesigns, 42; counteracted by negativity, avoidance, ambiguity, 55, 61–65; craft as antidote to, 44; deflected by the *ficelle*, 75, destroys community, 123; dual meanings of, 23–24; economic sense of, 61; of formulaic plot, 41; of "helping," 59; innocence and, 24–25, 96, 104, 152; as keyboard, 22–26; and the machine, 8–13; overcome by

storytelling, 87; or racism, 150, 156, 161, 163; responsibilities of, 59; of the South, 96, 99, 203 n.86; Thomas Sutpen's, 25, 91–95, 98, 103–10, 113, 198 n.8, 205 n.6; of university knowledge, 106–7. *See also* Interest and design; and entries under Faulkner, William, and James, Henry

de Vionnet, Jeanne. *See* James, Henry: *The Golden Bowl*

de Vionnet, Marie. *See* James, Henry: *The Golden Bowl*

Dewey, John, 1, 193 n.3

Dialogics: addressing "the other," 12–13, 15–16, 18, 21, 42, 44, 55, 80, 82, 98, 101, 120, 134, 141, 143–44, 147–48, 153, 161, 175–80, 188–92, 195 n.28; and composition theory, 196–97 n.40; as emphasis in contemporary theory, 21; and the *ficelle*, 73–78, 130–31, 146; and metadesigns, 40, 195 n.28; of metaphor, 88; and negativity, 139; and pedagogy, 196–97 n.40; and rhetoric, 197 n.40; and structure, 143; in theory of Mikhail Bakhtin, 16–21; and voice over vision, 47, 166, 155, 167–69, 187–92; and women, 82, 98. *See also* Bakhtin, Mikhail; Polyphony; Storytelling

Dialogue, 41, 79; between James and Faulkner, x; versus design, xvi, 208 n.15; as healing, 16; of hearing and telling, xiii, 85; as hermeneutic model, 2; of interest and design, 22; and lack of closure, 18–21; of literary critics, xi; narrators engaged in, xvi; promoted by *ficelles*, xvi, 78–79. *See also Ficelles*

Dickinson, Emily, 13, 16

Dilthey, Wilhelm, 193 n.1

Disinterest, 27, 57–58, 62; as antidote to design, 25–26, 198 n.7; as model for community, 25, 55

Doom. *See* Faulkner, William: *Go Down, Moses,* Ikkemotubbe

Dos Passos, John, 51

Dostoevsky, Fyodor, 17–21, 80, 86, 196 n.39, 202 n.58; *The Brothers Karamozov,* 196 n.39

Doubling, 19–20, 91, 98, 110

Dunn, Margaret M., 209 n.14

Dwight, Timothy, 6

Edel, Leon, 9–10, 20, 24, 26–27, 39–40, 53, 196 n.39, 202 n.49, 209 n.5

Edmonds, Cass. *See* Faulkner, William: *Go Down, Moses*

Edmonds, Mary McCaslin. *See* Faulkner, William: *Go Down, Moses*

Edmonds, Roth. *See* Faulkner, William: *Go Down, Moses*

Edmonds, Zack. *See* Faulkner, William: *Go Down, Moses*

Eliot, T. S., 41

Elliott, Emory, 3, 6–7, 12

Emerson, Caryl, 196 n.38

Emerson, Ralph Waldo, 6–7, 13–14

Epistemology, x, 22, 27, 75–76, 99, 104, 127, 146–47, 161, 178, 196 n.40, 205 n.2. *See also* Knowledge; Ocular metaphor; Problem of knowledge; Rorty, Richard; "Seeing"

Failure: and Faulkner's poetry, 35–36, 40, 60; and great writers, 51, 200 n.26; of James as playwright, 40–42; as theme and structure, 7, 30, 44, 71–72, 92, 97, 103, 113, 129–30, 167–69, 176, 178, 180–81 184–86, 189–92, 203 n.86; as victory, xii–xviii, 50–52, 58, 77, 81–82

Fathers, Sam. *See* Faulkner, William: *Go Down, Moses*

Faulkner, William: ambivalence toward Old World and Puritan traditions of, 3–8; and antidesign, 48; carpentry metaphor of, 7, 48; celebrityhood of, 39–42, and the Civil war, 28, 177; and closure, 3; definition of freedom within community, 191–92; and direct presence in fiction of, 102–3; and Dostoevsky, 196 n.39, 202 n.58; and experiments in form of, 36–37; and failure, 7, 34–40, 203 n.86; and freedom, 49–52; and hermeneutics, 1, 12, 198 n.8, 205 n.4; as humanistic novelist, 3, 48; and idea of character, 20, 42–43, 202 n.58; influence of Hawthorne upon, 29–30, 34–39, 198 n.8, 199 n.16, 200 nn. 24–25; influence of Henry James, Sr., upon, 27;

Faulkner, William (continued)
    influence of William James upon, 27;
    interest and design in, 22–26;
    interviews of, 20, 48–52, 181, 185, 196
    n.39; and lying, 48–49; metaphors of
    compared to James's, 152; and modern
    America, 10–11, 43–44; as moralist, 20,
    26–27; as poet, 30–31, 34–37, 40, 60,
    201 n.37; and reader's role as teller,
    102, 195 n.28; and revision, 44, 48–52;
    and the role of the artist, 20, 28–30,
    37–39, 49–52; southernness of, 26, 51;
    speeches of, 20; and technology,
    43–44; and theoretical context of
    dialogics, 16, 195 n.28, 209 n.7; and
    theory of art, 11, 196 n.39; and Tolstoy,
    202 n.58; travels abroad of, 49; World
    War I service of, 48
—, works:
    Absalom, Absalom!, ix, xii–xiv, 119, 150,
        168; avoidance in, 84; Charles Bon,
        xii, 85, 89–90, 94–101, 105, 107–11,
        206 n.12; Charles Etienne St. Valery
        Bon, 202 n.12; Jim Bond, 102, 110,
        113, 206 n.12; Clytie, xii, 100, 102,
        110–12, 206 n.12; Ellen Coldfield,
        105; Rosa Coldfield, 24, 86–91,
        97–98, 101–2, 104–5, 107, 111–12, 206
        n.12; community in, 86–87, 89,
        91–95, 98, 100–106, 109–10, 113;
        compared to The Ambassadors,
        xii–xiv, 53, 84, 97, 101, 103, 107, 110;
        compared to Dostoevsky's novels,
        18–19; compared to The Golden
        Bowl, 84, 119, 124–25, 146; Caddy
        Compson, 24, 110, 205 n.6; General
        Compson, 25, 89, 91, 206 n.12;
        Quentin Compson, xii–xiv, 18, 24,
        84–113, 153, 168, 175, 186, 190, 198 n.8,
        205 n.6, 206 n.12, 209 n.4, 210 n.18;
        conclusion of, 96–97, 99–100, 113;
        demon metaphor in, 86, 97; designs
        summarized by Shreve, 110;
        dialogics of, 85–87, 95–100;
        doubling in, 98, 110; and failure
        theme, xiv, 84, 90, 96, 98–99, 100,
        103, 113; Faulkner's direct presence
        in, 102–3; ghost metaphor in,
        88–90, 97; hearers and tellers in,
        84–85, 87–92, 94–100, 101; Millie

    Jones, 106; Wash Jones, 92, 95,
        105–6, 206 n.12; the lawyer as model
        for design in, 86, 106–8; Luster, 206
        n.12; Shreve McCannon, xii, 18,
        84–90, 95–110, 146, 175, 205 n.2, 206
        n.12, 209 n.4; names in, 206 n.12;
        narrators of, 100–103, 205 nn. 3, 8;
        negativity in, 84, 111; ocular
        metaphor in, 205 n.6; outline of,
        101–3; role of reader in, 85–86, 98,
        102–3, 113; role of women and blacks
        in, 98, 104–5; storytelling in,
        84–100, 103, 113; structure of, 53,
        84–86, 100–103; Henry Sutpen,
        89–90, 97–101, 107–12, 186, 206 n.12;
        Judith Sutpen, 89, 100, 110–11, 205
        nn. 6–7, 206 n.12; Thomas Sutpen,
        xii, 13–14, 24–25, 85–93, 91–95, 96,
        101, 104–6, 109, 111, 113, 119, 124–25,
        150, 167, 185, 206 n.12; Sutpen's
        design in, 25, 91–95, 98, 103–10, 113,
        198 n.8, 205 n.6; typology of, 102;
        voice over vision in, 109–10, 205 n.6
    "The American Dream: What Has
        Happened to It?," 43
    As I Lay Dying, 30, 43, 48, 87, 100, 175;
        Cash Bundren, 48; Darl Bundren, 87,
        100, 153, 175; Jewel Bundren, 30; the
        Rev. Mr. Whitfield, 30
    "A Bear Hunt," 210 n.18
    "The Bear," 12, 38, 152, 162, 165–68, 170–85
    "Delta Autumn," 152, 156–57, 166, 170, 180,
        183–87, 191
    "That Evening Sun," 10
    "The Fire and the Hearth," 151, 153, 158–65,
        187–89
    "Go Down, Moses," 152, 162–63, 183,
        187–92
    Go Down, Moses, ix, xiv–xviii, 10, 149–91;
        and addressing "the other," 158;
        ambiguity in, 171–72; ambivalence
        toward technology in, 11; Butch
        (Samuel Worsham) Beauchamp, 162,
        187–88, 190–91; Fonsiba Beauchamp,
        175; Henry Beauchamp, 158; Hubert
        Fitzhubert Beauchamp, xvii, 154–57,
        175, 180; James Beauchamp (Tennie's
        Jim), 184, 188; Lucas Beauchamp, xvii,
        150, 153, 158–62, 165–66, 184, 187;
        Mollie Beauchamp, xvi, xviii, 153,

158–63, 187–92; Sophonsiba Beauchamp, 154–57, 169, 175; comedy of, 156–57, 191; community in, xiv, 158–65, 167, 169–70, 173, 178, 181–83, 186–88, 191–92; compared to Dostoevsky's novels, 18–19; compared to *The Golden Bowl*, xiv–xviii; designs in, 149–53, 155, 158, 161, 167, 171, 173, 179–81, 184–86, 188, 191–92; de Spain, Major, 173; dialogics of, 158, 168–69, 175–80, 188–92, 209 n.7; "doing" in, 191; Cass (McCaslin) Edmonds, xvi, 153–54, 158–59, 165, 168–70, 172, 175–79, 184; Mary McCaslin Edmonds, 151; Roth (Carothers) Edmonds, xvii, 151–52, 158, 160, 162, 165, 185–87, 189; Zack Edmonds, 158–59; and epistemology, 161, 178; and failure theme, 150, 152–53, 163, 167–69, 171, 176, 178, 180–81, 184–86, 189–92, 209 n.14; Sam Fathers, 163, 165–69, 171, 173–75, 179–82, 185, 187; gambling theme in, 152, 154–57, 163, 180, 209 n.7; genealogical design in, 150–51, 179; hermeneutics of, 149, 151, 172, 187; historical design in, 150–51, 179; Boon Hogganbeck, 165, 173–75, 180, 182; hunting theme in, 152, 155–57, 160, 163, 165–87, 191; Ikkemotubbe, 165, 179; initiation theme, 168, 170, 172–73, 200 n.25; "interest" in, 156; knowledge, conflicts of, 167; knowledge , as mysterious, 172–73, 176, 178–80, 182; ledger mentality in, 158, 178–79; Lion, 165, 167, 173, 182; Buck (Amodeus) McCaslin, 155–57, 169, 175; Buddy (Theophilus) McCaslin, 155–57, 165, 169, 176; Isaac McCaslin, xv–xvi, 150–54, 157–59, 161, 163, 165–86, 188, 191, 200 n.25, 209 n.14, 210 n.18; L. Q. C. McCaslin, xv–xvi, 24, 149–51, 154, 157–61, 167–69, 171, 179–82, 184–87, 200 n.25, 209 n.5; Mannie, 163; marriage theme in, 152, 155–63, 165, 180, 184, 187; metaphors of, 151–52; moral theme in, 158; narrative structure of, xiv, 20, 84, 103, 149–53, 209 n.4; narrator of, 151, 172, 175, 180; negativity of, 149, 151, 162, 171, 175–76, 178, 180–81, 186, 191; negro spiritual in, xvi,

187–92; Old Ben, 163, 165–67, 170–71, 173–75, 180–81, 192, 200 n.25; openness of, 149–51; personal design in, 150–51, 167, 179; problem of ownership, 171, 176–77, 179, 182; racism as design in, 150, 156, 158, 161, 163–65, 173, 177, 184, 187; Rider, 161–64, 188; role of Indians in, 165–70; role of women and black characters in, 159–62, 164–65, 184–85, 188–91, 209–10 n.17; sexual knowledge in, 179, 182; Gavin Stevens, xv–xviii, 149, 152–55, 162–64, 187–91; suspense by omission in, 154; Tomey's Turl, 154–56; voice over vision in, 161, 168–69, 187; wilderness theme in, 166–87; George Wilkins, 160; Nat Wilkins, 160; Worsham, Miss, 188–91. *See also:* individual story titles, under Faulkner: "The Bear," "Delta Autumn," "The Fire and the Hearth," "Go Down, Moses," "The Old People," "Pantaloon in Black," "Was"

The Hamlet, 43, 149; Flem Snopes, 24

"The Hill," 38

Intruder in the Dust, 189

"The Ivory Tower," 35

A Justice," 210 n.18

Knight's Gambit, 189

"L'après-midi d'un faune," 35

Light in August, 150, 189; the Rev. Gail Hightower, 153

"Lion," 210 n.18

The Marble Faun, 30–31, 34–37

Nobel Prize Award Speech, 10–11, 50, 149

"The Old People," 151–52, 163, 165–70, 210 n.18

"Pantaloon in Black," 152, 157, 160–65, 175, 182

Pylon, 10–11

"A Rose for Emily," 10

Snopes, 43, 189

The Sound and the Fury, 34, 43, 87, 150, 158; Benjy Compson, 87; Caddy Compson, 205 n.6

The Town, 189

"Two Puppets in a Fifth Avenue Store Window," 35

The Unvanquished, xiv, 149

Vision in Spring, 34

—, works (continued)
"Was," xvi, 152–54, 157–59, 162, 166, 175, 184, 191
The Wild Palms, 149
Feminism, 1, 3, 21, 195 n.28, 196 n.40; and hermeneutics, 12–16
Ficelles, xii, xvi, 21, 55–58, 73–83, 96, 130–31, 146–47
Fish, Stanley, 196–97 n.40
Fitzgerald, F. Scott, 40, 198 n.8; *The Great Gatsby,* 12
Freneau, Philip, 6
Frost, Robert, 27
Fulwiler, Toby, 197 n.40
Fussell, Edwin, 200 n.21

Gadamer, Hans-Georg, 193 n.1
Garrett, George P., Jr., 35–36
Gollin, Rita, 199 n.20
Gostrey, Maria. *See* James, Henry: *The Ambassadors*
Grenier, Cynthia, 50–51

Hagopian, John, 111
Hawthorne, Nathaniel, ix, 6–7, 9, 46, 74; characteristic techniques of, 29; and characters' designs on each other, 199 nn. 19–21; and the Civil War, 28; compared to Lambert Strether, 24; compared to Waymarsh, 34; hermeneutics of, 27, 198 n.8; as influence on James and Faulkner, 27–39, 199 nn. 16–21, 200 nn. 24–28, 201 n.34; problems of authority in, 199 n.19; and the Unpardonable Sin, 199 n.19; wilderness theme in, 200 n.25
—, works:
"The Birthmark," 29
The Blithedale Romance, 26, 195 n.28; Miles Coverdale, 29; Preface to, 29, 46; Priscilla, 199 n.19; Zenobia, 199 n.19
Diaries, 32, 34
"Ethan Brand," 38
The House of Seven Gables, 30, 32
The Marble Faun, 30–31, 34–36
Mosses on an Old Manse, 31
Notebooks, 1, 32, 199 n.20
"Rappaccini's Daughter," 24, 38

The Scarlet Letter, 29–32, 201 n.34; Roger Chillingworth, 29; the Rev. Arthur Dimmesdale, 29–30; Pearl, 30
"Young Goodman Brown," 183, 200 n.25
Hawthorne, Sophia Peabody, 31
Hazlitt, William, 198 n.7
Heidegger, Martin, 193 n.1
Hemingway, Ernest, 40, 51
Hermeneutics, 1, 22, 75, 78, 82–85, 100, 111, 114, 143–44, 148–49, 151, 157, 161, 164, 172, 187, 205 n.4; in contemporary theory, 16, 193 n.1; definition of, x; disinterest and, 26; and feminism, 12–16; Hawthorne's concern with, 27; history of, 1, 193 n.1; as moral issue, x; of novel, ix–x, 7, 187; in pedagogy, 196–97 n.40. *See also* Richard, Rorty; and entries under James, Henry, and Faulkner, William
Heteroglossia, 88
Hightower, the Rev. Gail. *See* Faulkner, William: *Light in August*
Hirsch, E. D., 193 n.1
Holquist, Michael, 17
Howard, Roy J., 193 n.1
Howe, Irving, 14
Hutchinson, Anne, 4

Ian, Marcia, 208 n.15
Ibsen, Henrik, 41
Ikkemotubbe. *See* Faulkner, William: *Go Down, Moses*
Ilacqua, Alma A., 205 n.2
"Interest": authorial, 41, 85, 114–19; as cause of design, 24, 55; economic and personal senses of, 23, 56, 115–17; etymology of, 22–23; as keyword, 22–26. *See also* entries under James, Henry, and Faulkner, William
Interest and design, 22, 103–4, 108, 114, 156, dialogue of, 26; economic and personal senses of, 117; problems of, xiii–xviii, 39. *See also* entries under James, Henry, and Faulkner, William
Irwin, John, 205 n.6
Isle, Walter, 41

James, Henry: ambivalence toward Old World and Puritan traditions, 3–8;

architectural metaphor of, 7, 45–46;
and celebrityhood, 39–41; and
characters, 20, 203–4 n.6; and the
Civil War, 28; and closure, 3, 41, 44;
and community, 8, 14; compared to
Lambert Strether, 53–54; craft of, 8–13,
44–50; and failure theme, 7, 71–72;
and the *ficelle,* 73–83; and
hermeneutics, 1, 12, 198 n.8; as
humanistic novelist, 3; influence of
Hawthorne upon, 29–30, 198 n.8, 199
nn. 16–21, 200 n.28, 201 n.34; influence
of Henry James, Sr., upon, 26–27;
interest and design in, 22–26;
international point of view of, 9, 26;
international theme of, 53, 82–83; and
knowledge that comes "too late," 69,
90; metafiction of, 66–67, 195 n.28,
204 n.16; metaphors of compared to
Faulkner's, 152; and modern America,
9; as moralist, 20, 26–27; narrators of,
114, 204 n.13; need to connect with
audience, 41; playwrighting of, 40–42;
prefaces of, 44–47, 51, 54–55, 71, 74–75,
80; and problems of authority, 114;
reading of Russian literature, 196 n.39;
and relationship to William James, 27;
and revision, 44–46; and role of the
artist, 8, 28–29, 69; and "seeing," 45,
65, 126, 131–34, 137; and theoretical
context of dialogics, 16, 195 n.28;
treatment of love, 206–7 n.4, 207–8
n.15; and voice of characters, 47
—, works:
The Ambassadors, ix, xii–xiv, 21, 26, 33,
47, 53–83, 97, 101, 110, 115, 120,
131–32, 143–44; ambiguity in, 65, 69;
avoidance in, 64–65; Miss Barrace,
57, 62, 64–65, 71; Mr. Bilham, 59,
61–62, 64–65, 68–70, 83; characters'
syntax in, 64–65; compared to
Absalom, Absalom!, xii–xiv, 53, 84,
101, 103, 107, 110; compared to
Dostoevsky's novels, 18–19;
composition of, 53–55; conclusion
of, 53–54, 58, 61, 73, 78–83; designs
of characters in, xiii, 57–61, 76;
Jeanne de Vionnet, 76, 204 n.24;
Marie de Vionnet, xii, 56–59, 60–63,

66–70, 72, 75–77, 80–82; economic
metaphors in, 60–61; failure theme
in, xiv, 53–55, 58, 60, 62–63, 67–69,
77, 81–82; feminine versus masculine
values in, 82–83; the *ficelle* in, 73–83;
Gloriani's garden, 69, 71; Maria
Gostrey, xii, 55–58, 61, 63, 65–66, 70,
73–83, 130–31, 147, 188; "interest" in,
55–58, 77; international theme in,
82–83; the "Live" speech of, 69–73;
and "Living" theme, 53, 60, 69–73;
narrator's limitations in, 55, 64; Chad
Newsome, xii, 24, 55–59, 61–63,
65–72, 77, 82, 124; Mrs. Newsome,
xiii, 24, 53, 57, 59, 61, 63, 67–70,
75–78, 81–82, 107; Paris, xiii, 58–60,
62–63, 69, 77; Jim Pocock, 57,
59–60, 62, 70–71; Mamie Pocock,
57, 59, 71, 83; Sarah Pocock, 57, 59,
62–63, 65, 67–70; Preface to, 47,
54–55, 71, 74–75, 80; public versus
private worlds in, 66–67; retreat
from design of, xiii, 57; river scene
of, 68–69; role of women in, 75–83;
"seeing" in, 65; sexual knowledge in,
69–71; Lambert Strether, xii–xiv,
24, 33–34, 47, 53–55, 57–58, 60–63,
65–66, 68, 70–83, 81–83, 97, 101, 107,
120–21, 123, 131, 148, 188, 204 n.6,
208 n.15; view of the machine in, 83;
voice over vision in, 80–81;
Waymarsh, 33–34, 58, 60, 62, 70–71;
Woollett, Mass., 47, 53, 57–58, 60,
62, 67, 69–70, 77; *Woollett Review,*
76, 107
The American Scene, 9, 115
"The Art of Fiction," 24
The Aspern Papers, Preface to, 137
The Awkward Age, 41
The Beast in the Jungle, 74, 143–44, 178;
May Bartram, 74, 143–44; John
Marcher, 143–44, 178
The Bostonians, 41, 199, n.19, 209 n.5
"Daisy Miller," 30, 46; Daisy Miller, 46,
148; Preface to, 46
"The Figure in the Carpet," 41, 202 n.58
The Golden Bowl, ix, xiv–xviii, 21, 26, 29,
44, 54, 74, 81–82, 114–48, 195 n.28;

The Golden Bowl (continued)
     ambiguity in, 136–39, 142, 145, 147;
     American city, 82, 134, 136; Bob
     Assingham, xvi, 130–32, 142, 145–46;
     Fanny Assignham, xv, xviii, 74,
     116–21, 124–25, 127, 129–32, 136,
     138–39, 142, 145–47; Lady
     Castledean, 116, 135; community in,
     125, 134–37, 148, 206–7 n.4;
     compared to *Absalom, Absalom!*, 146;
     compared to *The Beast in the Jungle*,
     143–44; compared to Dostoevsky's
     novels, 18–19; compared to *Go
     Down, Moses*, xiv–xviii, 153;
     conclusion of, 147–48; dangers of
     knowledge in, 145; designs of
     characters in, 115, 118–34, 206–7 n.4;
     dialogics of, 125–27, 133–34, 136, 208
     n.15; disinterest in, 125, 143; "doing"
     in, 129, 140–41; drama metaphor in,
     146–48; economic metaphors in,
     115–17, 123, 127–28; failure theme in,
     129–30, 135, 138–42; the *ficelle* in, 82,
     124–25, 146–47; the golden bowl in,
     116, 124–25, 128–31, 133; "helping" in,
     130, 140; hermeneutics of, 143,
     206–7 n.4; "interest" in, 114–19;
     metafiction in, 132, 139, 141–48, 207
     n.4, 208 n.15; metaphors in, 116–17,
     142, 208 n.16; narrator's evasiveness
     in, 27, 138; negativity in, 139–42,
     206–7 nn. 4, 13; "possession" in,
     118–19, 128; power as subject in, 114;
     Preface to, 44, 51, 114; Prince
     Amerigo, xiv, xvi, 82, 116–35, 138–41,
     144–47, 208 n.15; reification in, 207
     n.4; role of the reader in, 119, 137;
     role of women in, 208 n.15; "seeing"
     in, 126, 13–34, 137; sexual knowledge
     in, 132; Charlotte Stant, xv–xvi,
     xviii, 82, 116–36, 138, 140–42,
     144–47, 208 n.16; structure of,
     xiv–xv, 20, 114; title of, 129;
     treatment of love, 206–7 n.4, 207–8
     n.15; Adam Verver, xv–xvi, 81,
     116–27, 131–41, 145–46; Maggie
     Verver, xiv–xviii, 29, 47, 54, 65, 73,
     82, 115–27, 129–42, 145–48, 153, 178,
     195 n.28, 206–7 n.4, 207–8 nn.15, 16;
     voice over vision in, 127, 129, 137
Guy Domville, 41

Hawthorne, 28, 31–34
"Hawthorne" (*Library of World's Best
     Literature*), 201 n.28
"Hawthorne's French and Italian
     Journals," 200–201 n.28
"Ivan Turgenev's Virgin Soil," 196 n.39
"The Jolly Corner," 7
"The Lesson of the Master," 39, 41, 62
"The Other House," 41
"The Papers," 39
The Portrait of a Lady: Isabel Archer, 40,
     148, 204 n.6; Madame Merle, 46,
     204 n.6; Gilbert Osmond, 39–40,
     46, 204 n.6; Preface to, 45
Prefaces, 26. *See also* individual entries
The Princess Casamassima, 41; Preface
     to, 46
"The Real Thing," 41
Roderick Hudson, 26
The Sacred Fount, 26
The Spoils of Poynton, 41
The Tragic Muse, 41
"The Tree of Knowledge," 39
The Turn of the Screw, 7
What Maisie Knew, 41; Maisie, 148
The Wings of the Dove, 24, 26, 46, 74;
     Kate Croy, 24, 247; Merton
     Densher, 24; Susan Stringham, 74,
     Milly Theale, 24, 46, 73, 148, 199
     n.19
James, Henry, Sr., 26–27
James, William, 1, 27, 40, 193 n.3
Jehlen, Myra, 187
Jones, Millie. *See* Faulkner, William:
     Absalom, Absalom!
Jones, Wash. *See* Faulkner, William:
     Absalom, Absalom!
Joyce, James, 42

Knowledge: and absence of, 62–64;
     ambiguity, 65; artistic, xiv; avoidance
     of, 64–65; and celebrityhood, 39; as
     communal, 133–34, 149; and
     community of author, narrator,
     characters, and reader, 26; conflicts of,
     167; as dangerous, xiii, 17, 29, 81, 94,
     128, 145, 163, 190; as dialogic, xiv, 15, 17,
     79, 81, 86, 134, 137, 196–97 n.40; as
     imperfect, 54–55, 129–30; James's and
     Faulkner's self-consciousness about, 8;
     leads to inaction, xvi; as mirror of

nature, 2; as offered by the *ficelle*, 73–83; in pedagogy, 196–97 n.40; as personal design, 149; private versus public, xiii; problems of authority and, 33, 39, 41, 196–97 n.40; Puritans and, 4; in racism, 161; as recognition, xii, and "seeing," 65–69, 99, 126, 131–34, 137, 205 n.6; sexual, 69–71, 132; and suspense by omission, 154; as "too late," xii; and voice over vision, 15, 127, 155, 161. *See also* "Design"; Epistemology; Hermeneutics; "Interest"; Ocular metaphor; Problem of knowledge; and Rorty, Richard

Kohler, Dayton, 10
Krook, Dorothea, 136
Kuhn, Thomas, 1

Lamar, Lucius, Q. C., 209 n.5
Lawrence, D. H., 14
Lee, Vernon, 40
Leitch, Vincent, 193 n.1
Lewis, R. W. B., 14, 200 n.21
Lindbergh, Charles, 43
London, Jack, 40
Longfellow, Henry Wadsworth, 140
Lubbock, Percy, 204 n.13
Lukács, Georg, 14

McCaslin, Buck (Amodeus). *See* Faulkner, William: *Go Down, Moses*
McCaslin, Buddy (Theophilus). *See* Faulkner, William: *Go Down, Moses*
McCaslin, Isaac. *See* Faulkner, William: *Go Down, Moses*
McCaslin, L. Q. C. *See* Faulkner, William: *Go Down, Moses*
Machine, the, 83, 123; destroys wilderness, 167; opposed by craft, 44; problem of 8–13
Mailer, Norman, 40
Mailloux, Steven, 196–97 n.40
Maimon, Elaine, 1
Mallarmé, Stéphane, 36
Mannie. *See* Faulkner, William: *Go Down, Moses*
Marble faun: as image of the artist, 30–31, 34–37, 69, 162
Marcher, John. *See* James, Henry: *The Beast in the Jungle*
Martin, Terence, 29

Marx, Leo, 11–12
Matthiessen, F. O., 53, 199 n.17
Mellow, James B., 200 n.24
Melville, Herman, 6–7, 21, 30–31, 199 n.19, 200 n.26; "Hawthorne and His Mosses," 200 n.26; *Moby-Dick*, 12, 200 n.26; *Pierre,* 200 n.26
Menippian satire, 17
Meriwether, James B., 49
Merle, Madame. *See* James, Henry: *The Portrait of a Lady*
Metafiction, ix, 31, 53–54, 57–58, 66–67, 78, 84, 95, 108, 141–49, 157, 195 n.28
Metaphor, xvii, 13, 16, 88, 116, 142, 152, 155, 208 n.16
Michelson, Bruce, 200 n.27
Miller, Daisy. *See* James, Henry: "Daisy Miller"
Miller, J. Hillis, 197 n.40
Millgate, Michael, 49, 209 n.14
Minter, David, 198 n.8, 205 n.7, 207 n.4, 208 n.1
Morozova, Tatiana, 196 n.39
Morris, Wesley, 164
Morson, Gary Saul, 196 n.38
Mueller-Vollmer, Kurt, 193 n.1

Narrative techniques. *See* Ambiguity; Avoidance; Dialogics; Metafiction; Negativity; Polyphony; Storytelling
Narrators: James's and Faulkner's described and compared, xvi–xvii, 100–103, 114, 151; in community, xvi, xviii, 26, 44, 102–3; as evasive, 27, 158; as limited, 55, 64
Negativity, 61–64, 73, 95, 110–13, 128, 136, 139–42, 161–62, 171, 175–76, 178, 180–81, 186, 191
Neohumanism, 1, 196–97 n.40
Nettels, Elsa, 58
New Criticism, 193 n.1
New historicism, 1, 21
New World, the, xiii, 3, 7, 10, 12, 31, 53, 77, 81–83, 123, 136
Newsome, Chad. *See* James, Henry: *The Ambassadors*
Newsome, Mrs. *See* James, Henry: *The Ambassadors*
Norton, Anne, 13–15
Novel: as anticanonical, 17; carnivalization of, 17, 209 n.7; and closure, x, 18–21;

Novel (continued)
    community of, 20, 101; contrast of
    American and British, 19–20; history
    of, 17; as polyphonic, 17, 19–20, 55, 84,
    151; problems of authority in, 26; social
    reality of, 17. *See also* Bakhtin, Mikhail;
    Narrative techniques; and entries for
    James's and Faulkner's individual
    works

Oates, Stephen, 203 n.86
O'Connor, William Van, 208 n.2
The Octopus (Frank Norris), 12
Ocular metaphor, xvii, 2, 45, 66, 81, 127, 137,
    155, 161, 164, 205 n.6. *See also* "Seeing"
"Ode on a Grecian Urn" (John Keats), 177
Old Ben. *See* Faulkner, William: *Go Down,
    Moses*
Ong, Walter J., S.J., 193 n.1
Oppenheimer, Robert, 43
Osmond, Gilbert. *See* James, Henry: *The
    Portrait of a Lady*

Palmer, Richard, 193 n.1
Pastoralism, 12, 36, 38
Peirce, Charles, 193 n.3
Phenomenology, 1
Plato, 49
Pocock, Jim. *See* James, Henry: *The
    Ambassadors*
Pocock, Mamie. *See* James, Henry: *The
    Ambassadors*
Pocock, Sarah. *See* James, Henry: *The
    Ambassadors*
Point of view: problems of having, xiv. *See
    also* Ocular metaphor; "Seeing"
Poirier, Richard, 3, 7–8, 203 n.6
Polyphony: in the novel, 17, 19–20, 55, 84,
    151. *See also* Dialogics; Storytelling
Porter, Carolyn, 13–14, 205 n.6, 207 n.4
Pragmatism, 27
Prince Amerigo. *See* James, Henry: *The
    Golden Bowl*
Problem of knowledge, ix, 84, 149; of the
    artist, 36–37, 114; becomes secular issue
    in nineteenth century, 27; definition
    of, 1–3; as interest and design, 22; as
    "Living," 73; "seeing" and, 73; as
    theological issue, 27. *See also*
    Epistemology; Hermeneutics;
    Knowledge
Puritanism, 3–8, 14–15

Reader-response criticism, 1, 196 n.40
Reed, Joseph, 86, 103, 176, 205 n.4, 209 n.4
Reising, Russell J., 195 n.28
Ricoeur, Paul 193 n.1
Rider. *See* Faulkner, William: *Go Down, Moses*
Rimbaud, Arthur, 36
Rimmon, Shlomith, 137
Rorty, Richard, 1, 16, 27, 66, 148
Rowan Oak, 43
Royce, Josiah, 193 n.3
Runyan, Harry, 201 n.42

Salmon, Rachel, 74, 143–44
Samuels, Charles Thomas, 58, 65, 127, 137,
    139
Schleiermacher, F. D. E., 193 n.1
Schneider, Daniel J., 141
Sears, Sallie, 207 n.13
"Seeing": as metaphor for knowing, xii,
    xvi, 65–69, 99, 126, 168–69. *See also*
    Ocular metaphor
Segal, Ora, 208 n.16
Seltzer, Mark, 206–7 n.4
Sensibar, Judith, 201 n.37
Sicker, Philip, 207–8 n.15
Slatoff, Walter J., 203 n.86
Slavery: in the American South, 85, 155, 157,
    169, 177
Snopes, Flem. *See* Faulkner, William: *The
    Hamlet*
Socratic dialogue, 17
South, the, 14–15, 24, 50–51, 86–91, 95–99,
    113, 151, 167, 185, 203 n.86
Stant, Charlotte. *See* James, Henry: *The
    Golden Bowl*
Stein, Paul S., 200 n.25
Steinbeck, John, 51; *The Grapes of Wrath,* 12
Stevens, Gavin. *See* Faulkner, William: *Go
    Down, Moses*
Stewart, Randall, 199 n.19
Stewart, Susan, 196 n.39
Stone, Phil, 35, 202 n.65
Storytelling, 84–100, 103, 113, 143. *See also*
    Dialogics; Polyphony
Standberg, Victor, 27
Strether, Lambert. *See* James, Henry: *The
    Ambassadors*
Stringham, Susan. *See* James, Henry: *The
    Wings of the Dove*
Sundquist, Eric J., 150, 186, 189
Sutpen, Eulalia Bon. *See* Faulkner,
    William: *Absalom, Absalom!*

Sutpen, Henry. *See* Faulkner, William: *Absalom, Absalom!*
Sutpen, Judith. *See* Faulkner, William: *Absalom. Absalom!*
Sutpen, Thomas. *See* Faulkner, William: *Absalom, Absalom!*

Technology and art. *See* Machine
Theale, Milly. *See* James, Henry: *The Wings of the Dove*
Thoreau, Henry David, 6, 198 n.8; *Walden,* 8, 11
Tick, Stanley, 298 n.2
Todorov, Tzvetan, 137, 193 n.1
Tolstoy, Leo, 202, n.58
Tomey's Turl. *See* Faulkner, William: *Go Down, Moses*
Transcendentalism, 31
Turgenev, Ivan, 196 n.39
Twain, Mark, 7, 21, 40, 49, 73

Verver, Adam. *See* James, Henry: *The Golden Bowl*
Verver, Maggie. *See* James, Henry: *The Golden Bowl*
Vickery, Olga, 202 n.58, 205 n.8
Vision: as metaphor for knowledge. *See* Ocular metaphor; "Seeing"
Voice: as metaphor for knowledge. *See* Dialogics; Polyphony; Storytelling

Waggoner, Hyatt, 85–86
Ward, J. A., 199 n.19
Warren, Robert Penn, 27
Waymarsh. *See* James, Henry: *The Ambassadors*
Weisgerber, Jean, 196 n.39
West, Nathaniel, 27
Wharton, Edith: *The House of Mirth,* 195 n.28
Wiesenfarth, Joseph, 207 n.10
Wilkins, George. *See* Faulkner, William: *Go Down, Moses*
Wilkins, Nat. *See* Faulkner, William: *Go Down, Moses*
Williams, David, 209–10 n.17
Williams, Raymond, 22–23
Williams, Roger, 5
Wolfe, Thomas, 51
Worsham, Miss. *See* Faulkner, William: *Go Down, Moses*
Writing across the curriculum, 197 n.40

Yeazell, Ruth Bernard, 64–65, 75, 78, 80, 130, 139, 145, 147
Yoknapatawpha County, 24, 42, 103, 149, 205 n.3
Young, Art, 197 n.40

Ziff, Larzar, 3, 16

This book has been set in Linotron Galliard. Galliard was designed for Merganthaler in 1978 by Matthew Carter. Galliard retains many of the features of a sixteenth century typeface cut by Robert Granjon but has some modifications which give it a more contemporary look.

Printed on acid-free paper.